Given to Alan Heidelberg
Christmas 1984

By~ Van Heidelberg

General Sherman's Son

JOSEPH T. DURKIN, S.J.

General

Sherman's

Son

New York

FARRAR, STRAUS AND CUDAHY

Preface

by John LaFarge, S.J.

Father Durkin's scholarly biography of Father Thomas Ewing Sherman came into being, like so many other books, as the result of a chance occurrence. In my autobiography, *The Manner Is Ordinary*, I quoted from a letter that my father wrote to me in the fall of 1905, shortly after I had entered the Jesuit novitiate at St. Andrew-on-Hudson, Poughkeepsie. In this letter Father referred to "that wild raid of Fr. Sherman, I believe on horseback, passing through the country which his father ravaged and desolated." In his characteristic bantering fashion he expressed the hope that I, as a Jesuit, would not follow Father Sherman's example.

My words of comment on Father's letter drew the attention of one of the Sherman family relatives, who had read them, and was afraid my language might cause a false impression as to Father Sherman's truly noble character. This led to discussions of the problem, and finally to asking Father Durkin to undertake the task of writing this biography.

For certain readers a question might quite naturally come to mind. Why relate the story of a Jesuit and a priest who had experienced such emotional and mental disturbance? What meaning could the average normal Christian draw from such a life? Why prolong a troubled tale by consigning it to print for future generations?

For many people no such explanation is needed. The story of Thomas Ewing Sherman is part of our country's history, part of—or a sequel to—a crucial phase of that history, to which today we pay an ever increasing attention. Whatever be our judgment as to the great figures of the tragic conflict of 1861-1865 and the subsequent decades, whether we esteem these personages or detest them, the contemporary mind wishes the entire story to appear. The life of Thomas Sherman, covering so many years and so many scenes and places, is an integral, even if a minor part, of that story.

However, quite apart from these strictly historical considerations, I believe, and many others of his own Jesuit brethren whom I have consulted believe, that the life-history of Father Sherman stands upon its own merits: both as to the personal caliber of the man himself, and as to the religious community through which he dedicated his life to God's service.

Father Sherman's life suffered, his biographer says, from "a tragic flaw." Unfortunately this trait was not foreseen at a sufficiently early period, and may have been helped by a certain confusion that seems to have stayed with him as to the difference between religious (or Ignatian) obedience, and the military model that appealed so vividly to his soldierly imagination. But "tragic flaw" is but a relative term. His life was emphatically not a tragedy. On the contrary, it was a striking example of how a great soul could seek and find God and devote himself to the good of his fellowman despite such an obstacle. It is a testimony to the clarity of the spiritual ideal that he never for a moment lost from sight, even though his conduct at times seemed to militate directly against it; to the intensity and depth of that total dedication to the service of the Divine Master which he renewed with the very last breath of his truly apostolic life.

It seems to me only fair to point out that Father Sherman's

career also testified to the cordial charity of his fellow-priests and the prevailing patience and kindness of his Jesuit Superiors. The Superiors' refusal to dismiss him, in fact their inability to dismiss him for acts, however vehement, for which he was not fully responsible, was itself a witness to the Society's total commitment—for better or for worse, in sickness and in health—to its own members.

I do not remember having met Father Sherman personally, but do recall the esteem and affection in which he universally was held. That the South, the Deep South, offered the final hospitality to the son of William Tecumseh Sherman is a symbol of the peace and reconciliation that we pray may come to all regions and all peoples of our country.

Campion House
New York City

Contents

Contents

General Sherman's Son

CHAPTER 1

Beginnings Are Endings

MAY 24, 1865, was a mild Spring day in Washington. The trees along the Avenue, the tender green of the banks of the Potomac, the early buds in the gardens of Georgetown—all provided a gentle and peaceful setting. But the city itself was buzzing with activity. The Willard, the National, and the numerous boarding-houses were crowded with visitors, and the sidewalks and streets were thronged with men and women in gay dress. The *National Intelligencer* was struggling to press with one of the most gaudy holiday editions in the history of American journalism. It was the second day of the review of the Grand Army of the Republic.

To young Thomas Ewing Sherman, a slim, grey-eyed, dark-haired, intense boy of nine, this was the greatest day in his life. His father, the hero of the day, would soon come riding down the Avenue. Tommy stood with his mother on the reviewing stand before the White House, next to the President, the members of the Cabinet, and other distinguished guests. Andrew

Johnson, a nervous, gaunt man in black, looked very serious. Secretary of War Stanton was fussily giving orders to the police controlling the crowds. Mrs. Grant had her arm linked tightly to that of her husband. Grant, impassive, stood staring straight ahead. Yesterday his Army of the Potomac had had its hour of glory; today the divisions of the West were parading. The triumphant forces of the Union were showing themselves for the last time in a blaze of splendor.

"They're coming!" The word raced along the lines of waiting spectators. Soldiers swung down Pennsylvania Avenue to the roar of the crowds along the curbs. Down the broad street marched the regiments and divisions of the tatterdemalion Army of the West. They looked ragged and shabby, the tough, grim, fighting men of the Fifteenth Corps, the Nineteenth Illinois, and the Twelfth Wisconsin—heroes of Donelson, Shiloh, Vicksburg, Savannah, Atlanta, and Chattanooga. With bands blasting, flags flying, with the proud prancing of officers' mounts and the flash of the sun off bayonets, the victorious army of William Tecumseh Sherman swept on grandly.

There were broken soles on the marching shoes of some, and holes in their faded uniforms, but to the shouting watchers they were the unforgettable reminders of a thin line of infantry that irresistibly took the summits at Lookout Mountain; of Prentiss holding off a force three times his size at Shiloh; of Mower making his lightning move at Memphis, and of Corse's handful who plugged the gap at Altoona. On they came with measured, disciplined swagger, the rough, hard-bitten battalions of the Army of Tennessee. Howard rode at the head of the Fifteenth and Seventeenth Corps. Slocum led the Fourteenth and Twentieth. Hazen, waving gaily to the ladies on the sidewalks, was in his place with the Fifty-third Ohio.

A girl broke out of the crowd and into the marching ranks

to throw a handful of roses at a young lieutenant. For a moment the men lost step as they boisterously cheered her. A middle-aged man leaped up on a stool and began to shout "Yankee Doodle." Spontaneously, hundreds of people picked up the battle song. A mounted captain of engineers had a wide bandage about his head; they cheered him hysterically as he passed. Some of the marching men had their arms in slings and a few of them were limping slightly. The crowds made them their special darlings as they went by. As the head of the column turned at Fifteenth Street, a group of women almost stopped the march as they ran forward to give baskets of food to the men of the Indiana contingent.

As visiting English journalists rightly observed, there was much over-emotionalism in the crowd's reaction and in the American press reports the next day. But the American people surely had an excuse. The long, bitter, tragic war was over; the Union was preserved. The great show of May 23-24 was a legitimate and harmless case of mass intoxication.

Now the Fifteenth Corps was passing by, led by Major General William Tecumseh Sherman. He swerved his horse out of the front line and rode over to the reviewing stand. He made straight for the woman and small boy beside the President. The crowd cheered wildly as they caught the drama of the incident. This was the hero of the march to the sea saluting his wife and son! President Johnson made him dismount and motioned him to come up. There was handshaking all around. (There was one exception which the boy noted; he would find an appropriate moment to inquire why.) Then Sherman took his place beside Ellen and Tommy.

This day was never forgotten by General Sherman's son. The sight of the victorious troops, the supreme honors accorded to his father, the very appearance of his father as the beau ideal of the triumphant, heroic soldier, the accolades to this hero— none of these impressions could ever fade, nor would they fail to influence in a decisive way his thought and ambitions forever.

When Tommy Sherman was barely five he had heard the firing of one of the earliest skirmishes of the war, the blocking by Federal volunteers of the attempt by Southern sympathizers to seize the United States arsenal at St. Louis. Men had been killed in the brief but sharp action, and his mother had tried to explain the meaning of the event to the child. In the fall of 1862, he had been taken by his mother to visit his father in the camp at Memphis. He had had a wonderful time: he had been allowed to sleep on the ground in a military blanket, and the company tailor had made him a uniform with corporal's chevrons.[1]

There had been also the early morning surprise visit of the General to his wife's temporary home at Lancaster, Ohio, in the bitter cold winter of 1864. Sherman, at that point of the war, was under a cloud. The Washington politicians were blaming him for the reverses in the West, and were generally dissatisfied with his record. As a result of the bitter criticism he was struggling with one of the spells of melancholy and discouragement that often came to him. He had snatched a few hours off to see Ellen, who always braced him up when he was in such moods.

Tommy had been awakened from bed to greet the General. How he had wondered at the vehemence, the roughness almost, with which his father had snatched him in his arms and kissed him. Although the General had stayed only a few hours he had talked several times very gravely with his son. Tommy could not recall much that he had said except that he would soon be a grown-up boy who would understand many things that were now too difficult for him. When the General left them soon after dawn that day he had gone to Chattanooga to begin planning his march across Georgia.

What the boy remembered most clearly, perhaps, was another stay with his father behind the lines at Vicksburg a few weeks after the city fell. That visit had brought to William Tecumseh Sherman a personal grief from which, possibly, he never fully recovered.

In mid-August Ellen had taken her children, Willy, Minnie, Lizzie, and Tom, to her husband's camp on the Big Black River. It had been, at first, a wonderful lark for them all. Tom was permitted to roam over parts of the now quiet battleground. He had received a half-serious reprimand from his father for talking too freely about military news to stray Confederates whom he would seek out for conversation. His older brother, Willy, stood beside his father during reviews, and he had been made an honorary sergeant by the troops of the Eleventh Engineers.

Then had come the sorrowful event. The General had received sudden orders to take his corps and relieve Rosecrans in the Chickamauga Valley, so Ellen and the children began their return journey to Memphis. As they were traveling up the river, Willy fell ill and died a few days later in his mother's arms.

It was a fearful blow to Sherman, whose military orders prevented him even from attending the funeral at Lancaster. He wrote a poignant letter of gratitude to the men of the Eleventh who had thought so much of Willy and who had mourned him so keenly. Then, a few months later, a very serious and sobering letter was sent by the General to Tom:

> You are now our only boy, and must take poor Willy's place, to take care of your sisters, and to fill my place when I too am gone. . . . Work hard to gain knowledge and health, which will, when you are a man, insure you all you need in this world.[2]

Tom now sensed that he had become dearer and more important in his father's eyes. "Whatever may happen to me," the

General had written to him on the eve of the march to the sea, "you are old enough to remember me, and will take my place. Don't study too hard as it may make you weak and sick. Play at all sorts of games. And learn to ride a pony this summer. . . . Also as soon as you are old enough you can learn to swim, to hunt and to fish. All these things are as necessary as to read and write."[3]

Repeatedly his father had given him the same admonition: "Always remember that on you now rests the care of our family. Minnie and Lizzie . . . will marry and change their names, but you will always be a Sherman and must represent the family."[4] Occasionally the exhortation would be more specific: "When you get old enough [you] can choose for yourself whether to be a soldier a Lawyer a Doctor or Farmer . . ." And, somewhat ambiguously: "I don't want you to be a soldier or a priest but a good useful man."[5]

There was another feature of the family history which the boy perhaps could not yet appreciate. Almost from the beginning of their married life his mother and father had been wanderers. After their wedding in Washington they had lived for a while in St. Louis, but had then moved to New Orleans. From the latter city they had shifted their residence to San Francisco, thence back to Ellen's old home in Lancaster, Ohio, and soon again, successively, to Leavenworth, Kansas, Alexandria, Louisiana, back again to Lancaster, and finally once more to St. Louis. Before Tommy was nine years old, he had lived in five different cities. The reason for these migrations was largely the energetic and wide-spread business ventures of Sherman. Even without the spur of these interests, however, he might have kept his family just as much on the move. He was basically a restless man, with a dislike for staying rooted.

Such a necessity of repeatedly "changing his base of operations," as he termed it, combined with another of his traits to keep Tecumseh Sherman under a constant and unwholesome tension. He felt toward his family an almost morbid sense of responsibility. His obligation to give them every possible advantage and comfort he accepted lovingly, but it also awed and frightened him. He knew that these periodical movings were not good for Ellen and the children, yet he felt compelled to make them. As a result, he carried a smouldering disquiet within himself.

In regard to one point, however, no Sherman or Ewing ever had any doubts, and the boy had already caught the attitude. His father and mother, like their own parents, had a passionate pride of family, an intense satisfaction in the name they bore.

It is difficult to recapture the feeling of reverence inspired in nineteenth-century Americans by their own particularized portion of the general tribe. One's family, with its associations and achievements reaching back through the generations, was a thing to be idolized. There was something so ineffably *private* in the special group of one's forebears and their living descendants. The cult was exemplified in such declarations as that of the New Englander who said that the United States in time of war could always depend on the alliance of his family; or that of the Virginian who recounted how the Federals had fought his family at the battle of Fredericksburg and lost. For the Shermans and Ewings the family was a sacred reality.

As Tommy Sherman later expressed it, his most precious legacy was the religious training imparted by his mother. In the 'eighties he wrote her: "Thank God, my dear Mother, you succeeded in turning my young imagination strongly to Him."[6] Her Catholicity was of the admirably paradoxical type that could be down-to-earth while aspiring to heaven. It had a strong masculine tone that manifested itself in constant acts of practical charity toward her fellow man. Though General Sherman was not a Catholic and never became one, he agreed that all their children should be raised in the faith of their mother. He felt a sincere respect toward priests and welcomed them into his home. As a military commander, he always saw to it that a Catholic chaplain was with his troops. Several Catholic bishops—such as Purcell, Ryan, and Cardinal McCloskey of New York—were his personal friends. A profound appreciation of the necessity and value of religion was an essential note of the Sherman tradition.

"Mama, why did not Papa shake hands with Mr. Stanton?" Tommy was referring to a small but significant incident that had occurred on the reviewing stand on the day of the General's triumph: Sherman had ostentatiously refused to give the conventional greeting to the Secretary of War.

Ellen explained to her son, in the proper terms, the unkind and unjust charges that Stanton had made against the General in the last days of the war. Stanton considered Sherman too "soft" with respect to the terms of surrender offered to General Johnston. He had high-handedly sent General Grant to relieve Sherman, an insulting gesture which Grant tactfully sidestepped. What Ellen did not go into, of course, was the fact of the General's extreme sensitiveness to the slightest adverse criticism of his actions. This, too, was a part of the heritage that would be passed on to the boy.

Tommy had been a sturdy infant at the moment of his birth in San Francisco on October 12, 1856. His weight, as Ellen had promptly reported to her mother, had been "ten and a half pounds with only one petticoat, a night slip and a light flannel shawl on." He had come into the world in the midst of what was practically a state of anarchy in the California city. The Vigilantes, enraged at what they considered a lax application of justice toward a murderer, had seized control of San Francisco. Since Cump—as Ellen always called her husband— was in charge of the state militia, the family received threats from the headstrong men who had taken the law into their own hands. But the crisis passed, and Ellen received a respectful note from an anonymous Vigilante, assuring her that the Shermans would not be harmed. Tommy, after the fashion of a small boy, felt a secret satisfaction when he learned that his first hours had been spent in the shadow of armed violence. As a grown man, he could say that the atmosphere of turmoil that surrounded his birth hinted at the future circumstances of his life.

Ellen had had with regard to the baby a feeling evoked by none of her other children——a conviction that "he would do some special work in the world." "Perhaps," she had remarked to her friend, Archbishop Purcell, "he'll even become a famous priest and some day preach in this very diocese."[7]

For the most part, Tommy's babyhood and childhood had been normal with some points, possibly, of special interest. He had been afflicted during the first nine years of his life with various illnesses that appear to have been chronic. When he was two years old he had recurrent spells of earache.[8] From his infancy he had been subject to attacks of severe ulcerated throat; this ailment would plague him periodically until he was thirteen.[9]

His uncertain health was such a great source of concern to his mother that only a few weeks before the Grand Review she had expressed her fear that the boy would not attain the age of manhood.[10] This foreboding was, as events proved, quite exaggerated, and to attribute any great significance to these childhood sicknesses would be unjustified. Yet the facts of his early medical history may have some relevance when placed in the perspective of his whole life.

Another circumstance of his first years may be worth mentioning: he was, at least until he was five, a very difficult child to manage. The term "bad" boy has a mitigated meaning when referring to such a tender sprout; but this is the adjective that Mrs. Sherman often applied to him."[11] "Our children," she writes to her husband in the spring of 1860, "are . . . with one exception . . . good," and the exception clearly is Tommy.[12] His father felt constrained a few weeks later to send the boy a stern letter of reprimand with a threat of forcing him as a penance to sleep in the stable.[13] The Ewing household at Lancaster, says Mrs. Sherman sadly, "have pretty much given Tommy up as an outlaw."[14]

As in the case of his illnesses, it would be captious to attach too much importance to what many would dismiss as a normal incident of childhood. It is, in other words, the nature of normal youngsters to be naughty occasionally. What strikes the observer, however, is the degree of worry evoked in two very level-headed parents by this childish defect in the boy. Whatever the extent of his juvenile faults, he apparently soon grew out of them. Mrs. Sherman reports in the fall of 1864 that "he is a good boy"; and she adds significantly, "now."[15]

Indeed, Tommy's "badness" may have been nothing more than an exaggeration of a trait he would always have—a marked positiveness of character, a determined will. This more respectable quality he displayed not infrequently. While the family (except the General) were living at Lancaster just after leaving Leavenworth, Tommy, age three, would, when annoyed at anything, declare that he would at once go back to Kansas.[16] One day during the same period he demanded suddenly of his mother, "Where is my Papa?" "In Kansas," replied Mrs. Sherman. "Well, I wish he would come back," said Tommy grumpily.[17] Mrs. Sherman could describe the domestic scene one day in these words: "Lizzie is cutting roses and Tommy is lording it over the girls downstairs."[18]

A third fact about the boy's early childhood (until mid-1863) was discussed by his mother in a letter to her husband: "You seem to think so much more of Willy than of Tommy that . . . [the other children of the family] perceive it. Poor little Tom was charmed—his eyes brightened and his whole face beamed happiness when he found you had mentioned his name with Willy's as one to whom the bullets were to be sent."[19] And a little later: "You will have to be careful about making such a distinction between Willy and Tommy. It will have a bad effect on Tommy. He notices it now and loses all ambition when he thinks of it. Willy prides himself on your preference for him."[20] This situation was, of course, made obsolete by Willy's death. It may, however, have persisted in another guise when Mrs. Sherman for years afterwards kept idolizing the memory of her dead son and continued to hold him up as an unsurpassable model of all that was good and fine.

A few days after the Grand Review the Shermans were given a reception at West Point. Tommy was all agog, like any boy, at the cadets' parading; and he was thrilled again at the honors accorded to his father. When later, on their way home to St. Louis, they stopped off at Notre Dame to see the Sherman girls who were at school with the nuns there, his main interest, after a perfunctory greeting to his young sisters, was the smooth ballfields of the older boys' school. Like all healthy boys, too, he derived a handsome pleasure from eating, and did full justice to the delicacies placed before him by the hospitable nuns.

After the victory festivities, the Shermans returned to St. Louis. They were to reside there until the spring of 1869. The General had been placed in charge of one of the five Federal military districts, the Mississippi section, including all the States north of the Ohio River and across to the Rockies. St. Louis was his headquarters, although he would often be called to make official trips through the vast territory committed to his charge.

The city's old French Creole culture, meticulous and ornate, was being transfused in the mid-sixties and 'seventies with the gusty spirit of the expansionist West. The typical St. Louisans were now no longer the slightly tired *noblesse oblige*-minded descendants of the aristocratic Empire, but careful, hard-headed businessmen and their competent wives. The General, a few years later, made this contrast between the Missouri city and the national capital: "St. Louis is of course dirty as compared with Washington, and the streets comparatively rough; but the difference is between an honest working community and a borrowing one. Here there is substance rather than pretension."[21] And further: "St. Louis is very smoky and dirty—has the same relation to Washington which a foundry has to a parlor; but the one is producing and self-maintaining, while the other is dependent on Luxury and will collapse, like the French Noblesse of 1789, on [at?] the first Grand Crash. . . ."[22] St. Louis, the General remarked, was "in the very heart of the U.S.," and an ideal location for the progressive businessman.[23]

Besides, the city was one of the main bridgeheads in the white man's penetration into the far west. The great transcontinental railroads were being thrown across the plains and over the mountains. St. Louis was one of the chief headquarters for this huge enterprise. Along with the railroads went the determined pioneers to stake out a civilization in the new lands. These forerunners of modern America were constantly passing in and out of the city. The famous scouts, too, like Kit Carson and Jim Bridges, came often to St. Louis to renew their supplies and exchange information regarding the vast virgin empire they were helping to open up. It is likely that young Tommy Sherman was one of those who listened to the reports of their adventures and their accounts of the fabulous opportunities to the westward. He would certainly be thrilled, also, by his father's talk of the serious Indian problem that must be solved before the American flag would be secure in the western country. This peril was real in the 'sixties and 'seventies and far from settled.

The Shermans' home life during these years was one of the most pleasant periods of their lives. There was always plenty of company in their large frame house on Garrison Avenue. Minnie was now enough of a young lady to supply her mother's place at times as hostess to the numerous friends—including officers of the General's staff—and relatives who dropped in. Tommy, though not yet in his teens, was proud of the way his sister conducted herself in receiving the guests on New Year's Day, 1866, while Mrs. Sherman was confined to her room with a headache.

There were song fests in the Sherman parlor, family trips to the theatre, skating parties and, on some evenings, family readings. This latter placid form of entertainment had survived the invasion of the vigorous new generation and probably reduced a bit the rate of their nervous prostrations, as the malady in those days was termed. With parents and children gathered in an attentive circle, Shakespeare and Dickens laid a chastening hand on the worldly ambitions and dollars-and-cents thinking of families on the make.

Tommy was at the Notre Dame nuns' school and was doing well in his studies. Mrs. Sherman could announce, with pardonable pride, that he would soon be leading his class. This triumph, she added, would be a bitter pill to "the Rebels [of St. Louis] who hate us so heartily."[24] He had acquired, while at home, the habit of practicing his reading by shutting himself up in a room and declaiming the text in a voice that could be heard a block away.[25] He wrote at least one very creditable Latin letter to his grandfather Ewing—no small achievement for a boy of eleven years.[26] He had been promoted two classes.[27]

Nor was he neglecting the other accomplishments of a growing young man. He loved to dazzle any given group of spectators by performing brilliant manoeuvres on ice skates.[28] He could now swim "froggy," and looked down on smaller boys who could swim only "doggy."[29] He would sing loudly if not well at the drop of a hat. His preference ran to such red-hot favorites as "I Feel Just as Happy as a Big Sun-Flower" and even the more sophisticated ditty about "The Charming Young Widow I Met on the Cars."[30]

Several times there came to the Shermans' a man who made a deep impression on young Tommy. He was the Jesuit priest, Father Peter De Smet, the missionary to the Indians. He was a devoted friend of Mrs. Sherman's, but he came mainly to confer with the General about the troubles in the west. He was of inestimable value to Sherman in handling the Indian situation. He was said to be the only white man who dared to walk unarmed among the semi-savages. He worked in close collaboration with Sherman's army posts in the interest of peace and justice to both parties—Indian and white.

The boy was fascinated by the combination found in De Smet the priest and daring pioneer of the wilds. He talked with the Jesuit whenever he could; his imagination kindled as he pictured this brave priest acting in his own way a powerful part in the political and military arena.

For a brief period in 1867 the Shermans visited the Ewings at Lancaster. Ellen's father, the great Thomas Ewing, felt the end of his days approaching and had asked his daughter to come with her husband and children to see him. He had played an eminent part in the momentous first three-quarters of the country's history. Born in the year of the establishment of the Federal Government, he had been admitted to the bar in 1816. He had been a friend of Webster and Clay and competed with them professionally in the courts. He had known John Marshall and had pleaded cases in the Supreme Court under Taney and Chase. He had been Secretary of the Treasury under Presidents Harrison and Tyler, and Secretary of the Interior under Taylor, the Chief Executive who had established that department. He had been a war-time adviser to Lincoln. He had been a true humanist as well as an outstanding lawyer. Literature was his first love and the solace of his declining years, and his conversation to the end was enriched by references to the masters of prose and poetry.

A thrilling opportunity was presented to the boy in 1868. He and Minnie accompanied their father on a tour of inspection of the Western army posts. They went by train and stopped at Forts Leavenworth, Laramie, and Sanders. Here, indeed, was a boy's paradise! Tommy was enthralled by the sight of the hard-bitten cavalrymen, the long-bearded hoarse-speaking scouts, the real cowboys, and their lumbering herds; and he tingled with pleasurable fear at the realization that he was within a few miles of savage red men. He was taught more about rifles than he had ever learned before, and he rode horseback, well chaperoned, to his heart's content. He was stirred to his boy's heart by the glamor of the open and dangerous West with its mounted United States guard to keep it safe. When they returned to St. Louis he felt for awhile cramped and "let down."

The Sherman ménage was soon to be on the move again. Grant, as one of the first acts of his Presidency, made Sherman General of the Army, with his headquarters at Washington. Ellen and the children wished, of course, to be with him at the capital.

The last few weeks of their residence in St. Louis were filled with preparations for the change. Tom, in particular, was pleased. He wrote to his father: "I will be glad when we go to Washington, for I always feel more at home where you are stationed."[31] He expressed his desire also "to enter some College at Washington about the First of May."[32]

To his studies at the sisters' academy in St. Louis he apparently was giving a great deal of attention. With a studied casualness he informed the General in early April: "Next Wednesday we will have a little exhibition at the College, and I guess I will be at the head of my class when we leave St. Louis."[33] And he added: "I will be glad when I have in the house in Washington a large room of my own, where I can study without being disturbed."[34] The latter observation may have been a side thrust at his new brother, Cumpy, who had appeared on January 9, 1867.

Meanwhile, home affairs were proceeding quietly. Cumpy was learning, with some difficulty, to speak. He found it rather hard to say, at his brother's and sisters' prompting, "Hurrah for General Sherman"; but he could manage such pronouncements as, "Brother Tommy is a good man" and "Papa is sick."[35] Minnie and Lizzie had been cultivating the young officers of General Sheridan's staff but were not quite satisfied with the results.[36]

Tommy had been reading one of the cambric tea novels of the period—a chromo by a lady writer, one Bina Pierce. He observes that it is "very exciting but a little too love-sick,"[37] which is probably more accurate criticism than most of the adult critics were awarding the book. He guesses that, notwithstanding this literary defect, Miss Bina will make a good deal of money— a suggestion that he was not invulnerable to the reigning spirit of St. Louis.

In the spring of 1869 the family entrained for Washington. For the next five years the national capital would be their home.

CHAPTER 2

Basic Training

THE SHERMAN HOME in the national capital was a heavy, placid, red-brick and brownstone pile in what would soon be the fashionable West End. An indication of its ample proportions is the fact that Mrs. Sherman at once decided they would not need the entire rear portion of the house, and consequently sought a tenant for that section. A footnote to the social and economic history of the times is the circumstance that they finally rented this part of the dwelling to a general.

The city itself, when the Shermans arrived, was in a period of transition. The older Washington had been much like a potentially comely matron who was either underdeveloped or run to seed. The well-laid-out streets and avenues of L'Enfant, with their really sumptuous trees, were like boulevards politely but vainly seeking a metropolis to adorn. The lack of adequate surfacing for these municipal highways was a constant hazard for vehicles that bumped and clattered along them. Some streets were not paved at all. It was not unusual for a horse and dray to be bogged in the mud in the center of Pennsylvania Avenue. The small, shabby stores in the business sections, the rather ramshackle wooden houses in the residential quarters, and the mostly unkempt and sometimes tawdry parks did nothing to enhance the appearance of the capital of the nation. The swampy land that disfigured the northwest section of the city, the absence of proper sewage facilities, and numerous other unhappy features, gave color to the charge that Washington was squat, dull, and frowsy.

There was, consequently, good reason why President Grant, in 1871, created a Department of Public Works, headed by the very competent and high-handed Alexander R. Shepherd, to rehabilitate the physical character of the city. To Shepherd, more than to any other, modern Washington owes its beauty. He has been accused of being a corrupt operator in municipal improvements. He certainly made himself rich (until the auditors came) while making Washington fair. He was not, however, corrupt. He was simply a man who could not permit the niceties—or fundamentals—of financial ethics to interfere with his plan of making the city splendid. From his later enforced exile he could look back with pride on the results of his work: the long, wide avenues now smoothly paved with asphalt or concrete; improved landscaping that brought into actuality L'Enfant's dream of a city of magnificent vistas; a proliferation of circles and parks embowered in shrubbery, flowers, and additional shapely trees; a further development of handsome public buildings and private residences to supersede the old horrors; the covering over of the old swamps and the installation of an up-to-date sanitary system.

Washington was now a pleasant and inspiring place in which to live. Federal officials, diplomats—American and foreign, and the numerous visitors, could enjoy, in their hours of relaxation, the National Theatre or Ford's Opera House; they could lead their wives and daughters through the marvels of the Smithsonian or the Botanical Gardens or go to the Corcoran Gallery of Art or regale themselves with the Marine Band concerts on the White House lawn, or astound their guests with the magnificence of the refurbished Capitol or the unfinished Washington Monument, boasted of as the highest in the world. There was also, needless to say, an endless round of official and semi-official receptions, dinners, and parties.

Rather surprisingly, the social atmosphere was largely determined by the Westerners. Washington would always retain much of the character of a Southern city; but the energetic, serious-minded democracy of the Mississippi and Ohio valleys had established itself in the life of the capital and provided some starch for what might have been otherwise the languid social fabric of the city. Frequently remarked, too, was the fact that there were fewer really poor people in Washington than in almost any other American city. Even in the case of the Negro population the average of material well-being was not as low as might have been expected.

General Sherman, when he was not away on some official mission or journey, rode to his War Department office daily in the one-horse street car that passed near his house. His wife had plenty to do in running her household. Following the custom of the Washington housewives, she walked or drove several times a week to the Central Market, with her basket under her arm. She must have admitted that this institution—it covered two square blocks and was supplied by the farmers and dairymen of Maryland and Virginia—was unparalleled in St. Louis. Besides these normal duties she participated generously in the religious and philanthropic activities of the city.

Minnie had become increasingly the co-mistress of the Sherman home and was one of the belles of the capital. Ellie and

Rachel were boarders at the Georgetown Visitation Convent school, while Lizzie was a day student there. Tom had entered the Jesuits' college at Georgetown.

The Sherman home was a gathering point for distinguished visitors. Generals Sheridan, Meade, and Thomas, and Admirals Porter and Dahlgren were frequent guests. Members of Grant's cabinet, the Supreme Court justices, representatives of the diplomatic corps, and shining lights of Congress were familiar figures in Mrs. Sherman's reception rooms.

The lady of the house was on sufficiently intimate terms with Hamilton Fish, the Secretary of State, to tease him about her Irish flag, flaunted from one of her doors on St. Patrick's Day. Sir Edward Thornton, the British Ambassador, and his wife remarked privately—a compliment that would have surprised Henry James—that the Shermans were the most civilized people they had met in America. When the son of Queen Victoria, Prince Arthur, met Minnie Sherman he was greatly captivated, even though—on her mother's orders—she declined to dance a waltz with him. Mark Twain had sat in the General's parlor and filled the room with cigar smoke.

Most of the people who frequented the Sherman's receptions constituted a rebuttal to the usual strictures on the culture of the Gilded Age. With some exceptions, the men and women who were received by the General's wife were representatives of a society that had blossomed out of a tradition of living based on respect for character. Personal integrity was their aim and the touchstone of their actions. It is, of course, impossible to excuse the corruption of the age of Grant; but the error of some historians has been to extend the immorality of a few to the society as a whole.

Nor must we underestimate the generally wholesome influence of the European diplomatic corps on this society of the 'seventies. Although the Americans could scarcely be expected to admit it, the young republic had much to learn from the older culture. There were some of the finer graces of civilized living that had weathered the storms of the Atlantic only in the persons of such men and women as were living in the embassies in the developing West End. Perhaps in no respect was the dependence of America on Europe more evident than in this matter of civilized manners.

Periodically the whole Sherman family dined with the Grants at the White House. These were private parties including little Cump, who sat at the President's table in a high chair.[38] The Sherman girls were always amused at Mr. Dent, Mrs. Grant's father, who lived at the White House and loudly announced to all visitors that he was and would always remain a staunch Democrat.

Although Tom was busy with his studies at Georgetown during most of these days, he participated to a great extent in the family's social activity. He probably came into contact with more of the famous men of the period than did any other American boy of his age. The boy was, at the same time, fond of the things that fourteen-year-old males should normally cherish. He was good at the games that enlivened the college yard. He rode horseback whenever he could. He played billiards—always, of course, at home—and often brought home some of his classmates for a song fest, with his sisters only too happy to assist at the piano. He raised chickens in the back yard and had a grape-vine and pear-tree garden of his own. He loved to handle a gun and regretted the restrictive influence exerted by the city government on the use of such weapons.

During the periods when his father's official duties took him away from Washington, Tom took over some of the General's domestic functions. He was making a really brilliant record in his studies at the college; but, despite his close attention to his books, found time to supervise such projects as the reflooring of the family barn—it had become so muddy that the cows had to be kept in the yard—and the putting up (by his own hands) of a partition across the rear of the stable to make private winter quarters for the chickens. When Ellie and Rachel had permission for a holiday, Tom was always most willing to call at the convent for them and drive them home in the Sherman carriage or do anything they desired. One of his mother's secret satisfactions was Tom's sincere devotion to his sisters. For Lizzie he would have, to the end of his life, a special affection.

That even at this early age he was not destitute of a degree of subtlety is evidenced by a delicate hint he sent to his father (then traveling in Europe) one Christmas Eve: "You remember we got Mama a kneeling bench for a surprise Christmas gift. . . . This took about all the money that we three [presumably Ellie, Rachel, and himself] could scrape together, and so we could not give one another any nice presents. I had $40.00 of chicken money, and now I have not a cent left."[39] He seems, indeed, to have been maturing rapidly. "I have quit reading novels for the present," he informed his absent father in the spring of 1872, "and whenever I have spare time I read something for my own improvement."[40] More than once he urges his father to keep a careful diary of his journeys—this for the sake of future historians.[41]

He is interested in politics. At the beginning of the presidential campaign of 1872 he likes Greeley's chances; and he adds that "Mama of course is a Greeley *man*."[42] He went to a session of the Congress: "If it had not lasted so long it would have been very interesting."[43] His comments on the Washington setting are always sensible if sometimes uncomplimentary. The city, he tells his father who has been away for some months, is being rapidly improved with miles of wooden and concrete pavement all over the area.[44] But Washington in late spring is "about the hottest and dullest place in the country."[45]

The General wished his son to be self-reliant. He once instructed Tom—then fourteen years of age—to travel alone by railroad to Des Moines and join his father there. This was to be done under two conditions laid down by the General: first, that Tom should convince his mother that he is man enough to make the trip unchaperoned; and, second, that he return to Georgetown in time for the opening of his classes, since, as the General warns, a good start in learning is everything.[46]

In the late summer of 1871 the boy was given a further chance to exercise his sense of responsibility. He chaperoned Minnie on a trip to their cousin, Mrs. Ellen Denman Lynch, at Syracuse, New York. He was much impressed by the importance of this duty. Poor Minnie, who like a lady never said a word about it, was burdened by her brother with all sorts of unnecessary formal courtesies on the journey. He also despatched to his mother a telegram informing her of their safe arrival. On this visit he had a gay time with his cousin John Lynch, hunting, fishing, and swimming.

Despite the evident effort to act "grown up," the note of the small boy frequently breaks through. He requests his friend Colonel J. C. Audenreid (then traveling with the General in Europe) to "save your small change for my coin collection."[47] He thanks his father for sending them some Spanish candy: "We all like it, but it is so rich that we can only eat a taste at a time."[48] He concludes one of his letters to the General: "Please excuse the trifling nature of my letter. But as the news of the country reaches you by newspapers, and as the girls tell you about the family, all that is left for me is to speak of the horses, the chickens, and myself."[49]

One day in late March, 1872, the General, still in Europe, unburdened himself to his son on the subject of education in general and as relating specifically to Tom. "I am not satisfied," he wrote, "that Georgetown is a college with Professors skilled in teaching modern sciences that in spite of all opposition are remodeling the world, but your Mama thinks Religion so important that everything else must give place to it, and now that you are big enough to think for yourself, you must direct your mind to the acquisition of one class of knowledge or the other."[50]

Logic, mathematics, and the natural sciences, the General believed, embraced knowledge of things and of laws as they actually existed. The languages and moral studies on the other hand, contemplated men and objects "in the artificial situations arrived at by experience or tradition." He felt that the former class of studies should be given the primary place in schools, while moral and religious training should be left to the home. He respected the Catholic religion and had no intention of shaking his son's faith in it. But Tom should leave to others also a free choice in the matter of religion. Though it might be true that the Creator has designed that all should have the same Faith, He Himself has left every man liberty to select his own religion. It was the General's conviction that all religious beliefs, if sincerely held, are equally good.[51]

It was because of this desire of the General's to broaden his son's knowledge in all possible fields that he offered to the boy a splendid opportunity in the summer of that same year. He suggested that Tom should come over alone and join him in Paris in mid-July. As he explained it, "I would ask one of the girls to come but I am pulled and hauled about so that I cannot attend to a lady, but you will not only be able to take care of yourself but of me also."[52]

It was rather an undertaking for a boy of sixteen, but Tom

was enthusiastic. Firmly escorted to New York by his mother and sisters, he embarked on the Cunard liner "Russia" on July 3 and proceeded to enjoy himself on his first ocean voyage. The son of General Sherman was sure to be well taken care of by everyone on the big steamer. Tom had practically the freedom of the whole ship, and was insatiable in his desire to meet and talk with officers, passengers, and members of the crew.

There was a happy reunion with his father in Paris, immediately after which the General announced to Tom that he wished him to take a few days' journey alone to Geneva. This, explained the General, would provide the boy with samples of Swiss lakes and mountains to be treasured in memory. On arrival in the Swiss city, Tom was to inquire for General Caleb Cushing, Mr. Francis Adams, Mr. William M. Evarts, and some other eminent gentlemen.[53]

Tom complied with this plan and again rejoined his father, who remained in Paris, a week later. The General remarked that his son moved amid the new scenes with the utmost self-possession. "I believe," he concluded, "that Tom would be fully capable of traveling all over Europe alone."[54] Indeed, Tom's ardor to see the world was, in one respect, too forward even for the General: "He would be willing even to embark in [sic] dinner parties, but I think it best for him not to associate too much with older people."[55]

As they passed over to London, Tom predicted that the English capital could not possibly please him as much as had the French metropolis. A few days later, they were honored by a visit from Archbishop Manning.[56] The General, who had a sincere respect for all churchmen, was much interested in meeting one whom he termed a great ecclesiastical statesman. The three of them, as they sat there easily in the General's hotel quarters, would have been a fit subject for the Shermans' friend, the painter Healy.[57] Tom's thoughts, as he gazed at the rugged, practical, and sometimes choleric champion of the Church, can only be surmised, but it is not unlikely that for the boy Manning's appeal was that of sheer power, the capacity implicit in the churchman for controlling and dominating large issues. It was a type of mastery that would always fascinate Tom Sherman.

They met the Prince of Wales and Princess Alexandra, who, Tom thought, was very pretty. The General was visited almost to exhaustion by English military and naval personages who would not forego the opportunity of talking with him. He was toasted, dined, and entertained at unconscionable length by the politically great. Tom enjoyed hugely as much of this as his father would let him take.

The General was a stimulating person to travel with, one of his chief traits being a bold and original and, be it confessed, a sometimes dogmatic manner of drawing conclusions from what he saw. He had, for instance, a very positive opinion with regard to the expansionist policy of Imperial Russia: "Tiflis was the old capital of Georgia but now all of the Caucasus . . . are swallowed up by Russia, which bears the same relation to the Old World that the United States does to Mexico, and the truth is that these small states were quarreling and fighting with each other so much that it was a good thing for Russia to absorb them, for now they have good roads, and live in peace instead of eternal war."[58]

A foreshadowing—a very small one—of a future conflict in the Sherman family is suggested by some remarks made by the General towards the end of the trip. Evidently a letter from Mrs. Sherman had made some comparisons between the Catholic and Protestant faiths not very complimentary to the latter. The General made a mild remonstrance: "I don't doubt your sincerity, but only fear that your zeal for your Cause absorbs all the better instincts of your nature and makes you see things through the colored lens you describe for me and others. I have afforded Tom every chance possible to conform to his Religion, and only want him whilst enjoying the widest privileges, not to question the sincerity of others."[59]

On another point, too, the General could not help showing his difference of outlook. Mrs. Sherman had reported the entrance of their niece Eleanor (daughter of General Hugh Ewing) into a convent. This step, observes the General, is quite natural for the girl, since all her education has tended that way. But— "I certainly do not wish [Ellie and Rachel] to follow their cousin into a Convent, but to grow up qualified to make good wives."[60]

The travellers finally embarked for home in mid-September. Tom could say that again in a new and wider sphere he had had more opportunities of meeting eminent people and seeing fresh scenes than usually came to a boy of his age.

Minnie had observed that Tom "dreaded a quiet summer."[61] She was referring to that of 1872, happily featured by the European trip; but this foreboding on Tom's part extended, doubtless, to the June-September period of the following year. Therefore, in the last days of June, 1873, a plan for dispelling summer ennui was formulated by Tom and two of his young friends. They would make, on horseback, a tour of some of the more interesting portions of Maryland and Pennsylvania, with their primary objective being the investigation at close range of a coal mine.

They left Washington on July 3, and would cover about 700 miles before they returned five weeks later.[62] Mrs. Sherman considered the start of the journey as being sufficiently important to be enshrined in an entry in her diary: "W. H. Dennis and Charley Bradley went with him—the former on Minnie's horse

'Roy.' All started from our door. The Bradleys, Bartleys, Evers-fields [?] and Shermans all on the side-walk, some in smiles and some in tears. Sue B, Cumpy and I rode an hour with them."[63]

Their route was through Hagerstown, Altoona, Lockhaven, Wilkes Barre, Mauch Chunk and back to Washington. Sixteen or twenty miles a day was their average rate of progress until Roy developed a sore back and had to be traded—at a pecuniary loss—for what an unsympathetic bystander termed a "moon-eyed" mare. As they passed through Frederick on the Fourth of July they were greeted by the juvenile population, who exploded multitudinous fireworks in their honor. At Lockhaven their caval-cade was mistaken for the advance guard of Van Amburgh's circus that was being eagerly awaited by the inhabitants.

Their sense of observation was sufficiently keen. They were impressed by the fact that almost all over the Pennsylvania countryside buildings were being erected. They were pleasantly surprised to find that they did not encounter on the road "any really abandoned characters." All whom they met had their good qualities and were kindly disposed toward the travelers. They were interested to learn how the Quakers had accidentally dis-covered the value of anthracite coal. The first users of the fuel had tried it in their hearths and found it would not burn. In disgust, they had left it there to smoulder untended—and had found that this was exactly the way to secure excellent results. Tom insisted on telling of Charles Lamb's Chinese, who dis-covered by a somewhat analogous method the virtue of roast pork.

They were awed by what they termed the "omnipresent Pennsylvania railroad." It seemed that everywhere they went the railroad followed or preceded them. No quiet valley, they felt, and no sylvan retreat was safe from its long lines of track and loud screaming locomotives. It was impossible to fly from it in the state. It haunted their very dreams. They had heard strange stories about the great corporation. For example, they were told, the branch which ran from Altoona to the mines at Bellefonte had been erected at the expense of the country people and the owners of the mines. The Pennsylvania Railroad had then assumed possession and now ran the line as part of their general system. Thus, according to the natives, the corporation had secured a paying branch in a locality where it could not afford to build one.

They were induced to reflection by the casual attitude of the Frederick people with respect to the old battlefields around the town: "The sternest lessons of war seem to leave light traces, and are soon forgotten. It is easy to understand how in a few years after the bloodiest contest a nation is ready to plunge into another of equal fury."

Their sense of humor did not desert them. They listened soberly to the farmer who informed them that the land around Muncy, Pennsylvania, was so flinty that when a man died they had to blast a grave out of the rock with dynamite and bring in dirt from the next county to cover the corpse. At a place called Jersey Shore they encouraged (by drinking his beer) a gallant Dutch tavern keeper who was holding out against the local-option dry laws by flourishing both a federal and a state license.

The climax of the trip was their breathtaking descent into a coal mine near Wilkes Barre and an exploration of miles of low, black tunnels underground. For a long time, Tom could not forget the white, stark face of a sixteen-year-old boy in miner's dress at the bottom of the pit.

But the weather was warm and their thoughts were turning toward home. As Tom later remarked, "The novelty of the thing was worn off." Wherefore, on August 9, Mrs. Sherman could note in her diary: "Tommy got home today . . ., having come in by the War Office and stopped to see his father. . . . I missed seeing the party come in. . . . When I drove to my door Tommy came running out to take me in his arms. All very happy."

The fall of 1874 was an important one for the Sherman family. Minnie, who for a long time had been favored by the law of averages, became the wife of Lieutenant Thomas William Fitch, of the United States Navy, in one of the most elaborate weddings ever witnessed in Washington. Mrs. Sherman was determined to show the capital what an imposing affair a Catholic marriage could be. She showed them, indeed.

The Jesuit church of St. Aloysius was crammed with notables. President Grant, most of his official family, generals and admirals in abundance, the diplomatic corps, and eminent folk like the Drexels of Philadelphia, Chauncey DePew, Dr. Orestes Brownson, and many others, graced the occasion. The ceremony was performed by Mrs. Sherman's venerable friend, the 80-year-old Archbishop Purcell, flanked by the leading clergy of the diocese. Bishop Wood of Philadelphia sat in the sanctuary and Archbishop Bayley of Baltimore sent his sincere regrets at not being able to be present. The crown of the occasion was the solemn pontifical Mass, celebrated by the Archbishop.[64]

A. T. Stewart, the New York merchant prince, sent the bride a $1,000 point-lace handkerchief. From the Khedive of Egypt, an old friend of the General, came a gift of a diamond necklace insured for $80,000.

The wedding was front-page news. The Washington *Chronicle* led off with a six-point headline: "Our Minnie: The General's Daughter: The Sherman-Fitch Wedding: Brave Men and Handsome Women: A Gorgeous and Brilliant Display of Bridal Presents."[65] Frank Leslie's *Illustrated Weekly* contributed a full double-page line drawing of the reception. The Philadelphia

Item practically wrote an ode on the Archbishop's appearance: ". . . mitre studded with diamonds and having a large cross of emeralds and rubies. . . . Leans on his golden crozier a grand old shepherd coming forth to bless his flock. . . . Vested in rochet and tunic of rare and old lace; around his neck and depending down his breast was a stole of cloth of gold. On his feet were the sacred sandals. . . ."[66]

An unidentified minstrel named Fritz composed a rhymed commentary that was sung in the streets on the night after the wedding:

> And Grant was there and Phil[67] was there
> And all the sojers in town were there;
> The ladies were there, bedad they were,
> And all had flowers in their hair.
>
> The Priests stood by, all robed and serene,
> And the grandest Archbishop that ever was seen;
> The Pope he wrote that he would have come,
> But important business kept him home.[68]

Tom was one of the groomsmen. When, after the ceremony, he brought to the Archbishop the honorarium of a fifty-dollar gold piece offered by Mr. Fitch, the venerable prelate good-humoredly told him to keep it for himself.[69]

CHAPTER 3

At Yale

THE GRADUATION exercises at Georgetown College in 1874 were marked by their usual splendor. As the Washington *Chronicle* recounted, "The attendance was the largest ever before seen at any of the [Georgetown] commencements, and the glad and smiling faces of the parents [not to mention, of course, the graduates] . . . were pleasant to behold."[70] The young gentlemen who were to receive their degrees were escorted across the campus by the Marine Band and seated conspicuously on the stage in Mulledy Hall. Four of them then proceeded to deliver in dignified succession the addresses of the day. The last orator was Thomas Ewing Sherman of the District of Columbia.

Tom's subject was "Science and Religion." He declared that there was no real conflict between what he termed these two kinds of knowledge. He awarded due credit to the great accomplishments of science, and criticised religious men for their fears that the findings of science would undermine the truths of religion. But, most emphatically, he upheld the claims of religion and theology as being far superior in value to science. The former disciplines dealt with God and man's relations to God. Science, notwithstanding its high worth in its own field, confined itself to infinitely less important matters.[71]

Another feature of Tom's address merits passing attention. It was, in regard to substance, an ordinary school-boy effort. It abounded in sweeping generalizations and was meagre in proofs. But, as it stands today in the Georgetown College archives, it testifies to a virtue that the old conservative college training, with all its defects, undoubtedly possessed. The speech is distinguished by a polish, beauty, and maturity of style that college teachers of today seek vainly, for the most part, in their students. The style of the composition was, for a boy of eighteen, quite remarkable for its correctness and grace.

The current question regarding Tom was, naturally, what would be the next step in his education? There was no outward evidence at this time that he had decided on a future career. The General, if asked, would have probably suggested the law; but the General, apparently, was not being asked.

It was determined, therefore, with Tom's ready concurrence, that he should continue his general, fundamental education. Very important in his father's mind was the necessity of a thorough broad intellectual training as the best possible preliminary to the undertaking of more specialized professional or business studies. Typical, moreover, of the science-oriented views of the eighteen-seventies, this fundamental course must be, the General urged, a scientific one.

As to the particular college to be chosen, the General had no doubts. The new Sheffield School of Yale University was pre-eminent at this time in the field of engineering; and its curriculum comprised, in its early years, an excellent course in general science. Tom would never plump for the engineering profession; but, while making up his mind about his future, what could be better than a solid grounding in what his father considered to be the most essential learning for conditioning and equipping the mind—the empirical and theoretical knowledge of nature and natural processes?

The selection of Yale had for the General another important attraction: the great university would present to his son a further opportunity for association with the kind of young and older men it was so helpful for him to meet. Yale was also an intellectual center where Tom would come into contact with the most vital thought of the day. Georgetown, in the General's eyes, had always been in this respect decidedly provincial.

So, by mid-September, 1874, Tom was settled in a "respectable" boarding house within a short distance of the Sheffield classrooms. (The adjective was applied at that period to any lodging that cost more than twelve dollars per week.) The first letter he received from his father included the reminder that the chief benefit to be gained by his stay at Yale was his association with the young men who would be the future leaders of the country.[72]

Tom seems to have been largely oblivious to the special tenseness in the intellectual and emotional weather of the university at this time. Not only was science elbowing the old humanities out of the classrooms; a more basic struggle was taking place. The old conservative religious tradition, supported by the Scottish "common sense" philosophy was being challenged by the new and dazzling world view of the Spencerians. The contest was dramatized in the sharp opposition between the university president, Noah Porter, and the brilliant head of the economics department, William Graham Sumner. The issue was, can the Christian theology and philosophy be reconciled with the positions taken by Spencer and Darwin? The latter, it seemed, must in the minds of men be awarded precedence. Could there be effected a combination with the old views, or were the latter doomed?

We look in vain for any observations of Tom with respect to this struggle. Apart from a few incomplete attacks he makes on the theory of evolution, he does not refer to the contest that has always been regarded as being the biggest fact on the intellectual scene. The omission tempts one to wonder whether the impact made by Spencer and Darwin at Yale in the 'seventies was as great as the history books claim. His silence—and he was not usually silent about momentous things happening around him—may be a witness to the continuing vitality and strength of the old tradition.

Tom carefully kept his father informed about his studies. He was receiving a good course in quantitative chemical analysis with much laboratory work. In agricultural chemistry he has had a dozen lectures relating to the composition of soils. In another series of lectures in metallurgy he has learned the practical methods of extracting the metal from the iron ore and the processes of manufacturing wrought iron and steel. There was ample instruction in the assaying of all types of ores.[73]

He says that the regular course work requires very little hard studying. Indeed, he would have much time on his hands if he did not undertake some private work of his own. He has been spending many hours in reading the essays of Macaulay and the works of Milton, Cowper, and Thompson. He thought he needed a little poetry to counterbalance the dominantly practical nature of his studies.[74]

The curriculum at Sheffield is, rather surprisingly, not wholly devoted to scientific subjects. Tom is keenly enjoying a course in Shakespearean criticism and one of constitutional history. The liberal arts, it would seem, had not yet completely abandoned the field; or, more exactly, they had not yet been asked definitely to leave.[75]

It is evident that, even with the addition of his self-chosen readings in literature, he feels he has not enough to do. There was, apparently, no driving of students at Yale during this period. Accordingly, before he had been at the university two months he is thinking of supplementing his regular studies with a post-graduate law course! It does not appear that his object in doing this was to prepare himself as a lawyer; he seems merely to be eager to learn something about a field in which he felt an intellectual interest.

He is no uncritical or passive recipient of professional attentions. He tells his father what he does not like about the Yale methods of teaching: "The system of lectures in which we are taught in political economy, constitutional history, and some other studies is very unsatisfactory to me. You are kept in a constant strain writing rapidly to catch what is said, and then there is an unusual amount of mere copying to get the lectures into proper shape to be presented. This copying is not study, and is of very little benefit, while it consumes a great deal of time. Besides, the lectures cannot get over half as much ground as a text book would. Nor can a student pause in a lecture to judge what is important for him to put down."[76] He complains also that the Yale professors do not encourage original thinking in their students.[77]

His proposal of entering the law school (while not dropping any of his other courses) he had first made in October, 1874—as we have already seen. Then, in September, 1875, he brings it up again with his father.[78] It is clear that at this time he has not decided to become a lawyer but only to study some law.[79] It is equally plain that his father is quietly trying to induce him to determine on a law career. If, says the General without seeming to push Tom too much, *if* he wishes to study law he can secure him an excellent place for study in a law office in St. Louis.[80] Meanwhile, urges the General, he should read Blackstone and Kent, both of which are indispensable to a lawyer.[81] Tom steadily declines to commit himself any further than to say he *does* wish to study law. He is still uncertain that he will assume it as a profession. The General, however, talks more and more as if the decision has been made. By early November, 1875, Tom's views on the matter have changed. He has been working hard on Blackstone but feels the need of an instructor, and he wishes to learn more about modern law.[82] He has, apparently, finally made up his mind: he will become a lawyer.[83] There followed an exchange of views between father and son as to the plan to be followed. Tom's wish was that he should enter the law school at Yale and complete his legal course there. His father gently disagreed. The better procedure, thought the General, would be to take one year of legal studies at Yale and then come down to St. Louis and finish his preparation in the law office of their good friend, Col. Henry Hitchcock, and at the Washington University Law School in St. Louis. In this way, Tom would secure a better training. The lecture system at the Yale Law School was inferior to that of Washington University; also, it would be to Tom's advantage later to have studied in the locality where he was to practice as an attorney. To this modification of his original plan Tom at once agreed. He announced to his father in mid-November of the same year: "I will enter the Yale Law School then in [next] February, and without neglecting my regular studies in the Scientific School I will try and keep up with their [the Law School's] Junior Class so that I may be able to enter the Senior [Law School] Class in St. Louis next year.[84] This schedule was actually put into effect; but Tom was a glutton for work. In the following May he will inform his father that, while continuing his graduate work in both the law and scientific schools, he would like also to enter the senior year of the Yale liberal arts course and graduate with them!

He mingled easily with his fellow students and was well liked by them. He referred later to his fellow-boarders as being "as nice a crowd of fellows . . . I ever knew."[85] He would have preferred to live in a dormitory "so as to be more with the fellows." His customary initiative displayed itself in his efforts to establish a debating society among the Sheffield men. The attempt failed, due, he complained, to the stranglehold exercised on college activities by the student secret societies. These organizations he blasted in terms foreshadowing the strictures later to be delivered by Woodrow Wilson at Princeton: "The boys are so divided up into cliques by their miserable little secret societies that nothing open and manly can find any favor among them. I am heartily disgusted with their whole system which prevents good feeling, causes jealousies and bickerings, wastes time and money, and does no good whatever. I am very glad now that I was not foolish enough to join one of these societies."[86] He felt that the societies encouraged "foppish feelings."[87] His participation in sports and exercise was rather meagre and, it would seem, directed by a sense of duty to his health rather than by inclination. He rowed a little and took regular but rather superficial exercise in the gymnasium. That he was only mildly affected by the current enthusiasm for college baseball is hinted by his remark (it would have evoked derision from the legendary Stover) that the game between the Yale and Harvard nines was a "pretty" sight.[88] He loved to attend the theatre. One of his frequent companions in this enjoyment was the future Chief Justice and President, William Howard Taft. Both of them became noted for their loud and wholesome laughs—an accomplishment that induced a theatre manager in New Haven to offer them a fee to sit in the front row three times a week.[89]

He was in constant contact with young men of wealth and considerable social standing, and he frankly tried to keep up with them in dress and expenditure. So much so, indeed, that the General addressed to him some homilies on the dangers of extravagance. These exhortations never named him personally, but they stated universal truths of economy in such suggestive language that Tom caught the point. The General received from his son this careful defense of the latter's position on the question of spending: "I am sorry I am unable to say I will be economical; for I am quite sensible of the fact that none of your boys knows what economy is, as we never have had a chance to earn money, to feel its real value. I am living, as you know, with a dozen fellows who are pretty well off, dress well, and spend quite a good deal. . . . I try not to be extravagant, but between extravagance and economy, it seems to me, there is a long margin. College is a poor place at best to learn economy. . . ." The apologia concluded with a delicate thrust: "When a boy comes with a name and social position that make him generally known he is apt to spend about as much as anybody else."[90]

The General had also warned Tom about "looking on every pretty face as the *only* angel."[91] Tom replied that he had not yet met any angels but had seen plenty of pretty young ladies.[92] He was later to admit that he paid an extra visit to the house of a Doctor White, of New Haven, because of that gentleman's very handsome daughter.[93] There were a few special families near the campus or farther "in town" with whom he became quite friendly. He would love to recall in after years the many happy evenings he spent with the Robinsons, the Ropes and Bremners. He was, without being boisterous, the life of every party or evening "sociable." He was a witty conversationalist, his singing was a delight to any lady accompanist on the piano, and he could talk gravely and interestingly with the older folk. He was not a snob, but he was constantly being reminded of his privileged social position. "You had better call on the President [Grant]," his father instructs him casually, just before one of the young man's brief visits to Washington.[94]

It is clear that at this time the General was much harassed with financial worries. He had been forced to sell his Washington house and to borrow money—"a thing," as he confided to Tom, "I hoped *never* to do."[95] Mrs. Sherman does not share her husband's horror with regard to this necessity and, says the General, "she sometimes thinks me severe when I am outspoken on the point."[96] He is deeply concerned about the high taxes that place such a burden on property holders like himself, and he fears the possibility of a sharp reduction in his Army salary.[97] "I want to prepare in advance for this and therefore want no undue extravagance [on the family's part]," he warns Tom. As the year 1875 draws to a close his pessimism about the country's economic future increases his worry about personal financial prospects: "Do study economy [he writes to Tom], for I see hard times ahead. Things are out of joint and you must observe that the whole Country is effected [*sic*]. It is the reaction from the heavy Expenses and losses of the War. The Nation, States, and individuals borrowed vast sums of money, and pay day is coming. I believe Congress will further reduce the Army, and may include me. Don't breathe a word of this but it is among the probabilities."[98] Implicit, and often frankly stated, in all these forebodings is the fact that he is relying heavily on Tom to help him in carrying the family burdens. More and more, as his son's period of schooling turns toward its conclusion, the General is looking forward to the time when he can place much of the family's financial management into his son's younger—and perhaps more capable—hands. Tom had not been at Yale two weeks before his father struck this note:

I want to give each of the children a good education and the equivalent of $10,000 on starting out on their own hook. This is the best I can promise and it will require economy and self denial on my part to do this! You are now old enough to help me and to understand the Mathematics of the situation.[99]

Not all the General's letters to his son were, however, on this sobering theme. He frequently confided to Tom his thoughts on the great political issues that faced the country. To receive from an eminent General of the Union a severe indictment of the Republican Reconstruction program was of no small advantage to a young student of history.[100] To watch the progress of corruption in the Federal Government through the eyes of an observer on the scene was an excellent opportunity for a young man in Professor Walker's class of political science.[101] In his correspondence with Tom, the General analyzed with great completeness—if with some natural bias—the problems arising from the determination of Congress to reduce the prestige of the Army in times of peace.[102] Close contact of this sort with his father's observations and opinions constituted an important part of his education. Occasionally, too, the General would declare himself on educational theory. One of his early pieces of advice to Tom is somewhat puzzling. He feels that practice in quantitative chemical analysis is useless for a possible law career; but the study of agricultural and mineral chemistry is very helpful for a future lawyer.[103] He approves of Tom's debating society but warns that the oratory of fifty years before is now out of date: "There must [now] be substance without too much flourish. To have something to say and say it clearly and effectively is the oratory of the present day."[104] His educational credo he summarizes thus: "But after all the habit of study and to know where to find specific knowledge when needed is the great object of preliminary education."[105] Tom was to apply well the second part of this injunction; the first part he was never to learn thoroughly.

Tom transmitted some exhortations of his own to his nine-year-old younger brother, Cump. The latter had sent to New Haven a sample of his artistic work—an elaborate painting of a ship that he called the "Warbash." Tom compliments the young artist and apologizes for the slight tear that the "Warbash" had suffered while lying on his desk—"But you know that the more exquisite a painting is, the more delicate any work of art is, the more liable it will always be to meeting with unlucky accidents of this sort. I hope the Warbash can be successfully mended, for it would be a shame to have a leak in such a noble vessel."[106] Cump should practice his reading and writing and should study the insects he finds in the backyard. (Cump, as a matter of fact, was finding more enjoyment in eating them.) He should not, however, adopt the profession of an artist without consulting his father, who might have some objections. He tells Cump of his *humiliation* at beholding the St. Louis University baseball team lose twice to the University of Yale nine.[107] Only rarely does a serious note creep into Tom's letters to his small brother:

There are more girls than boys in the family, so we two boys will have to do our best to keep up the honor of the Sherman name, as the girls will lose that name in due time, as Minnie has done.[108]

Tom continued to show that he was anything but lazy in his pursuit of knowledge. Toward the end of his Junior year in the fall of 1876 he submitted for his father's approval the new plan notable for its daring if not for its practicality: he proposed to enter also the senior class of the liberal arts course in the following year and, while not reducing in the least his other commit

ments, graduate with them in June 1877! He would thus be
carrying, in his last two semesters at college, the scientific course,
the course in law, and the course in the liberal arts.[109] The
General, who—from his military experience—knew when to
draw in his lines, vetoed this plan. But Tom would have tackled
the task with the greatest confidence.

During his last months at Yale, Tom's thoughts were fixed,
naturally, on his graduation day. He was writing a senior thesis
on the very inclusive topic of "Arsenic and Its Relation to the
Law." He would seek to show, in this provocative study, the
lawyer's need in certain cases of a knowledge of poisons and
their effects. He asked his father to suggest some books that
might throw light on the subject. The General, obviously taken
aback by the request, discourages him from "buying several
costly books for a single essay" and suggests that he look for "a
single work that would give the required information."[110] He
adds, in a spirit not always imitated in our day, "I would hardly
call on yr. uncle [Senator] John Sherman except in some extreme case, when the book cannot otherwise be found, for he
ought not to send away books from the Congressional Library."[111]
He also makes the intelligent observation, "I don't see that [the
thesis topic] gives you much room for original thought and
composition, which is generally better than old matter recom-
piled—yet I trust you will make the effort and be satisfactory to
those who will be your judges."[112] In addition to his required
work, Tom is also trying for some prizes. He explains his reasons
for making the extreme effort: "What ambition I have comes
from the fact that I am known as General Sherman's son."[113]

This last stretch of his Yale days may have aggravated a physical affliction that had begun to bother him. Just after the preceding Thanksgiving Day, he had reported to his father that
he was not doing much law reading since he was having diffi-

culty with his eyes.[114] He had repeated the complaint shortly before the Christmas holidays.[115] As a matter of fact, he would be near-sighted for the rest of his life. He was looking forward to going home. "In about two more months," he wrote to Cump in late April, "I will graduate and after that I hope we will not have to be a thousand miles apart during the next few years. . ."[116]

The General, who had never quailed before Confederate gunfire, succumbed to some trepidation as the time of the Examination approached. The ceremonies extended over three days; and, evidently, the General could not get Tom's essay subject out of his mind. He wrote to his son the following careful note: "I understand that your Exercises consist mainly [merely?] in reading [on June 27th] the treatise on Arsenic in its relation to Law, but that the Diplomas are to be conferred in due form on the 29th. If you *really* want me there on the 27th . . . I will try. . . ."[117] Tom could scarcely fail to catch the implicit appeal. However, as it turned out, the General bravely sat through the three days. All the Shermans were very proud of Tom as he received his diploma from the hands of Dr. Porter.

CHAPTER 4

A Change of Plan

Two years after he had left Yale and gone to live in St. Louis, Tom Sherman was guilty of an act that a soldier like his father could never fully forgive; he deserted his post and turned his back brutally on his family. This was the General's verdict on a decision put into effect by his son in the early summer of 1878. What were the circumstances that persuaded the devoted father to this harsh judgment?

In the summer of 1876 the family fortunes were in a precarious state. The General was Chief of the Army and was living in Washington with his wife and the younger children. Ellie and Rachel were still boarders at the Visitation Convent; Lizzie was at school in New York; little Cump was not yet in his teens. Minnie and her husband were occupying the family house in St. Louis, and with them was Tom.

The financial worries which had plagued the General for several years were greatly increased. The heavy taxes that were burdening the whole country were practically drying up the income from rents on which he depended essentially for the support of his dear ones. His living expenses, including the high costs of the entertainments and other social activities his official position required him to sponsor or share in, were beyond his margin of safety. Moreover, the determination of Congress to reduce the size of the Army and to cut the salaries of Army officers was threatening to choke off his basic source of livelihood.

As he sat uneasily in his office in the War Department during those two years and thought of what might happen to the wife and children he loved so passionately, and for whom he felt a responsibility that rode him day and night, the heart of William Tecumseh Sherman felt real trepidation. The months went on, and the future grew progressively more dark. Each month, as taxes rose and as he felt his official status less and less secure, the way out of his financial impasse seemed more and more impossible to find. Aggravating his situation was another kind of family crisis. Minnie and Mr. Fitch were manifesting some traits that no one had ever anticipated. Soon after Minnie's marriage there had been a minor dispute concerning the fabulous necklace sent by the Khedive. Mrs. Sherman had insisted that the diamonds should be divided equally among Minnie and her sisters. Minnie had sharply and most surprisingly objected, but had finally yielded; everybody believed that the squabble was over. Now, in the spring of 1877, when, as a necessary anchor to windward, the General wished the Fitches to maintain the St. Louis house, Minnie was determined to abandon it and set up housekeeping on her own.[118]

One bright ray of light, or—to change the metaphor—one strong support for the General at this dark period was his eldest son. Tom had come down from New Haven in late June, 1876, and had set himself up as a paying guest with the Fitches in St. Louis. Within two weeks he was managing, like an experienced hand, all his father's business affairs, while at the same time he was studying law in the office of Col. Hitchcock and at Washington University. He administered with a sure touch and practical wisdom far beyond his years his father's properties in St. Louis and elsewhere. All questions of rents were under his control. "Do the best you can with the Shidy place," his father instructs him in the fall of 1876, "and if you can find a tenant do so on your own judgment and dispense with the Land Agent, who is always a Nuisance."[119] He took care of all tax payments. On the basis of his close observation of the market he successfully dissuaded the General from selling some of the family real estate holdings.[120] He kept in close touch with his father's banking operations and frequently advised him on interest rates with a view to cautious speculative ventures. He was on the alert, too, for any good opportunity for speculation in land.[121] The General urges him to "experiment" with the properties in St. Louis—"The same causes which exist there exist everywhere in the U.S. . . . Now property is low, and everybody who has money puts it in Bonds and Mortgages; but soon these too will fail and then property will rise."[122] The family insurance policies, the premiums on which the General sometimes forgot to pay, were finally placed in his son's care.

The General came to depend more and more on Tom. If a tenant was in default with rent, it was Tom who determined whether the delinquent was to be pushed or carried along. If some cash was needed urgently, it was Tom who negotiated with the bank. If a quick purchase of realty or anything else had to be made, Tom put it through in his own way. All problems of maintenance and improvements of the family properties were left in his capable hands.[123] When a family squabble threatened over the disposition of the old St. Louis house, Tom was the umpire who made the ultimate determination.[124] Again and again the General uses the phrase in his letters to Tom: "You may do what you please . . . always sure that I will approve of anything. . . ."[125] And all this Tom seemed to be thoroughly enjoying. He had always had an intense and far more than ordinary love for his mother and sisters and small brother. Now he was actively showing his affection by protecting their helplessness.

Indeed, relatively helpless—or, at least, in need of considerable help—they were. His mother was now aging and ailing. Ellie, Rachel, and Lizzie were still mere teen-age girls, while Cump was a boy of twelve years. The General, never adept at handling money, was held down in Washington by his official duties. Congress, he confided to Tom, was bent on reducing the Army establishment and cutting officers' salaries. If this policy was triumphant the General would be severely pressed to support his family. Bitterly he wrote to Tom, "It is simply shameful that our pay and our Army organization should depend on the very men we whipped 12 years ago. Such however is the measure of a Representative Government."[126] High taxes, furthermore, were so lowering property owners' profits as to render real estate almost a liability.[127] Insecurity and lack of confidence was a constant feature of the money market. "The Country is full of trouble," declared the General, "and no one can say what he will do to others, until he knows what others will do for him. I don't know if my April notes will be paid, and until I do I will resolve on nothing."[128] But, with Tom at his side, the future could be faced with courage. "I can manage here [in Washington]," the General wrote to him, "with you all established in St. Louis, till the date of Retirement, 62 years of age, now only 5 years off. Meantime you also will be firmly established in business. . . . There is not a Shadow of doubt of your professional success in due time. . . ."[129] "By moderate industry, faithful attention to details, you may become early in life a lawyer of repute, and moderately prosperous."[130] There was, indeed, every outward indication that Tom was enthusiastic about his legal studies and that he was looking forward to a career at the bar: "As for my studies, I am more and more interested in them."[131] Again he says, in February, 1878, ". . . I appreciate the fact that I will have to keep steadily at work in future, at least for a number of years."[132] "Our studies [in the Hitchcock law office] progress regularly and steadily," he tells his father just before Christmas, 1876; "I have very little to do at the office except study my regular lessons, and Mr. Hitchcock is very kind in helping us [students] and explaining doubtful points."[133] Each morning a specific amount of reading is assigned by Mr. Hitchcock, usually from forty to fifty pages. In the afternoon at four o'clock the students are questioned on this material. Tom manages also to insert into his daily schedule an hour of study in history.[134] He has an understanding with Ellie that he is not to be called on for escort duty, "since parties and the law would hardly agree."[135] He certainly speaks as if he intends to make St. Louis his home for many years to come. He was trying to hold on to the family's old St. Louis house by temporarily renting it: "My feeling in giving it up was this, that I was giving up a present enjoyment for the sake of future happiness, for, living in St. Louis, I shall always look forward to the time when some part of the family or the whole family will be gathered into the old house."[136] Another trait of his thinking at this time is evident; notwithstanding his large independence in acting for the family he maintains his deep respect for his father's wishes. "Whatever our council of war determines upon [about living arrangements for the future]," he assures his father, "we will of course do nothing definite without notifying you and having your sanction."[137] All circumstances considered, the General might indeed comfort himself with the conviction that his son was settled in his life work.

Then, in mid-May, 1878, came the bombshell: Tom announced to his parents that he would enter the Jesuit novitiate. To his father he had given not the slightest warning. The extent of Mrs. Sherman's foreknowledge is doubtful. The General's reaction was at first one of stark disbelief. When he finally realized that his son was in earnest, his grief, anger, and bafflement scarcely knew bounds. There was a brief and stormy scene with Tom, and a last-ditch appeal by the General to his old friend, Cardinal McCloskey of New York. When the latter supported Tom's position the afflicted father dropped all protests and accepted the blow from which he would never fully recover. "He was the keystone of my Arch," the General declared later, "and his going away lets down the whole structure with a crash."[138] To his daughter Minnie he confided:

Tom's course . . . has embittered me more than I ought to write. I try to check my feelings against him personally but cannot against the cause of his action, the Catholic Church. I realise that all I held most dear and whom I have tried hard to provide for liberally are not mine, but belong to a power that heeds no claim but its own; who takes unfeelingly . . . my son whom I had trained to assist me in the care of a large and expanding family.[139]

Her brother, he told Ellie, who should have been her help and protector, has "shrunk into a Cloister."[140] On the eve of Tom's departure to England (where he would make his noviceship) his father had declared: "If Tom sails tomorrow he leaves us forever and casts his lot among those with whom I can have no intercourse."[141] In more systematic fashion the General explained his attitude in a letter to his friend, Major Henry Turner:

I don't want to hold anybody to my standard, and I don't suppose I am always right, of course you and I look at Tom's case from an entirely different standpoint. You can and do believe that God reveals His will to man on earth, and that when he does man must and should act accordingly, that what Tom called a vocation was such a call, and that his only duty was to obey. With such a faith, the conclusion is logical and sound. But I don't believe that at all. I believe God governs this world, with all its life, animal, vegetable and human, by invariable laws, resulting in the greatest good, though sometimes working seeming hardships. The idea of a vocation from God seems to me *ir*religious and I would look for the inspiration of a vocation in the opposite quarter (the Devil). When anybody assumes "vocation" their reason & all sense ceases and man becomes simply a blind animal. My idea of God is that He has given man reason, and he has no right to disregard it. I believe Tom could serve his God and his Church better at St. Louis than shut up in a Cloister in England. I think he owes his own sisters Ellie and Rachel the attention & duty which a brother alone can give at this period of their lives. I think he owes me some return for the time, money & affection I have bestowed upon him and to have deferred action until I could have reconciled my feelings & plans of life. Therefore I fear Tom has committed a sin so great in the eyes of God that no amount of penance can possibly wipe it away. By acts of positive goodness, action—and not penalty—he may make amends.[142]

What were Tom's feelings as he made the most crucial decision of his life? Such queries halt before the impenetrable barriers of a man's most secret thoughts. In the first place, he must have been fully aware of how his act would appear to his father. If he had struck the General in the face he would not have hurt him as much. It was, in the General's eyes, sheer treason—Tom, though he might rightfully sacrifice himself, could not rightfully throw off his duties to others.[143] "Why," cried the distraught father in his agony, "should he desert me thus, and leave me convinced that his whole life had been a deception?"[144] Also, loving those dear ones as the young man did, so intensely, and realizing as he did their very real helplessness without him, what emotions must have torn Tom's heart? To Minnie, who may have been his favorite sister, he bared his soul: "I felt overwhelmed by Papa's grief. . . . My step seems rash and hasty to all who do not know what it is to watch and wait and hope and pray and doubt and despair until a young heart grows old and can face anything to attain its object—especially when that object is God."[145]

Mrs. Sherman related how he broke the news to his sisters: "He seemed to feel so badly at seeing . . . Lizzy cry, and dreaded so that Ellie would cry that I told her last evening. . . . You will never know how much he suffered."[146] His mother could see him "falling away in flesh and strength day by day."[147] What were the motives that could override these powerful pulls? "We can have no will," he would write to his mother years later, "than that of our Heavenly Father."[148] From the novitiate he elaborated on his motives to Minnie:

> People in love do strange things. . . . Having a vocation is like being in love, *only more so,* as there is no love so absorbing, so deep and so lasting as that of the creature for the Creator. What a grand thing it is always to be as it were shooting straight at one's mark, living every hour, performing every action in direct preparation for the great hereafter.[149]

Perhaps, in the last analysis, the answer to all these questions is simple: he was trapped—splendidly trapped—by an ideal that his father himself had taught him—that a soldier and a soldier's son should devote himself without reserve to the leader with the right to command him.[150]

It must be conceded that Tom handled the matter, at least in its preliminary and critical stages, in a strange way. As he admitted afterward, "The plain truth is I had no common sense in me at the time."[151] His mother he told of his great decision only two or three days before he informed his father.[152] But his attitude could be blamed on broader grounds. On his own plain testimony his decision to be a Jesuit had been reached "conclusively," as he put it, in the spring of 1874. This had happened while he was at Georgetown College. He had then gone to Yale, agreed to all his father's plans for a legal career, and completed his law course at St. Louis. Not once had he given any indication of his real aims in life. On the contrary, he had consistently spoken and acted as if he was firmly determined to be a lawyer. In 1877 he had expressed his hopes of living in St. Louis for several years more. He had habitually referred to the prospect of practicing law there for the indefinite future. When twitted by his father for attentions to several young ladies, he had parried by assuring the General that it was "too early" for him to consider marriage, and that when he did so he would consult his father's wishes. This was, by any standard, ingenuous.

Up until a month before he announced his decision he was actively directing the family business affairs and launching business plans that would fructify only in the following year or even later. "I shall be slow I hope in taking any step that might possibly add to your cares and burdens," he had assured his father.[153] And he had added: "I know that I should be very ungrateful to Providence and to you if I did not appreciate the many advantages I possess, in having my time free for study, in having a charming home and abundance of everything that a man could want; and I assure you I am as happy and contented as I ever want to be."[154] It is indeed difficult to reconcile this assertion with his statement of June 4, 1878 that he had been waiting and hoping and praying and doubting and despairing during the past four years. Then suddenly, without warning, in mid-May, 1878, he dropped everything. His father, as we have seen, accused him of deception. Whether the charge was true or not, it is easy to understand how the General could make it. A saint might suggest a solution for this puzzle of a young man's motivation. The value of God and the things of God (the saint might say) are superior to anybody or anything else in existence; but to make men understand this is one of the most difficult tasks in the world. Only, perhaps, by such an agonizing wielding of the knife against those he loved so immensely could Tom Sherman act out this truth.

Since he had been ordered to make his noviceship at Roehampton, England, he sailed from New York on June 5, 1878.[155] A little less than six years before, he had embarked from the same port to meet his father in Paris.

CHAPTER 5

The Noviceship

"PEOPLE IN LOVE do strange things. . . . Having a vocation [for the priesthood] is like being in love, *only more so*, as there is no love so absorbing, so deep and so lasting as that of the creature for the Creator."[156] This observation, written by Tom Sherman a few months after his arrival in England, was part of an effort to explain his sudden decision in the spring of 1878. But it was more than that: it suggested the main objective of the Jesuit noviceship. The theory is that if a man has caught the fascination of Christ the problem of sanctity is more than half solved. There must be, of course, in the noviceship, a rigorous training in asceticism. But if Christ has captured a man's heart the practice of the ascetical virtues will inevitably follow.

The purpose of the noviceship is to begin the formation of the kind of Jesuit which St. Ignatius of Loyola has described in what he called the "Sum and Scope" of the rules of the Society: "Men crucified to the world and to whom the world itself is crucified . . . new men . . . who have put off their own affections so that they may put on Christ." The attainment of this high end is sought for particularly by means of the "Long Retreat," the thirty-day period of seclusion and strict silence during which the novice "undergoes" the *Spiritual Exercises* of St. Ignatius. These *Exercises* are much more than a series of meditations. They comprise a profound soul-searching in the light of the life and character of Christ, a whole-hearted effort to inflame one's soul with a passionate personal love for Christ and a boundless enthusiasm for His cause.[157]

One of the central points of the *Exercises* is the meditation called "The Kingdom of Christ." It seeks to evoke, on the part of the exercitant, a total offering of himself to the Divine Leader and the quest for souls. We may speculate as to how Tom Sherman would take the challenge that St. Ignatius puts before him: "But those who wish to show themselves as pre-eminent in the service of the Divine King will not only offer themselves totally to the work but, by acting against their own sensuality and against their love of the flesh and of the world, will make an offering of higher value and greater moment." The oblation is then specified as follows: "O eternal Lord of all things . . . I affirm that it is my will and desire and firm determination . . . to imitate You in bearing all injuries and all vituperation and all poverty. . . ."

One might suppose also that Tom Sherman, as he was at this time, would not quail at the final self-abnegation demanded by the *Exercises:* "Take, O Lord, and receive, all my liberty, my memory, my intellect and all my will, whatever I have and possess. All of them You gave me; to You all of them I restore. They are all Yours; dispose of them as You will. Only give me Your love and grace; these are sufficient for me."

To the noviceship routine Tom made his adjustment quickly and easily. It all took place in the Roehampton building that looked like, as indeed it was, an English country house stripped clean, within and without, for action of a sort not usually occurring in English country houses. (The oak panelling of the great hall and the rich woodwork of the stairways had been, after some discussion by the Jesuit superiors, retained. From the walls and ceilings of what had been the dining room of the mansion had been deleted the realistic paintings of Angelica Kauffman, after no discussion whatever. The Roehampton house, dismantled and reduced to a subdued key, suggested a sporting duke converted to piety and attired in sober garb.)

There were special reasons why Tom's adaptation to the new life might not have progressed so smoothly. In the first place, he was not a malleable boy, but a mature man with formed habits. The necessary regimentation and restraint and the continual submission to orders might have been expected to constitute for him particular hazards.

The contrary, however, was the fact. Here his affection for the military ideal aided him. He regarded the noviceship as a period of training for a new and higher type of soldier's life. "My position now," he wrote to his mother, "quite corresponds to that of the cadet in the army."[158] He used a military phrase to describe the filling up of the noviceship roster: "We have had several new arrivals. . . . Christ's army is rapidly recruiting."[159] A basic part of the soldier's code is obedience and self-control. The principles and practices of Roehampton, in accord with this philosophy, struck a familiar and agreeable note in Tom's soul.

One of his first letters to home described his general condition as estimated by himself: "I am in good health and first rate spirits, feeling cheery about all things." In spite of the fogs and rains, he liked the climate: "It is bracing and mild in summer, and [he adds significantly] the soft light I find very agreeable to the eyes."[160]

By his fellow-novices he was looked on as one of the most likeable and gayest of companions. He was the wit and chief entertainer at the novitiate picnics, and a generous contributor to the physical labors required for such outings. He never lorded it over his younger companions, yet they found his conversation, enriched by his experience, fascinating and instructive. A democratic trait he would always possess revealed itself in his delight in talking (at the proper time and under the proper circumstances) with the coadjutor brothers, those members of the Order who were not destined for the priesthood but for other essential offices.[161]

He was appointed special guide—or "angel," as the noviceship term was—to the newly arrived Henry Van Rensselaer, from New York City.[162] It was good to have another Yankee to talk to about the latest news from one's country. The two of them discussed also—with due charity and tolerance, of course—the linguistic and other idiosyncrasies of their English fellow-novices. The latter, as Tom generously remarked, had probably much to be amused at in the Americans' manners.[163]

To his directors he was gladly and affectionately submissive, and, in regard to the observance of rules, he was meticulous. The novices were required, outside of times of recreation and a few other occasions, to address each other in Latin. This prescription applied even to mealtime unless special permission was granted to speak in English. Far from regarding the obligation as onerous, Tom derived a particular amusement from his own and his companions' not always successful efforts to translate such terms as beefsteak and apple dumplings.

Roehampton had a compact truck garden, known as the Wall Garden, tended by the novices. This work Tom liked best. It reminded him of his fruit orchard at home in Washington in the summers of 1869-1874. On holidays the novices disported themselves in various simple but thoroughly enjoyable ways. "Villa" day was the term applied to a holiday when the young men adjourned to various picnicking spots in Richmond Park, immediately adjoining the novitiate, and indulged there in mild relaxations. Cricket was one of the institutions of the English that appealed to the internationalist in Tom. He soon learned to play it passably well.

Tom's deepest reaction to the noviceship was summed up in the observations he had made to his mother on the eve of the Long Retreat. While he had been referring specifically to the thirty-day trial of prayer and self-reformation, he might have been speaking of the two years as a whole:

Tomorrow begins our long retreat, part of which consists of a careful drawing out of the life of our Redeemer, which is made as real as possible in order to prepare us for the long years of patient labor we young Jesuits have to go through simply as a preparation—years which may not unfittingly be compared to the years spent in the carpenter shop at Nazareth. At the end of ten or twelve years of preparation the Jesuit again makes the *Exercises* before entering on the ministry, but in the meantime he keeps looking back at his long retreat, drawing from it many lessons of obedience, patience, humility and the many virtues that are so much needed to sustain the soul in religious life. You may imagine, my dear Mother, with what feelings I am looking forward to this grand spiritual experience, and you know how much I trust to your good prayers to help me well through this, at once the grand trial and the great cause of happiness in the life I have undertaken."[164]

One slight worry bothered him: his eyes had been giving him trouble for at least the past four years, and by this time he was quite near-sighted. The defect had forced him to reduce the length of his reading periods at Yale and while studying in St.

Louis. The ailment was not serious, but it would be for him a constant minor preoccupation.

Tom's noviceship duties lessened not at all his affection for the dear ones at home and his interest in all their affairs, large and small. His letters to his mother are, after the fashion of novices, quite "spiritual" in tone. He wishes her, in his Yuletide letter of 1878, not only a Merry Christmas but a joyous one— "for which I know that the pleasures you will long for that day and which I shall beg God to reign [sic] upon you, will be all interior and hidden. Joy in union with the divine heart of the Infant Saviour and in the hope of that never ending Christmas when we hope to stand in his unveiled presence, united with Willie and Charlie and all the loved ones gone before, singing praises for all eternity before Him Who came to show us the way by living a hard, plain, prosy, dull, and suffering existence."[165] The lighter touches, however, he does not neglect. His sister Ellie's social triumphs give him great satisfaction: "Tell her I fully expect to hear of her making more than one convert out of her numerous conquests of this winter, and if she does not I shall lose all confidence in her charms."[166] He wants Lizzie to know that *he enjoyed making her Southern trip with her*—a reference to her recent visit to friends below the Mason-Dixon line.[167] Cump had written him a letter that expatiated on the virtues of the capacious Sherman backyard. "How consoling a thing in life to have a fine backyard!" Tom comments to his mother; "we must have marriages and deaths to split up families, but provided junior members have fine back-yards to exercise in. surely life cannot be said to be without its joys. Cump has heard perhaps that silence and control of the tongue is a virtue of people in religious life, and he is both philosopher and Christian in apportioning the length of his letter to my vocation. . .".[168] He gives Cump an account of a trip he had made to the famous preparatory school at Eton where they saw the boys wearing their stovepipe hats and very short coats.[169] Minnie and her children are much in his thoughts. "You may be sure," he writes to her, "I visit in fancy the Windsor flats [where they were now living] not unfrequently, and see Willie and Eleanor playing about the nursery, Tommy in his cradle and their sweet mother busy with her needle. But my visits, even in fancy, are very brief ones, and as for giving any substantial evidence of them in the shape of letters—you might as well expect Will [her husband] home in time for dinner as expect a Jesuit novice to write letters often; and both Will and the novice have good excuses for tardiness—he because he is working hard for you and the little folks, I because in the service in which I have enlisted one expects to be always kept busy and never to have one's way either."[170] He is anxious to know how Minnie likes the society of St. Louis: "There is a difference, I fancy, between the *Matron* in society and the winters of '69, '70."[171]

On his clear horizon at this time the one dark cloud was his continued estrangement from his father. He confided to his mother after he had been at Roehampton four months: "I spoke with Fr. Rector about Papa's having forbidden me even to write to him; and Fr. Rector seemed to think I ought not to accept such a prohibition, but should write occasionally notwithstanding. What do you think about it? My feeling is that it would only irritate Papa to hear from me, and would do no good. In justice to me, however, I think Papa would read something about the Jesuits, and I want you to get him Fr. Ravignan's work on the Institute of the Society. You would no doubt be interested in the book yourself, and perhaps it would be better if you should read it first and then give it to Papa, telling him I want to have him read it so that he may know what sort of life I have embraced, and what are the motives, aims, and hopes of the Jesuit. He will soon feel that I am not the tool of others in any other sense than the military one."[172] (Tom was constantly to stress to his father this latter point: he was, as a Jesuit, under the orders of other men, but it was the kind of subordination that should be familiar and even congenial to a military man.) His policy of not sending any letters to the General Tom modified as the months went on. He tells Minnie in the early spring of 1879 that he has ventured to write to his father but has little hope of receiving an answer: "It is my intention to keep on writing occasionally to him, knowing that eventually he will soften in his feelings towards me, as time dims the remembrance of the disappointment and sorrow caused by my so sudden and unexpected announcement."[173]

What would have been, probably, the main lines of the profile that, as the period of training drew to a close, the Master of Novices at Roehampton might have made of Brother Thomas Ewing Sherman? The estimate, we may speculate, would be something like this: "An ardent idealist. The concept of Christ the Supreme Leader and that of the Kingdom of Christ appeal to him as inspiriting motives he has always dimly felt. A natural leader among his fellow-novices; he draws them gently along with him, never dominates but always smoothly persuades them. Universally liked and greatly respected by the novices. As to humility, all that could be desired. Feels a special satisfaction in obedience. He is a man of prayer.

"We would like him a little less tense. He does not seem to anticipate any difficulties in the religious life and may be too much shocked and cast down by them when they come. He is still, of course, in his 'novice's fervor' which, while a desirable stage of his spiritual progress, keeps him in rather a rosy and joyous haze—or daze. Just now he finds everything so easy! He has an unusually developed imagination. He says he has no consuming desire for a life of study, but recognizes its importance for his future apostolic work. He is probably better fitted for an active apostolate among people than for the life of a student or teacher. He has exceptional ability as a speaker."

To this analysis some additions may be made. Tom had developed a keen sentiment of loyalty to the Jesuit Order. He had always had an unusual facility for arousing in himself an intense devotion to any group or organization in which he found himself. This inclination it was that had caused him particularly acute suffering when a few months before he had felt himself obliged to sever his immediate ties with his family. As he learned more about the great history and traditions of the Society of Jesus, and became intimately acquainted with the spirit of gallantry and selflessness that distinguished the Company at its best; as he recalled, on the very English soil where they had acted out their splendid drama—the martyr-priests Campion, Southwell, and the others—he was thrilled at the honor of belonging to the same shock troops of Christ, as he was wont to call the Society. Much of the powerful love he had felt for his family, and much of the deep pride with which he had regarded it he transferred to what, in his mind, was a knightly band of priest-fighters for Christ.

But, in evaluating his spiritual development at the point it had reached in 1880, was there anything to be said on the debit side? The answer must be in the affirmative. His military concept of the religious life may have been tinged with a great deal of unreality. After all, that life does simply not have the same type of glamor and thrill that marks the military life, under some of its aspects and in some circumstances. He may not have ever faced the question, How shall I act when ordered to do work that seems to me to have no relation to a gallant crusade for Christ and souls? How well can I live this life when it becomes at times, to use the terms he applied to the life of Our Lord, "plain, dull, humdrum?" The fact is that during his noviceship he was never crossed by a superior. How would he take it when the opposite situation should arise? Nor in his noviceship was he ever given a task that he really disliked; the whole idea of the noviceship was congenial to him. How would he act when, later, he would be told to do work that he very much disliked? Furthermore, he had always been a proud young man. To what extent was he deceiving himself when he declared so confidently in the meditation on the Two Standards that he wished to be looked down on by all for the sake of Christ?

The period of his noviceship drew to its close. He would soon be returning to America; and not the least of his joys as he looked forward to the next stage of his life as a Jesuit was a bettering of his relations with his father. He was able to tell his mother in early May, 1880, that he had received a "nice" letter from the General. "Please thank him for me," he urges her. "It gave me great comfort as it was much milder in tone from the last one I received. I shall write again soon but not as often as you suggested. I really think letters stir up the old disappointment, but I feel that I must get one [off?] before returning to America. . . . I thank God things are not as bad as I feared."[174] A month before leaving England he wrote thus to his father:

My dear Papa: I was very much pleased at the receipt of your last letter because it showed me that I had misunderstood or exaggerated what you had said in previous letters, and that I need not have been so timid about writing again. I have received my orders for next year and . . . am to go to Woodstock in Maryland to make up my Philosophy [studies]. . . . I shall . . . reach Washington about August 25th. Mama has invited me to make her a visit, and I am quite in hopes you will be in Washington then and that I may catch a glimpse of you. . . .[175]

He reached New York in late August. His home-coming senti-ments he expressed in a letter to Minnie: "How delightful it is to be in one's own country again. I liked England very much but America much better."[176] The visit to his father in Wash-ington came off beautifully: "Papa has let his grand heart get the best of past disappointment, received me most affection-ately, and shows no signs of displeasure. I have taken my meals at the hotel with him, am staying at the house, just rode with him to the Smithsonian, and would even be going to the Circus with him tonight if he was not taking a party of young girls, with whom of course a young religious could hardly go. In a word we are good friends again, and that is a great happiness to both of us."[177] He picked up Rachel from the Visitation school and travelled with her to the family's summer home at Altoona, Pennsylvania, where there was a joyous reunion with his mother and sisters and Cump. Before leaving for Woodstock he could not resist writing again to his father:

My dear Papa: I cannot let you cross the continent before send-ing my thanks for the pleasant visit I had in Washington, and your kind reception of me, which I had no right to expect! I could not help seeing that it cost an effort on your part to overcome the repug-nance my strange dress naturally excited, and I can't tell you how gratified I was to find that your generous affection had the upper hand so entirely. . . . You know that my heart is in my calling and that I care very little now for what the *world* says or thinks, but the assurance I have that we are good friends again is a thing I confess I craved for and prayed for and so I feel at this moment that my keenest earthly desire has been satisfied.[178]

The General's attitude had certainly warranted these relieved feelings on Tom's part. Yet the wound was still in the General's heart. Tom, in the midst of his joy at his cordial reception, had remarked that his father was "quieter in manner towards me than he ever was before, at least so it seems to me."[179] To Minnie the General revealed the still-smoldering embers of his repugnance to his son's course: "Tom is in fair good health and still is on probation. I understand he is under orders of the Chief Jesuit at St. Louis and I suppose the Order provides for him. He is to go to some college in Maryland called Woodstock. It is simply amazing to me that a young gentleman with such possibilities should voluntarily subject himself to such an obsolete and worn out old order of priests. It has been abolished in about every Catholic country."[180] Mercifully the General had now concealed these sentiments from his son. So Tom could say to his father as he set off for Woodstock, "I shall go to my studies with a light and cheery heart after the delightful visits I have paid to you and the rest of the family."[181]

CHAPTER 6

The Spirit of Woodstock

ALTHOUGH IT POSSESSED a few of its own special tonalities, the seminary in the meadows of Baltimore County, Maryland, was substantially like other institutions of its kind. It was an advanced training school for aspirants to the priesthood, in the spirit of Jesuit ideals.

A minor but pervading note in the atmosphere of the college is important for its relevance to the Tom Sherman story. The young seminarians were marked by a profound sense of *esprit de corps,* the realization of their being bound closely and affectionately to each other in a spiritual enterprise of the highest worth.

Almost everything they did was calculated to induce this sentiment of deep togetherness. They rose together at 5:00 A.M., made their hour's meditation or mental prayer, and together went to the altar to receive Holy Communion. Together they sat in class; together they walked to meals; they went on their holiday excursions or played their games together; together, even though separated by the walls of their rooms, they studied at their desks at stated hours; they knelt together in the half-darkened chapel just before bed-time; and, in the unique night-hush at Woodstock after 10:00 P.M. when only the crickets and an occasional long-drawn-out train whistle could be heard, the whole House laid itself down to sleep together—the small compact group (less than 200) of earnest men whose devotion to a common spiritual ideal and whose common ambitions had made them a close-knit family, joined together, as the Jesuit rule-book said, in the charity of Christ.

It is a valid surmise that this profound spirit of fraternity Tom Sherman never imbibed. The failure was not due on his part to any conscious or deliberate fault. Indeed, he conscientiously followed every rule, gave himself generously to Woodstock life in most of its aspects, was a good companion, and yielded to none in his affection toward the Society of Jesus. His spiritual life, with an exception to be noted, was beyond reproach. What, then, was his deficiency that caused him to miss the wholesome contagion of the Woodstock spirit?

From his earliest years Tom Sherman had been formed to think and act in large terms. His environment had always been the nation, the greatest war of the nineteenth century, and the most eminent personages of his time. He had joined the Jesuit Order in the conviction that he was, in so doing, embarking on a spiritual campaign that was momentous and, of course, in this he was correct. The difficulty was, however, that in fixing his eyes so intensely on the crusade, and placing it so constantly in the setting of national and world political and social forces, he could not appreciate such apparently lesser values as a fraternal feeling linking a band of seminarians. He never fully conquered, despite his undoubtedly sincere efforts to be a good Jesuit student, an impatience at what he regarded as a not highly important period of mere preparation for his real work for Christ.

We see him almost painfully arguing with himself that this long preparatory period is necessary and that he must not wish to hurry toward the goal of active ministry. But his self-admonitions in this regard never seem fully to convince him. Hence any strong realization of the affectionate tie that bound himself and his fellow-scholastics together was, for the most part, lost on him. To this criticism he would probably have answered, in very sincere surprise, that such a realization was a luxury to which, amid his ambitious planning ahead of work for Christ, he had never adverted.

Tom himself has described the general aims and character of the three-year course of philosophy at Woodstock. "My principal study here," he informed his father, "is rational philosophy, beginning with a thorough drill in logic which is helped by a review of pure mathematics. Our lectures, recitations, and disputations in logic are in Latin. . . . Every definition is well weighed, every proposition brought to the crucial test of being proved by plain syllogisms, and so, slowly and patiently, beginning with the simplest and most evident principles, just as in Geometry, we try to build up the house of human knowledge and to refute sophists, transcendentalists, etc. It is a capital training for the mind. I already begin to feel the beneficial effect of having to prove my assertions. . . ."[182]

A later scholar has explained in more detail the rationale of these studies, with particular relation to philosophy. What is sought, he says, is knowledge that is integrated. When knowledge has this quality it is also profound. One sees deeply into a truth when one sees it in its relationships to other truths, in all its premises and conclusions, in all its applications to life. A deep knowledge, therefore, is of its nature wide, well nourished by fact, well structured into a system of knowledge. Actually, therefore, the Jesuit theory does not condemn a wide knowledge, but only a knowledge that is scattered and disorganized. The means employed at Woodstock for achieving this academic ideal is the so-called Scholastic method. This latter does not mean the "mysterious art of correctly contradistinguishing the minor of a hypothetical syllogism, both of whose premises are negative propositions." It is, rather, a technique for the pursuit of organized knowledge through the natural human method of collaboration of mind with mind, and the clash of mind upon mind. It is the pursuit of truth by the combined activity of professor and pupil, and of pupil and pupil. Collaboration and clash are of the essence of the method. These take place, first, in the classroom (referred to, cutely, as clashroom), where the first element of the technique comes into play—the method of questioning (*methodus quaestionis*). The collaboration and clash are continued outside—the interior wrestling with authors and with one's own difficulties in private study, then the collaboration of informal discussion, then the clash of disputation, and finally the collaboration and clash of communal research in the seminar.[183] Obviously, the procedure is, in the broad sense, scientific. There is, when it is used properly, nothing narrow or exclusively dogmatic about it.

For the implementation of these objectives there were, during Tom Sherman's 1880-1883 sojourn at Woodstock, some professors who were only average in ability, method of teaching, and professional knowledge, and a few who were really great.[184] From her beginnings in 1869, when the college had been only a large barracks-like structure on a slight rise of land in the Maryland backwoods overlooking what was really a large creek called the Patapsco River, her teaching of philosophy and theology had been carried on by priest-professors from Rome and Naples such as Camillus Mazzella and Aemilio de Augustinis. The method of this Italian group was conservative. Its opponents accused

them of being intellectually timid and lacking in legitimate tolerance, but the charge was probably too severe.

In those pioneer days Woodstock enjoyed neither telephone
nor telegraph communication with the outside world. The mail
and food and other supplies were brought bi-weekly by the
B. & O. railroad train that paused briefly and testily at the station-
less whistle-stop opposite the college and across the rickety bridge
that spanned the river. The scene was scarcely inspiring as one
stood in the morass before the house and gazed unbelievingly
down at the Patapsco shallows. The partitions between the students' rooms at that time were so thin (it is reliably reported)
that a man could hear his neighbor brushing his hair. The water
supply was dependent on the variable energy of a mule named
Catharina who tramped the treadmill that operated the pump.
It was in this primitive setting that Fathers Mazzella, de Augustinis, and their colleagues had instructed the original Woodstock classes. In the case of the first-named savant, at least, the
cramped classrooms, lighted on dusky fall and winter afternoons
with oil lamps, must have brought back contrasting memories
of the spacious halls of Rome.

In Tom's time at the college one of the most eminent members
of the faculty was Father Benedict Sestini, former astronomer
in the service of the Pope, and world-famous mathematician. To
him was due largely the interest in contemporary positive science
that marked the Woodstock spirit during these years. One day
in 1880 he assembled his class in the chapel (from which the
Blessed Sacrament had been removed) to demonstrate the
pendulum experiment to prove the earth's rotation on its axis.[185]
He painted on the ceiling of the library an exact (for the time)
map of the planets and stars. (It is no proper part of this history
that one of the elderly coadjutor brothers, perceiving a large,
vacant space in one section of Father Sestini's map, added, in a

spirit of uninstructed cooperation, a big pink star to fill up the vacuum.) In Father Sestini's small astronomical observatory, set up on a small knoll beside the greenhouse, there assembled with him on clear nights two or three of his students to apply mathematical lessons to the stellar movements. It was one of the noteworthy facts about early Woodstock that all the natural sciences were given much attention. The geological collection of the college evoked high praise from a distinguished visitor, Dr. David C. Gilman, president of The Johns Hopkins University.

There must be in every seminary of students for the priesthood a teacher who is, beyond all others, a radiating center of good cheer. In Tom's days at Woodstock the need was met by the jovial Italian professor of moral theology, Father Aloysius Sabetti who, within a few years, would be regarded as one of the outstanding moralists of his time. Even to a part of the Woodstock routine that was not notable for sparkle Father Sabetti brought a gleam of light. Presiding at the periodical seminars on moral theology he would lighten the rather heavy atmosphere by punctuating the discourses of the participants with some remarks sufficiently humorous, at least, to keep awake a Woodstock audience at two o'clock in the afternoon.

Tom appreciated at least theoretically the worth of his studies. As was to be expected, he compared the training afforded by Scholastic philosophy to that given to the military novice: "[People] seem to think that the primary object [of education] is to crowd dates, facts and figures into one's mind, and do not dwell sufficiently on the need of developing, training, drilling the faculties themselves just as soldiers are drilled and trained. With a trained faculty of reasoning a man can go on educating himself all his life; with a lot of facts and dates and his reason untrained, he is like a soldier with a library of tactics, but without a knowledge of the manual of arms."[186] It is a question as to whether the Woodstock professors of Tom's day fully applied this ideal. In the first place, some of them may have been apologists rather than true philosophers. They seem to have dogmatized more than they inquired. They depended more on vigorous assertion than on proof. It must be added, in their favor, that what they so aggressively asserted *was* truth; but they often neglected the careful, rational technique of the great Scholastic doctors who had, with scrupulous fairness, weighed in a jeweler's scale the least objection of their adversaries. The effect of this deficient method on the later professional work of the students might be the subject of an interesting investigation.

Tom seems to have been in excellent health and good spirits during these three years, 1880-1883. Rowing and swimming in summer and ice skating and long walks in the colder seasons he indulged in vigorously. "I never felt better," he tells his father in mid-summer of 1882.[187] "I came up to the College with a light heart," he assures the General at the end of a pleasant visit to home.[188] He is disinclined to ask for any uncustomary visiting permissions: "I did not come home this Christmas because the other men usually do not get leaves and there is no reason why I should be privileged, though on your account I have no doubt I could easily obtain the necessary permission."[189] He passes up the opportunity to go to Washington to be a sponsor at little Kathleen Ewing's baptism: "It was hardly worth while coming down . . . as I had been there so recently . . . Then I should have missed a couple of lectures, each of which, as you used to remind me, is like a link in a chain. Whenever I happen to miss one I feel the loss for some time after, as it is difficult to pick up the connection."[190]

In his studies, indeed, he was doing very well. An evidence of this is his being selected for one of the leading parts in the "disputations" of the fall of 1882. These full-dress academic affairs, held twice annually, were exhibitions of argumentative skill in the various fields of philosophy. Tom was the "defender" of a series of theses in Special Metaphysics.[191] He sat erect as a ramrod at his desk on the stage and spoke in clipped staccato phrases—all, of course, in Latin. His manner toward his fellow-students who offered objections to his theses was marked by a perfect courtesy and, at times, a dash of humor. He did not fear to add a few original twists to the conventional proofs of the philosophical positions he was upholding. His whole appearance was poised, assured, and commanding.

His continuing interest in scientific subjects, as well as his proficiency in that field, is proven by his winning the right to read the physics essay included in the spring disputations of the same year. His paper was entitled "Chromatic Polarization and the Wave Theory of Light."[192] He made a special trip to the Smithsonian Institution in Washington to study the most up-to-date method of arranging mineral collections.[193] He would always be alert to scholarly discoveries. He is much interested in a current hypothesis presented by a Johns Hopkins historian, to the effect that George Canning, the English foreign minister, was the originator of the Monroe Doctrine. At the time the suggestion was new and rather startling. Tom viewed it with favor.[194]

It is clear that even thus early in his career as a Jesuit he was regarded as a better-than-average speaker. At the reception given to Archbishop Gibbons at Woodstock in September, 1880, he delivered the main address of welcome.[195] He gave one of the two main speeches at the installation ceremony of the new rector, Father Joseph E. Keller, on December 8, 1881.[196] For the St. Catherine's Day celebration of November 25, 1880, he presented a "reading" of the "Pied Piper of Hamelin," the only feature of the kind on the program.[197] He contributed some articles to the seminary periodical, *The Woodstock Letters.* The most notable of these was his account of his 1877 trip with his father through the West.[198]

An important influence on his future thinking was his close association with the lovable and many-sided Father Charles Piccirillo.[199] The Neapolitan Jesuit had suffered much from the Italian liberals of the mid-century, and had developed, through hard personal experience, a deep appreciation of the dangerous challenge presented by liberalism (of a special variety) to the Church. To such a man, who had seen the Mazzinian and Cavourian ideas in action and who had known the leaders of the movement at first hand, the liberalism condemned by Pope Pius IX was a threatening reality that at any moment might transfer its attack to the Church in America. His long talks with Tom on the subject aroused in the latter's naturally crusading nature a profound conviction that the liberal philosophy, as described by his venerable friend, was an imminent peril to the Church in the United States. It was a conviction that he would never drop, and it would determine the course of much of his future ministry.

Another fact about his professor was sure to appeal to Tom. Father Piccirillo had not only been a victim of the liberals' attacks; he had been an important director of the Catholic countermovement. For several years he had been an editor of *Civiltà Cattolica,* the Jesuit monthly that took the lead in fighting back at the new heresies. He had been an intimate adviser of Pius IX, and had been sent by the Pontiff as an informal ambassador to the Belgian government for the purpose of dissipating some of the latter's misapprehensions regarding papal ideas on constitutional monarchy. Father Piccirillo, in other words, had been a part of large historical events; he had grappled, on a stage as wide as Europe, with philosophical and theological questions of vital importance to the Church; he had been in personal contact with the protagonists in the great conflict. To Tom Sherman, in cloistered Woodstock, Father Piccirillo provided an outlook on stirring and momentous issues of the Church universal.

In one respect Tom did not derive as much benefit as he should have from his conversations with Father Piccirillo. The Italian exile had an unquenchable sense of humor. He would relate numerous comic incidents of his early life in the Society, with a quick, bird-like covering of his face with both hands to hide his chuckle at the climax of the story. As a young scholastic he had been fond of rehabilitating with paint brush and carpenters' tools whatever living quarters would be assigned to him. In order to make the most of this proclivity the Father Minister[200] would change him to a new room every few weeks. In the course of a year at the college of Naples he had had twelve different bedrooms. As a novice he had been about as much of a terror as could be suffered in such a decorous environment which does not provide for terrors. On one occasion he had received by mistake in his laundry bag a shirt of prodigious size. He had scandalized his fellow-novices by prancing along the corridor with the over-sized garment trailing along behind. On seeing a brother novice whose effort to maintain a modest and humble cast of countenance (as the Rule prescribed) had led him to look merely glum, Brother Picci had remarked audibly, "My, how ugly you look!" When ordered to make a public confession of his breach of charity, young Picci had accused himself, much to the merriment of his audience, of "telling Brother — how ugly he was."

All this was good, clean and, after all, very sedate fun, and Tom undoubtedly enjoyed hearing about it. He might even, given the proper stimulus, have done some of these things himself. But at Woodstock he strictly rationed his naturally ebullient sense of the comic. He was, most of the time, holding himself in a bit too tightly, although, paradoxically, he seemed to be able to do it without undue strain.

That he controlled his sense of humor too rigidly was, in the last analysis, not a fault of immense importance. Another feature of his reaction to Woodstock life may, however, deserve more careful examination. It must not be forgotten that Woodstock was a training school. Naturally, therefore, the students were—necessarily and legitimately—subject to a closely woven network of rules. To Tom Sherman, frequently, this type of reasonable restriction might appear to be a quibbling over trifles. He would gracefully obey the regulations, while remaining intellectually unable to view them as seriously as his superiors wished. One must remember that he was a mature man who, before he joined the Order, had had the experiences of a man of the world. He had grown accustomed to living with and being a participant in the spacious affairs of a large part of nineteenth-century political and military society. To translate his former ways of thinking into the simplicity of a seminarian who would worry over a breach of some trifling rule was extremely difficult.

Even at Woodstock the great voice of the world was, through his epistolary contacts with his family, breaking in upon him. He followed, by means of the newspapers and his correspondence with his father, the Congressional fight on the compulsory retirement bill which threatened the financial security of the General and his loved ones.[201] He approved his father's refusal to accept the Republican nomination for the Presidency.[202] He discussed with his father the political troubles of the General's friend, the Khedive of Egypt.[203] He was worried about the growing trend toward universal suffrage in the country.[204] He was, in a word, keenly alive to the swirling currents of national and world history, much of which touched his own family. It is not surprising if the question as to whether he should be permitted to go to supper a half-hour earlier or rise from bed an hour later should appear to him to be rather unimportant in comparison with these greater problems.

He had been raised, it is true, in an atmosphere that glorified military obedience. But, somehow, the military bloom and savor did not, in his view, distinguish the multitudinous and meticulous orders that were part of the life of a Jesuit seminary. He could sense the soldierly note in a regulation that obliged a private to black the shoes of a sergeant; he could not see a parallel in a rule that sent him to the door of one of his superiors to ask permission for toothpaste. What he did was to conform outwardly—and he did it scrupulously—but with only a half-assent of his mind. His attitude seemed to be: "I will follow these rules in the interest of the great Cause, but, for the life of me, I cannot see their utility." The maintenance of this position was not without its attendant tension on Tom's part; but he handled the tension with easy control and it gave him no major trouble at this time.

One source of real anxiety in Tom's soul had, after a brief flare-up, subsided. Toward the end of his first year at Woodstock he had made a candid admission to his father: "To be frank, dear Papa, I often feel doubtful about writing. Your last letter was so sad in tone that it made me feel I was only stirring up the past. If we could only 'let the dead past bury its dead' I should never hesitate to obey my inclinations and write freely, but I suppose that that is easier said than done."[205] But a few months later he could write to the General: "I must thank you again for that letter. It did my heart good to get it, and I have been a happier man these past few days than for some time before."[206] And, sometime afterward: "A feeling came over me very pleasantly during my visit that we are not so far apart, after all, together with a hope that as I grow older and less boyish, we may become yet more closely drawn together. As I can never have a family of my own, I shall remain more strictly a member of your little circle than if I were to marry and become absorbed in other affections."[207]

The improved feelings between himself and his parent emboldened him to ask the latter's intercession on behalf of the rector of the Jesuit college at Las Vegas, who desired some old army muskets for the military training corps at that institution, and, if possible, a military instructor. The General supplied the rifles, with a drill sergeant thrown in.[208]

His constant interest in the family has suffered no diminution. He urges Cump, now a student at Yale, to take an outing whenever the chance occurs. Cump is to remember also how much a young man is shaped by circumstances and companions and "how much it takes to make a gentleman." As one defect spoils a picture, so one glaring fault mars a character.[209] He gives some pretty grave and weighty advice with respect to his sister Rachel who is now a young lady: "With a little push and encouragement [she] could become a woman of solid culture, but she needs to be encouraged and directed. Our girls are satisfied too soon in the matter of education and when they get to be mothers they have little to give their children. I hope her social duties will not so engross her as to prevent her mental advancement."[210] To Minnie and, of course, to his mother, his letters were full and tender.

The most important aspect of his Woodstock years was, naturally (or supernaturally) enough, the development of his interior or spiritual life. This side of his growth was marked by some distinctive features.

For Tom Sherman the pursuit of spiritual perfection (which, as a Jesuit, he was bound to maintain) was never, as it is to some, a basically comforting experience, replete with the deep emotional satisfactions that come from a loving union with Christ. Rather, in his case, the ascetic enterprise was a stern fight for the advancement of a soldier's cause. It induced the soldier's impatience to conquer the enemy by the best and quickest means. There was, he thought, no time for the luxuries of divine consolations felt in one's heart. The struggle was grim, the time was short, and he must blast his way through to the goal—the triumph of God's Church by the winning of souls.

He kept no spiritual diary but, if he had done so, he would probably have echoed the fighting phrases of St. Ignatius' *Spiritual Exercises* without their tender references to Christ. He would have written much about the Kingdom but little about the King; much about the wiles of Satan but little about the attractiveness of the Saviour; much about battles but little about tranquil communion with the divine Leader for whose fascinating loveliness the battles were fought. His spirituality was, in a word, always helmeted and shod in campaign boots—which are, admittedly, good in their place, but singularly inconvenient for walking through a spiritual garden of peaceful joy, as, occasionally, it is well for the neophyte to do. This attitude would change later, but very slowly. It was different from his noviceship reactions.

The young Jesuit, after his course of philosophy, is assigned to a high school or college to teach a few years before entering on his theological studies. So, as mid-summer of 1883 approached, Tom and his classmates looked forward eagerly to this next stage of their careers. The great question was, where would each be sent? Tom was appointed to St. Louis University as teacher of classics and physics. He left Woodstock in mid-August to assume his role as instructor of youth.

CHAPTER 7

The Young Teacher

A spare, straight-backed, dynamic, and very earnest young man in a black cassock stood before a group of twenty boys in one of the old classrooms of St. Louis University and talked about the evils of Socialism. His audience was less than appreciative. In the first place, it was two o'clock of a warm spring afternoon and the students were much more concerned with the evils of confinement. In the second place, Mr. Sherman, first-year teacher, was lecturing over their heads. Moreover, at this moment he should have been explaining a chapter of Xenophon, the proper subject of the class; but Mr. Sherman was off on one of his frequent detours.[211]

As the lethargy of the pupils increased in proportion to the vehemence of his words, Mr. Sherman grew progressively and obviously nettled. Perceiving this, the class became more interested—not in the substance of the lecture but in the happy opportunity for baiting, with due restraint, a teacher. They bestirred themselves to assume even more elaborate postures of weariness; some of them even yawned audibly; they stared ahead glassily. There were two choices open to Mr. Sherman: he could fume, or he could admit to the boys that there was indeed in the situation an element of boredom. Fortunately for himself, he did the latter. The class paid him tribute with a collective friendly laugh.

His first months as a professor of physics, English, and Greek had been, like the session above described, spotty. He had been wrestling (not too successfully) with the teacher's primary problem, communication. To watch him in action was to understand why this was so. "We shall now," he would announce, "take up that great speech of Edmund Burke 'On Conciliation with the American Colonies'". But the students would not be treated to much of Burke's oratory; they would, instead, be lectured to—rather brilliantly but in far too-advanced style—on the wisdom of a limited suffrage for the United States, a policy which Burke would probably approve but which he had not touched on in the address in question.

There were days when Mr. Sherman would stride into class, drop his books on the desk, and talk vigorously for the whole period on the necessity for American representative government. Under other circumstances this might be quite appropriate; the difficulty in Tom's case was that he would be giving the lecture to his group in physics. Even when he stuck to the point, he could rarely get down to the linguistic and intellectual level of his teen-age mid-Westerners. Moreover, it appeared he was too impatient to make the effort. He told them he was training them to think like men. What he forgot was that, in order to achieve this end, he himself must think like a boy.

Yet, by a kind of wholesome osmosis, his classes did in fact derive much benefit from what an unsympathetic critic would term his rambling. If he rambled, he led them into some ex-

tremely important by-ways. After one of his free-wheeling performances, a student with a fresh gleam of enthusiasm on his
face would ask him for "a lot of books on that." It would be a
tribute of the kind a teacher loves.

Even while they sat at their desks with puzzled eyes as his
abstract and difficult phrases swept by, they felt a new respect
in their souls for knowledge and intellectual verve as embodied
in their teacher. He was not instructing them but he was often
inspiring them. If Herodotus and Addison were being crowded
out of the classroom, the great world of provocative ideas of all
kinds was elbowing its way in. That is what happened every time
Mr. Sherman pulled up anchor and made for the open sea of
speculation.

There gradually dawned on him, during his second semester at
St. Louis, that he was not, in the ordinary way, a teacher of boys.
One reason for this was the fact that he did not particularly like
this kind of work. He loved to talk to a prepared and receptive
audience, and what he had before him at St. Louis (as at any
other average college) was an audience whose attention had to
be bargained for and continually recaptured. He was, constitutionally, not at home in an educational clinic.

Accentuating—though it need not have been so—this incompatibility was the fact that Tom Sherman's outlook was, as
indicated before, already exceptionally mature, deeply serious,
and engrossed with the largest issues of the contemporary world.
He differed sharply from his fellow-scholastics in being not a
boy a few years out of high school, but a formed man, already
enriched by a great deal of worldly experience. His interests were
not bounded by the walls of his present living quarters and his
classroom. This can be shown from some of his later letters
which, however, reflect the attitudes of his first St. Louis period
as a teacher.

His uncle John Sherman was, in 1886, in the race for the presidential nomination. Tom was naturally paying no small attention to this possibility, and had the opportunity occasionally of learning at first hand from his distinguished relative some of the complicated workings of national political rivalries.[212]

His observations on his father's professional fortunes are not those of callow youth. "It is a shame," he declares to the General, "that the Government is so shabby in its parsimony as not to allow you the slender courtesy of hiring a single clerk for your convenience, but you know it is the old story and it would not do for you to be an exception to the rule, else we might have to modify old axioms and change our view of republics. The nation goes on 'booming,' caring little for the individuals to whom it is most indebted."[213]

He was in frequent touch with the men who had played eminent parts in the recent history of the country. He kept himself informed of current political affairs not merely through newspapers but by means of conversations with his father's many friends who were in the midst of the great events. It was not strange that such serious preoccupation with the most weighty issues of the time should have lessened his capacity to become interested in the comparatively narrow world of a Jesuit teaching scholastic.

But, to counterbalance his limitations as a professor, he possessed a saving grace which was evident to anyone who watched him with his boys. After muddling pretty badly a class lecture, he would say very simply to the students: "Gentlemen, I regret extremely that my explanation was not clear. I appreciate your courtesy in bearing with me." Only a teacher who was so obviously a gentleman, with a so evident instinctive considerateness for others, could have done this safely with a group of teen-agers. But Mr. Sherman, as even his severest critics among the students conceded, was above all a gentleman with a delicate concern for the feelings of those with whom he dealt.

"My dear sir," he would say regretfully to an erring boy, "the rules require that I should give you a punishment." It might be said that he deserved the "reprimand" administered to the teacher who was told that he respected the boys too much. He once declared that he thought that the highest task on earth was to "make men intellectual, cultured, refined."[214] Of this ideal he was undoubtedly a model.

Nor did it detract from his influence over his young gentlemen —as he preferred to call them—that, after a not-too-successful class period, he could take an active part in their ball games in the college yard. His love of outdoor exercise would never desert him. With his accurate throwing arm or fleet catching of fly balls, he often modified the less happy impression made on the students by a somewhat opaque classroom presentation of an English author.

The summer vacation period of 1884 was for Tom a time of even more enjoyable outdoor exercise and relaxation at the pleasant Jesuit house in the Wisconsin lake region where the scholastics recruited the energies they had partially left in St. Louis' and other classrooms. This holiday was, however, for Tom, mingled with some work of a type that he relished thoroughly— the writing of articles on current political and social questions. These essays were published during the next few months in various journals and were beginning to build for him a modest literary reputation. It must be admitted, of course, that the Sherman name provided an incentive for publishers to accept these early flights of his muse; but the articles had considerable merit in themselves.

The Sherman name! As he had reminded Cump more than once, they must never forget that they were sons of such a distinguished father. Not only did Tom never forget it; he luxuriated in it. He exhorts Cump that the shadow of a great name is "exacting and a spur to effort."[215] One of his most solid satisfactions was to hear himself referred to as General Sherman's son. When, one evening in 1884, he was present at a reception given for the great Matthew Arnold, Tom's interest was centered as much on General Sherman, who introduced the famous literary man, as it was on Arnold himself.[216]

One is tempted to recall the effects of such father worship on some other sons of record. Often the results of extreme idolizing of a parent have not been altogether wholesome. He was, deep down in his soul, under tension; and it may have had some relation to his fierce devotion to the man he worshipped so much. There was an additional fact that might have interested a psychologist: Tom could never forget that, by becoming a Jesuit, he had given this venerated father a wound from which the latter had suffered gravely.

More time was available to him in that summer of 1884 for a pleasure to which he always looked forward—visiting the numerous family relatives and friends. He was always welcome at his cousins', the Hoyts, whose children regarded him as another romping playmate. His characteristic ability to get down to the level of young people everywhere except in a classroom was clear to anyone who dropped in at the Hoyts while Tom was riding piggy-back or producing a wild-West show with the small fry.

Every now and then his religious superiors would express some mild concern at the frequency of his indulgence in these visits. Tom would probably be unable to understand the reason for their worriment. He felt that to be a human being was to be sociable. To mix with people was a necessity for him. And it was when he was in a circle of relatives or friends that his natural charm blossomed forth most beautifully.

With ease and a kind of sweet simplicity he could entertain with gay conversation a roomful of guests. It was said of him later that he "was always hungry for a parlor." He might have replied that this was a natural consequence of his having been, in a sense, raised in one. Something fine and delicate he had caught from the informal receptions and parties in his parents' home in Washington and St. Louis.

His second teaching year at St. Louis was, perhaps, his most effective, and in a very important sense his most fruitful. While retaining his post as head professor of physics, he was given full charge of the Freshman ("Humanities") class, and, in addition, was prefect of the debating society and chief librarian of the college.

For the main work of the Freshman class—the development of the students' ability to write good prose—he was very well equipped. His own writing style was smooth, polished, and clear. He could compose more-than-ordinarily-good verse.* It was (to repeat) a virtue of the old liberal arts training that it inculcated a sensitivity to form of expression. It stressed rhetoric, the ideal of the forceful and beautiful word. It emphasized structure, architectonic art applied to poetic or prose composition.

The effectiveness of the system is proven by what can fairly be termed the remarkably high stylistic quality of the student essays and verse efforts of those days. In their written productions the boys, it must be conceded, did not say much; but they said it with a literary grace and force that college students have today for the most part lost. Possibly the most important contribution made by Tom as a teacher was in this field. He could inspire and train his boys to produce comely prose because he himself could write in that fashion.

It might be argued that the Jesuits, in striving so strenuously

* See Appendix A at the end of the book.

for this goal of "writing or saying it beautifully," neglected other aspects of the pedagogical enterprise. One might say, for instance, that the method did not produce men who were widely read and widely informed. Whatever the validity of the charge, the choice made by the Jesuits was frankly in favor of the art of communication. They felt, moreover, that they were not unduly slighting the duty of imparting to their students factual knowledge proper to a college course.

It is significant that Tom's successor in directing the class of rhetoric some years later at Detroit was Father Thomas A. Hughes, one of the really fine writers of the Missouri Province and, for eight years previously, head of the postgraduate course at St. Louis. Possibly, to this part of the college curriculum were assigned teachers whose ability was considered to be above the average.

Tom's handling of the undergraduate debating society at St. Louis brought, paradoxically, more benefit to himself than to the students. A representative session of this organization would witness Mr. Sherman holding the floor for long periods and flailing at the fallacies of Martin Luther, Henry George, or Karl Marx. It must be said that in directing the St. Louis University debaters he gave himself a great deal of forensic practice. Not that the returns to the students were completely nil; they would unconsciously imitate—when he gave them a chance—his direct, electric manner, and as he did so often in his classroom digressions, he would open up to them highly significant issues they had never considered.

In helping the boys to prepare their speeches he himself read widely, an exertion that strongly appealed to his ever-questioning and thirsty mind. He would be criticized years later for ranging broadly but not profoundly in his thinking. The germs of this deficiency might have been perceived in these early years.

He was fearlessly outspoken in regard to questions that involved his feelings; which explains the mild furors caused in some St. Louis quarters when his debaters—obviously following their coach's instructions—said some rather harsh things about the South in questions touching the Civil War. While Mr. Sherman's orators were not exactly waving the bloody shirt, they had no time for the cooing doves of moderation. At every debate Tom himself would add a few—and sometimes more than a few—highly decisive words to sum up what he considered to be the right side of the argument. Almost every time he did this at one of the society's public exhibitions he trod on some of the audience's toes. He justified this procedure by an appeal to the edifying but often expensive principle that forthrightness of speech is more precious than diplomacy. He would never, indeed, to the end of his life, acquire the habit of thinking in shades and discriminations. He was urged by his academic superiors to go ahead a bit more gently. He made a real effort to heed the admonition, but only succeeded in going ahead.

In addition to his work with the boys he gave occasional lectures to other audiences. He addressed the local Catholic Historical Society on the subject of Father Marquette. He talked to the novices at Florissant on "American Imperialism" which, incidentally, he warmly approved. He spoke to the Negro congregation of St. Elizabeth's church on "America and the Negro."

But the academic year 1886-1887, his last period as a scholastic at St. Louis, was not for Tom a peaceful time. The "status" of the preceding summer had altered his teaching assignments.[217] He would no longer handle the physics class, and for his Freshman group was substituted what was equivalently an eighth-grade "preparatory" section. This looks very much like a demotion. The reasons for it are not clear.

An incident at the mid-point of this year indicated a continuing friction between Tom and the minutiae of the Jesuit rules. Into the community refectory he strode one evening with his usual dignified air—a half-hour late for dinner. Afterwards he was quietly reprimanded by the Father Minister. Good order demanded, said that official, that faculty members should come to meals on time. But, Tom demurred, he had been busy with class work and had felt he should finish it. The Superior was totally unsympathetic to this excuse. Tom meekly submitted to the correction, yet the sting of it went deep.[218]

He showed no outward signs of rebellion, but in his heart he simply could not understand how a trifling regulation (as he regarded it) should be considered as being more important than his duties as a teacher. This was the type of conflict that was dulling his enthusiasm and energy even while he loyally fought against the tendency.

Retaining still his post as Chief Librarian, his interest in the newest worthwhile books was evidence of his progressive outlook. Constantly he was urging his students to read great literature; such admonitions were, at the time, not frequent on the lips of the average teacher. He took care to stock the library with good books on the fine arts. One of his favorite arguments was that appreciation of the finest paintings and sculptures is a means to a deeper realization of the beauty of the divine. He succumbed, however, to the error of most Catholic educators of his generation—he slighted the representative works of the adversaries of the Catholic position.

Whatever his deficiencies as a teacher, he was, in respect to one all-important point, outstanding. The object of Jesuit education is not, exclusively, to produce candidates for the priesthood, but the achievement of that end, in particular instances, is always regarded by the Order as a specially consoling reward of their labors in the classroom. Besides, the development of an unusual number of priestly vocations by a teacher is commonly viewed as a tribute to his own character as a man of spirituality and to his knack of inspiring his students to imitate this quality.

Tom's record in this respect was remarkable, especially if compared with the previous output of priestly vocations at St. Louis University. From his class of 1884, four entered the Jesuit novitiate at Florissant. From his class of the year following, seven became Jesuits and two entered the secular priesthood. The previous yearly average from 1829 to 1879 had been, for the whole Missouri Province of the Society, two candidates for the Order and one for the secular seminary.[219] This would seem to be, to a degree, at least, indicative of Tom's influence over his students. Another point is worth considering. The attracting of boys to the priestly life requires definite qualities in the magnet. No worldly or unspiritual teacher can normally exert this power. Tom Sherman at this period must have been a man of prayer and union with God if he produced this kind of effect.

The only real lack in his spiritual life was, as before, warmth and the desirable type of tenderness of devotion. The motive that kept him faithful to his obligations as a Jesuit was to him the rigid military one of duty. There was still a coldness and hardness to that motive, even while it made him exemplary and regular in his practice of prayer. He was always, figuratively, in his exercises of piety, clicking his heels, saluting, and standing on guard for Christ, when the Lord would have welcomed just as well a simple, affectionate conversation.

Toward the end of the school year of 1885 Tom made a request that, in a Jesuit's life, is rather unusual. He asked to be changed from his post at St. Louis. His reasons for so doing may be surmised from the above account of his difficulties with those who were set over him. He later supplied, though vaguely, another motive for his seeking a transfer: "Here [at Detroit] I am free to speak my mind as openly as I please. In St. Louis it was always more or less dangerous to do so."[220] He is referring, probably, to the occasional unpleasant reaction at the latter place to some of his frank criticisms of the Southern position of 1861-1865. He was nothing if not a staunch Republican. Not all the people of St. Louis were so firmly Unionist. Whatever the reasons for his shift of residence, he was assigned at the end of the spring semester of 1886 to teach at the Jesuit college in Detroit.

The change was a tonic to Tom's morale. He would never be an expert college teacher, but he came closest to being so as he threw himself into his work with renewed energy in the congenial atmosphere of the University of Detroit.

He was charmed with the general atmosphere of the city. In mid-winter he found Detroit "perhaps doubly agreeable . . . at this season when it wears a joyous aspect with its many sleigh-bells, heavy furs, and almost Russian splendor. I have never been in the midst of so many bear skins, and it takes a little time to adjust one's feelings and fancies to universal runners instead of wheels. So far, it seems to me like a romance—sledges of wood, coal, hay and beer make the commonplace romantic, and the bracing air, tingling to one's finger tips is a perpetual incentive to exercise and a living commentary on Northern vigor."[221]

He seemed to be deriving a deeper satisfaction from his work: "I am toiling day and night for others. . . . I am never sorry that I have devoted my life to the good of others. To make men intellectual, cultured, refined, I hold to be the highest task on earth. That task is mine."[222] Constantly he sought to inspire his students with his own keen intellectual interests. The ideal he set before his brother (who was then dutifully trudging his way through St. Louis University) was what he thought to communicate to his boys: "Your ambition must be to be a man of thought and your happiness as well as your success will be in the field of the intellect."[223] His admonition reveals incidentally, of course, his own inclinations toward the intellectual life, with the qualifications previously noted.

He felt that he had a "finer body of students" than at St. Louis.[224] "Most of my scholars," he added, with his tongue in his cheek, "are taller men than myself so perforce I must treat them with respect."[225]

Since his main duty was now the handling of a class of rhetoric he had even more opportunity than at St. Louis to form his students to sound habits of expression, both written and oral.

In other respects, Tom's teaching methods during this year were progressive and imaginative. For the study of political science he organized a class as a debating society and had them engage in spirited arguments on the Constitution.[226] From his friend General Poe,[227] then engaged in supervising the great engineering project of the Sault Saint Marie locks, he secured official government publications on various topics of interest and made his students study them.[228] "Please tell General Poe," he had written to his father even before his teaching period had begun, "I shall be very glad to get any definite information about the Light House Board and its work, the Internal Revenue Service, the improvement of the Mississippi, in fact any reports or pamphlets . . . relating to National improvements of any kind. Next year I am to begin my career as a teacher and I have great faith in the broadening effects of general information."[229] (Here, it may be noted, he was filling in the oft-remarked gap in the Jesuit curriculum at this time—precisely, "general informa-tion" and its "broadening effect.")

In teaching history he utilized his close connections with

some of those who had contributed in an important way to the making of the national story. First of all there was, of course, his father. The son of General Sherman could describe the March to the Sea by adding personal recollections of his own to the account as given in his father's *Memoirs*. These latter he himself had helped to edit. All this imparted naturally a sense of immediacy and reality to his lectures on the Civil War. He could, from knowledge gathered at first hand from his father, correct the details of the Cyclorama of the Battle of Atlanta that was being presented at a down-town theatre. The picture, he frankly told one of the men in charge, was not true to the facts; it represented the terrain before Atlanta as being free of trees and underbrush, whereas actually the ground about the city had been thickly wooded; nor had General Sherman been as near to the front-line action as the artist had placed him. The curator had begged him not to let the public know of these poetic licenses but, we may be sure, Tom pointed them out to his boys, to their edification.[230]

When he discussed in the classroom the current political situation in the country he could draw on conversations he enjoyed periodically with his uncle, Senator John Sherman, who was at the center of things in Washington.[231]

He had definite ideas—formulated long before his sojourn at Detroit—as to the value of military training for college boys: "It was news to me [he writes to his father] that there are thirty officers detailed as [military] instructors in different colleges, but I can easily understand the wisdom of such a policy. National spirit will always be associated with the national arms, and we need something concrete, something sensible to remind us of the fact that we are a nation. I should like to see all schools flying the national colors and adopting other similar means to impress the important fact on the youthful imagination."[232]

The virtues of the military man would always have for him a powerful attraction, and we may be sure that he held this model up before his boys: "Surely there is something . . . in the profession of arms which carries with it lofty courtesy, fineness of perception, delicacy of touch and knightliness of disposition; qualities which win admiration even from those who are furthest from sharing the ambition that helps to maintain these traits in the soldier's character."[233] Never, of course, did he stop here, at what was after all a naturalistic concept of virtue, no matter how high. His advice to Cump when the latter was at Yale makes the all-important addition: "Never let your A Kempis get covered with dust, or your Beads grow rusty. We've got more wisdom than Yale knows and we must not be robbed while being enriched."[234]

Only once, in a letter to his mother, does he hint at a personal fact that later in his life would not be unimportant. He tells her, toward the end of his stay at Detroit, that his health is good; but it is so because he has, so to speak, been "pacing" himself in his teaching work and other activities: "I have not fasted at all this Lent and am as strong as when the year began, a thing I have never yet been able to say after seven months teaching. I am learning to save my ammunition, a most important lesson for a teacher. Pupils are quite willing to see a man exhaust himself while they sit passive. I can gauge myself now and am rarely ever fagged after class."[235]

In thus avoiding undue physical and mental strain he indulged, very moderately, in that popular nineteenth-century palliative, the cigar. "I must thank you [he writes to his mother] for yielding to the masculine weakness which ladies wonder at and which only as a teacher have I yielded to. I don't know how it is but most men in our age feel the need of sedatives and stimulants both. I never smoke more than twice a day."[236]

A high point during his Detroit period was in the early summer of 1887 when he was regaled with a two-weeks' visit from his mother. She installed herself in a boarding house overlooking the College, so that she could be as near as possible to Tom, and they had a fine time together, "riding, excursioning, calling out together and indulging in that sort of amusement and gaiety which is compatible with three-score years on one side and the cassock on the other."[237] Detroit was, at the first blush of the warm season, quite different from what it was in winter. It is now a "restful quiet dreamy sort of place," and it made on Mrs. Sherman an impression "particularly charming."[238]

His time of "regency," as the young Jesuit's first experience as a teacher is termed, was completed with the scholastic year 1886-1887. In the following September, after a very pleasant vacation with his brother scholastics in the lake region around Milwaukee, he returned to Woodstock College to begin his studies in theology.

CHAPTER 8

Ordination; Death of A General

The [theology] course is prodigiously long for us young Americans, though people abroad seem to think little of half a lifetime spent in serious study. We have such a long line to defend and such a series of enemies to guard against that I suppose it is necessary to dig pretty deep lines before opening fire. After all, I feel myself very much of a novice in theological matters, having given most of my life to lighter studies, so I can't afford to become impatient for awhile if I am kept out of active work to ground myself more thoroughly in solid knowledge.[239]

This estimate of his second three-year period at Woodstock, written toward its close, is probably indicative of his reactions throughout the whole time. He had a high appreciation of what he termed the "depth and difficulty of theology as the wide reaching character and tangled labyrinth of revealed truth investigated by human reason."[240]

His realization of the demanding nature of one branch of his studies was heightened by his constant awareness of contemporary advances in science: "Every scientific and physiological discovery opens up a whole fresh field of moral questions."[241] But any yielding to impatience at this time of slow and laborious work as a student would, he thought, convict him of what he castigated as "incompleteness and shallowness, the curses of our age and country."[241a]

He must have succeeded fairly well in following these edifying injunctions, for he was chosen to be one of the chief participants in the theological disputation of the winter of 1889. To this triumph there was attached, however, a slight mystery and a slight tarnish. He was not the first one chosen for the honor. He was a substitute for a Mr. Clark who, in turn, had taken another man's place. But the possibly too generous Mr. Clark had, in the succinct language of the diary of the theologians' beadle, "broken down" on the eve of the disputation, and Tom had filled in the breach.

Even though he thus received the assignment on the rebound, he did the job very creditably. His fellow students probably thought that he handled himself more like an aggressive debater than as a calm expositor. It was only the Latin, one might suspect, that prevented his retorts to objections from being snappy. What his hearers could not clearly understand then was that he was constitutionally a competitor whose idea of explaining a truth was to flaunt it like a flag.

The performance was symbolic of the two main benefits he derived from his theological studies: a blazing loyalty toward Catholic truth, and an intensification of his fighting style in defending it. If he engaged in a classroom argument against the Arians, it would not be for him a mere academic exercise. The Arians would be the enemy on Missionary Ridge or the heights of Fredericksburg, and the classroom would be, figuratively, full of battle smoke.

His saving grace would be always another result of his Woodstock course: he learned his theology exactly and had it always available for immediate use. In the history of his life this fact must always be stressed. Those who in after years would not be enthusiastic about his methods would watch him with grudging admiration on more than one occasion as he sat in a Jesuit recreation room and tossed off, easily and always accurately, the answers to difficult dogmatic or moral questions.

Some of his keener critics would detect the flaw in his armor: his theological knowledge, like that of some of his teachers, was memorized—remarkably so—rather than assimilated profoundly by his intellect; and he was utterly lacking in originality of speculation. It was a limitation from the viewpoint of scholarship, but it was a superb gift for an apologist; and, clearly, it was the latter that he wished to be.

No sooner had Tom returned to Woodstock in the fall of 1887 than he perceived a difference in the atmosphere. He was now no longer on the philosophers' side of the house, but lived with the young men who, like himself, were within a few years of their ordination to the priesthood. The idea of ordination was like an aura that, wherever they went and whatever they did, enveloped them. They went to classes as they had done in their years of philosophical study, but now there was felt a new stimulus and a new dignity to the daily routine.

When they pored over their textbooks it was not merely a chore; it was, they felt, an immediate preparation for their ministry as priests. To class lectures in moral science there was an immediacy and practicality they had not found in their philosophical studies. These rules for guiding and curing souls were being learned for actual use in the near future. The daily exercises of prayer were now precious opportunities for acquiring the close union with Christ that a priest must have if he is to be an effective apostle. One knelt at his prie-dieu in the cold, silent hours of the morning in the expectation of drawing from the Divine Source of spiritual power some fresh inspiration for the solemn work ahead. One watched more carefully over one's faults; the priest of God must be, as St. Paul warns, unspotted from the world, a faithful minister of Christ.

He felt himself consecrated, set apart. He was very soon to be clothed with the sublime dignity of holding in his hands the Body and Blood of Christ. He was to be a marked man, segregated from the rest of men, for the purpose of carrying on the sacrificial function of the Saviour. The words of St. Ignatius' *Exercises* came back to him: "Men crucified to the world and to whom the world itself is crucified; men dead to the world that they may live for Christ. . . ."

The theologians were humbly conscious, as they walked along the corridors or sat in the refectory, or relaxed on the walks or playing fields, that their younger brothers the philosophers regarded them with a degree of reverence. There was even a touch of awe in the manner in which the future priests were addressed by their juniors on the other side of the house.

Of his deepest thoughts Tom gave to his dear ones at home occasional hints. "The feeble spark of boyish emotion," he assured his mother, "has grown to a passion for all that concerns His Mighty Kingdom and the eternal welfare of man. Meaner aspirations cannot come between me and the great Heart of all things."[242]

To his father he wrote frankly: "As for fame which to you seems to mean so much, in my mind it is associated with the rocky island where Napoleon fretted away his strong soul, not with happiness, peace, and contentment, or doing good to self or others. You and I can never agree because we start from different principles. I am always sorry that I have caused you disappointment, but I am never sorry that I have devoted my life to the good of others."[243] And his analysis of his own inherited character is part of his meditations: "It takes a deal of softening to take the kink out of some natures and I am not sure that we Shermans are the most malleable individuals in the world."[244] Whatever the family fault, however, "we . . . are sincere, open, simple, and affectionate. . . ."[245]

He manifests an increased sensitivity to the things of nature: "I have just been down to the greenhouse, where the azaleas, camelias and lilies are in full bloom; and it seems to me one little island of the tropics had found its way up into this dull lifeless half winter and half spring that makes all the woods so muddy and the country so uninviting. . . . Please tell the girls I thought of them at the greenhouse. They would enjoy and appreciate it so much more than we men who look at flowers very much as we do at dresses, as necessary encumbrances. It takes 40,000 plants to make our grounds look pretty in summer, so the conservatory is very crowded with its long beds of shoots and slips. I noticed a number of varieties of narcissus from Butin bulbs that were exquisite. It may interest the girls to hear of them."[246]

He saw, on an early spring morning, "the myrtle . . . blossoming in the midst of snow, and white tulips thrusting their heads up through a bed whiter than themselves."[247]

In other more important respects, too, his heart is easily touched. Somewhat later he refers to himself as being, on the occasion of a visit from Lizzie, "pale, . . . wan . . ., and bruised by others' grief."[248] (He had just heard of the death of their dear friend Alice Blaine.) He generalizes his pity for his ailing sister Minnie: "Poor women, what a burden is theirs and how little we really sympathize with them."[249]

No, he was not too solemn. A traditional feature of Christmas at Woodstock was a treat of eggnog enjoyed by the theologians in their recreation room. Mr. Sherman, we are glad to learn, each year directed the preparation of this beverage.[250]

He is still sufficiently fond of outdoor exercise to feel regret in refusing an invitation for a horseback trip in the following summer through the Indian country.[251] He skated on the precarious ice of the Patapsco whenever the chance occurred; and he went on all-day walks of fifteen or twenty miles.

Yet, despite these indications of his *joie de vivre*, the evidence hints that he was not participating in the social life and lighter diversions of the theologate even as moderately as he had done during his philosophy years at Woodstock. His name, for instance, does not appear on any of the programs of the house entertainments; he is not mentioned in any of the team rosters in the spirited games of ball which, be it mentioned in the spirit of historical accuracy, sometimes sent a theologian or two to the infirmary. It is possible that he was a bit over-serious. He would at this time have been incapable, one might surmise, of the light irony evinced by the philosophers' beadle who reported in his day book that "Reverend Father Provincial reappeared today and was again lost to sight in the afternoon."[252]

A circumstance which he passes over lightly may throw some light on these facts. During the late winter and spring of 1888—it was his first year of theology—he had a rather serious illness. An ailment which began as a blister in his ear developed into a severe mastoid condition.[253] He had fears for his hearing, though the dread eventuality of deafness never materialized. He was hospitalized for several weeks in Washington and for many weeks afterward was distinctly unwell. He refers to his sickness as having been a "close call," and believes that his life and hearing were saved by the prompt and energetic remedies applied by a skillful infirmarian at Woodstock.[254] He is particularly grateful, he says, when he recalls Mr. Conkling's case.[255]

Conceivably, this indisposition rendered him less inclined to engage in the lighter and gayer activities of Woodstock. It is preferable to leave wide open the question as to whether this medical fact is unimportant, or whether, on the contrary, it is highly significant for the story of his later life.

Even though his thoughts were mainly oriented toward his ordination he did not abate his keen interest in the great issues of the nation and the world. He would always love even the marginalia of important human events: "I have only to remind myself of Broadway to feel like rushing, bustling, hurrying and getting excited."[256]

His ardent Republicanism takes comfort in the thought that "we are sailing smoothly under the old party with no fear for the nation's honor and no danger of being ashamed of the trophies of the past."[257] Only the Republicans, he is sure, can govern the country safely.[258] He is watching closely the administration's handling of the Negro question. He predicts that President Harrison will succeed in winning over the younger generation of white Southern voters to an enlightened policy of political coexistence with their Negro fellow-citizens. Then, he thinks, both parties will make a strong bid for the Negro vote.[259]

His innate antagonism to any theory that attacked the rights of property owners is as strong as ever. He is enthusiastic about a recent pamphlet that has put Henry George in his proper place.[260] In an exhortation that indicates his affectionate admiration for his father (who, apparently, was feeling a bit discouraged at the time) he expresses also his thoroughly conservative political and social philosophy:

Your life is of such great value to many, to your family . . . to the old soldiers, to the Union, that I trust you will not tire of it. You are still a power in the land, a power for good, an influence in favor of liberty, conservative government, and all the best that American ideas mean to the world, and if you have no occupation in the vulgar and trivial sense of the word, you certainly have in a higher and nobler sense. You are in more ways than you know a sustaining influence to those who cherish the idea of the Great Republic as held by Hamilton and Washington, and you are as necessary to us or more so than the Duke of Wellington was to the cause of the British Empire.[261]

A pleasant footnote to history is embodied in a query he addressed to the General: "Did you succeed in keeping for Gen. Joe Johnson [Johnston] the office that you obtained for him?"[262] The reference was to the Confederate commander who, during the last year of the war, had been Old Tecumseh's most immediate and troublesome adversary.

He presumed to disagree with his father on an important point of constitutional procedure: "I am sorry you are willing to throw over the last two amendments, for, as they stand written, we must uphold them at any cost." He admits, however, that it is hard to defend what one's judgment does not approve.[263]

To family affairs he was never indifferent. There came to his attention, for example, a little difficulty with respect to his sister Rachel. The young lady was just "entering" society, and, it must be admitted, had been living pretty expensively. The General termed it extravagance and complained to Tom. The latter assumed the perilous role of mediator. He says he will have a very serious talk with his sister on his visit to home at the following Christmas time. But he puts in a good word for her. It must be remembered, he tells his father, that her position as the daughter of General Sherman requires that she should maintain a definite standard of dress and equipage.[264]

The confidence displayed by the General in Tom's judgment in this minor family crisis was an evidence of the improved relations between father and son. The old breach, if not fully healed, was becoming so. The old warrior would never thoroughly approve of the step that his son had taken; but he had learned to live with his regret and to do it gracefully.

From Detroit a few years previously Tom had written to the General: "It is certainly petty even to hint at old sores. I trust that as the years glide smoothly you may have every evidence from your children that they cherish you in their hearts and give you . . . love genuine, deep, and devoted."[265] Another letter of that earlier period had, from Tom's side, summarized the state of their relation:

I think you and I have been very sensible, everything considered. We have agreed to differ and what better can men do who are set each in his own way? The remembrance of the chat I had with you in St. Louis will be one of my most cherished recollections through life, though I suppose all of your children will be inclined to dwell on the thought of their father as he came back to the fireside in '65 with a nation's blessing and unsullied honor fixed upon him, when he read to them from Dickens, Scott, and Irving, with the simplicity and tenderness of one of those old Roman heroes—a Fabius, Cincinnatus, or a Scipio. But the years that bring tenderness are more precious to both generations, I take it, than those that win glory. In the field you are the world's, at the fireside you are ours and will have our deepest love and most sincere devotion always. Your children and grandchildren bless you and will hand down your memory as a precious legacy of natural nobility and a spur to upright living and manly acting.[266]

Any attacks on his father's honor angered Tom to the quick. One Logan had made some severe charges against the General. Writes Tom to his father: "I do not wish to wrong the dead but I do not wrong him by saying that my intensity of personal feeling prevents my forgetting his persistence in cherishing a grudge toward you. I shall try to be cautious in any manifestation of this feeling before others and so imitate as far as I can that magnanimity for which you are so highly and so justly admired."[267]

A further proof that all was substantially well between them was the fact that Tom felt free to criticise very frankly the writings of the General that the latter would submit to his son for that purpose. Tom was particularly severe on one publication of his father's which comprised an editing of some Civil War correspondence. He candidly gives a lecture to the General on the impropriety of giving to the public the private letters of other men whose permission for such publication has not been previously secured. His excuse for being so severe toward the work is, as he says, his knowledge that his father bears adverse criticism so well.[268]

Occasionally, it seems, the General would in his letters to Tom let slip a note of dissatisfaction. He could not see the utility of elaborate systems of theology. What God required, he believed, was a simple worship of the mind. Tom lightly parried the dig by saying that in such case his course of studies would be happily shortened.[269] At times, too, the General complained that he found it difficult to write about things that would interest his Jesuit son. This was an opening that Tom immediately seized, and in all sincerity: "You know very well that anything whatever which interests you must of course be of interest to me on that account if for no other reason."[270] Only once, and then most delicately, did the young seminarian attempt to draw his father toward the Catholic Church. He sent to him through Lizzie a book that answered some of the common arguments against Catholicism. The General was unimpressed.[271]

A deep sorrow would fall upon Tom before he would have the happiness of being made a priest. Barely seven months before his Ordination he received word that his mother had died. She had looked forward so eagerly to his great day and had embroidered with her own hands the vestment he would wear at his first Mass.[272] His feelings toward her had been all that could have been expected of a devoted son. She, on her part, had perceived his weaknesses and had never hesitated to point them out to him. Her admonitions might have been very valuable to him in the years to come. As he knelt by her coffin he remembered how she had always been so valiant. That virtue almost summarized her life.

Tom was not to receive the priestly powers at Woodstock, with his class. In deference to the last words of his mother, he would be ordained alone in Philadelphia by Archbishop Patrick J. Ryan, the long-devoted friend of Mrs. Sherman. The date would be July 7. As the day approached, there were two shadows that clouded the prospect as he tremulously looked toward it. The one who was so dear to him would not be there to see him made a priest. The other less-bright spot on his horizon was the dubious attitude of his father. Tom had written to him a few months before: "I believe I told you . . . that I am to be ordained priest next summer. . . . It is in fact the one decisive step of my life and determines my future for time and for eternity. I am no longer an enthusiastic boy, but a calm deliberate man in my thirty-third year, with my eyes open to all that is meant by the step I am taking, after eleven years of preliminary testing, training, studying and waiting."[273] A few weeks previously he had given a loving reminder to his parent: "Now that we have passed through such a bitter trial [the death of Mrs. Sherman] you are both father and mother to us all."[274]

But the General was not to witness Tom's ordination. It is not clear that he absented himself deliberately. The facts appear to confirm his plea that he must be in the West on official business on the day of the ceremony. He could promise Tom, however, that he would meet him in New York after the all-important date. One is tempted to wonder if it would have been impossible for the General to advance his schedule by this short span and add to his son's joy. We have a rather pathetic exchange of letters between father and son, the former insisting on his intention of seeing Tom as soon as possible *after* the ordination, and Tom striving valiantly to build up this meeting to the status of a substitute for the General's presence at the great occasion itself.[275]

As to the young man's deepest sentiments on the eve of the great step, we can only for the most part surmise. A remark he addressed to Cump a short time afterward may have summarized his most profound feelings: "To be a priest is a dreadful responsibility. Order is heaven's first law and man's last, and to restore it in a few spots of earth takes greater exercise of divine power than to create a million worlds."[276] Again to Cump he made an exclamation that was a commentary on the words just quoted: "How people, even Protestants, lean on a priest!"[277]

What he said also in a sermon a few years later probably paralleled his thoughts as he awaited the bishop's anointing hand in that June of 1889: "Our hearts are wrapped up in . . . Jesus Christ. . . . He is our Alpha and Omega, the beginning and the end of our salvation." Most assuredly, furthermore, would he have symbolized the great event in terms that were military. This was both the commissioning of the officer of Christ's army, and the real opening of the campaign for Christ's cause. This was the soldier receiving his battle orders. This was the fighting man's receiving word of his mission. Salute to the Leader and his crack corps!

All the family, with the two exceptions, were there in the chapel of the Philadelphia cathedral on July 7. It was a very private affair with Tom as the sole "ordinandus." In accordance with the Jesuit custom the ceremonies would last through three days. He would receive his subdeacon's orders on the first, deacon's on the second, and his priestly powers on the last. The first two stages of the impressive ritual set the solemn emotional tone for the climactic last day. As the young neophyte's sisters, brother, relatives, and old friends took their places in the chapel on the morning Tom was to be made, by the grace of God, a priest, they felt as only those can feel who are witnessing the solemn event.

The venerable Archbishop advanced to his place. A procession of priests came up the aisle, with Tom walking alone at the end. He wore over his black cassock the alb that his dead mother had made for him, and across his shoulder in the manner of a deacon was his stole. He carried in one hand a folded chasuble, and a linen cloth for binding his hands that were soon to be anointed with the holy oil; in his other hand he held a lighted taper.

He was, as the Philadelphia *Press* remarked, "quite composed, and, though worn-looking, . . . seemed to be quite strong and his movements were sure and quick. . . . His figure . . . only fairly tall and very slight, and quite without the natural wiriness that must always have been characteristic of his father. . . . But there is indomitable force expressed in his countenance, even under the veil of placidity that years of self-repression and religious meditation have placed over it. His deep sunken eyes are bright, even behind the glasses that usually cover them. His forehead is high and full. . . ."[278]

As the Archbishop began the Mass, the candidate, still holding the taper, knelt at the foot of the altar. Beside him stood his old friend of novitiate days, Henry Van Rensselaer, himself ordained only a few months before, and now acting as Tom's special attendant. On the altar as archdeacon was Tom's beloved teacher from Woodstock, Father Sabetti.

The Archbishop, having read the tract of the Mass, turned, sat down on his faldstool or portable throne, and facing the candidate who still knelt before him, said in Latin the momentous words: "Let him approach who is to be promoted to the order of the priesthood." "*Adsum!*" came the reply from Thomas Ewing Sherman of the Society of Jesus.

The archdeacon presented the candidate as being worthy. Then, as in a marriage service, the Archbishop asked whether anyone had anything to say against Thomas Ewing Sherman's ordination. No one spoke. The Archbishop then read the admonition:

Being consecrated, beloved son, to the office of the Priesthood, may you receive it worthily and exercise it in a praiseworthy manner. . . . That they may teach both in word and action, the ministers of the Church must be, in their faith and works, perfect; they must be rooted in the virtue of the two-fold love—that of their fellowman and of God. . . . Imitate what you teach. . . . Let your doctrine be the spiritual medicine of the people of God. . . . By your preaching and your example may you build up the house of God, that is, the family of God. . . .

The Litany of the Saints was chanted. During this part of the ceremony Tom prostrated himself on the floor of the sanctuary, with his head cushioned on his folded arms. Then he arose and knelt before the Archbishop. The prelate, standing erect in all the majesty of his apostolic authority, laid his hands on the candidate's head and spoke the following prayer: "Let us beseech, brethren, God the Father Almighty, to multiply His heavenly gifts on this His servant, whom He has called to the Holy Order of the priesthood; that, receiving this exalted sacrament in a worthy manner he may discharge faithfully all its duties with the assistance of divine grace, through Christ our Lord."

Afterwards the chasuble, the priestly insigne, was placed upon his shoulders, but held up as yet with pins. Then his hands, already anointed with the holy chrism, were bound and he touched a chalice and paten. The Archbishop continued the celebration of Mass, while the candidate retired to the sacristy, where his hands were unbound and the sacred oil wiped off them. He returned to the sanctuary, and from the Offertory onward, pronounced the words of the Mass with the celebrant. Before the "Agnus Dei" he ascended the steps of the altar and received from the Archbishop the kiss of peace. After the postcommunion he recited a profession of faith, and the Archbishop, placing both of his hands upon Tom's head, recited the prayer, "Receive the Holy Ghost. . . ." Then the chasuble was unfolded and freed, and as it fell about the priest the Archbishop said: "May the Lord clothe thee with the stole of innocence." The new priest promised reverence and obedience. With a parting admonition by the Archbishop to live holily, the ceremony was over. All except Father Sherman retired from the sanctuary.

They left him behind them, praying alone at the altar. His head was buried in his hands and almost pressed down upon the blue covering of the upper part of the prie-dieu. He remained so for three or four minutes. Then his old professor, Father Sabetti, came back into the sanctuary, whispered to him, and the new priest rose up and turned toward the people.

The Philadelphia *Press* has not done badly in its account of what followed: "Then for the first time it was observed how snow-white his face was. All the lines were drawn with the excess of feeling that had swept through him as he knelt in the silence of meditation. But like a cloud passing, the sign of agitation left him and his countenance resumed its old expression of calmness. There was a word and a whisper between him and his old mentor, and then Father Sherman smiled and made a motion to someone in the congregation. A woman came forward and knelt before him. She was trembling with emotion. He made the sign of the cross over her and spoke the words of a benediction. The woman was his sister [Minnie] Mrs. Fitch, of Pittsburg. She was dressed in deep mourning for her mother. . . . Other members of the family and old friends came forward and received the benediction. Among them were the priest's [other] sisters, his brother, and other relatives and friends."

There followed the breakfast given in his honor by the Archbishop, and a reception for a small group of intimate friends. Next day he offered his first Mass.

He had two more years of theological studies to complete. Returning to Woodstock after a happy reunion at home, he began one of the happiest periods of his life. It was, as he said so often, the Mass that made the difference—his daily privilege of offering the Mass. The half-hour of intimate communion with the Master in the early hours of the morning is a love-tryst in a sublimer key that only the priest can understand.

He received a number of invitations to write and lecture but preferred to keep out of public discussion till he had finished his studies.[279] He made an exception in the case of his old Alma Mater and gave a series of talks at Georgetown College in the fall of 1889.[280] He appears to have been much more interested in his father's lectures than in his own. He followed closely the General's public addresses through the newspapers and his sister's letters. "Your words," he wrote to his father, "which I read in print . . . have the effect always of a personal and direct message, and I always feel after reading them that I have had a breezy chat with you and am the better for it."[281]

Although he was for the time limiting his social contacts with the outside world, the change was only relative. Tom Sherman could never be a complete hermit. As a matter of fact, he was probably away from Woodstock much more frequently than any other of his fellow-priests.

He spent a Thursday in Washington with the Blaines, who

gave him some stimulating ideas on the Pan-American Conference and the prospects for a confederation of all the republics of
the Western Hemisphere. Tom was much in favor of the Western republics banding themselves together as, he pointed out, the
monarchies of Europe had done.[282] "I am much interested in that
conference," he writes to his father, "my head is buzzing with
statistics."[283] On this visit he kept his eyes and ears open. Mr.
Walker, he notes, is virtually running the State Department so
as to give Mr. Blaine more time for international affairs.[284]

On another trip to the national capital he had a conversation
with Admiral Daniel Ammen, who was engaged in the Nica-
raguan Canal project. Judging by the Admiral's possibly biased
account, the climate of Nicaragua was healthy and the conditions
of the work wholesome.[285] (Tom did not have the opportunity
of talking with Colonel Goethals or Dr. Walter Reed.) He had
also met in Washington some of his father's old generals.[286]

He continued his interest in the possibility of a more uniform legislation on marriage. He had observed the great conflict
in the laws of the several states regarding this important topic,
and he felt that national legislation would be far more desirable—"if our people were not so jealous of the national government."[287] In asking his brother Cump, who was now studying
law, for sources of information on the subject, he displays a
scholar's sense for the right use of the bibliographical tool: "You
can tell me the authorities anyhow and then . . . I shall know
where to go for information, and that is about all a man can do
in these days."[288] He has not forgotten the family. In order to
answer the letters that Ellie's children send to him he is obliged,
he says, to go back to a large block printing style of orthog-
raphy.[289]

He tells his father that the sacred memory of his mother has
now begun to make even more precious his filial communications

with his living parent: "I reread yesterday the little treasure of her letters, all that I have in the handwriting of our mother who is now our guardian angel, and your letter was a postscript to her devoted love poured forth so constantly and so unsparingly."[290]

For his final year of theology he was sent abroad to the Jesuit college on the Isle of Jersey. It was another opportunity for him to broaden his perspective. His love of travel was indulged by a few side-trips to the Continent where he doubtless was sobered by the unhappy condition of Church-State relations in France. In his future sermons and lectures he was to speak much of what he felt were the underground forces attacking the Church in all countries. Possibly he exaggerated the importance of these enemies of Catholicism. There was in his make-up a proclivity for assuming the sombre rather than the optimistic view wherever opposition to the Church was involved.

He returned to America in February, 1891, to meet one of the keenest sorrows of his life. His father had died on February 14, while Tom was still on the high seas. No human being had won his affection and worshipful admiration as much as the grand old warrior had done. And, now that the General was gone, the memory of his soldierly greatness would be, if possible, an even stronger influence in Tom's life.

A *carte de visite* photo of General William Tecumseh Sherman and his son, Thomas Ewing Sherman, taken in 1865 by J. Carbutt, Chicago photographer. The wall maps and desk appear to be part of a painted background.

Opposite, top: Thomas Ewing Sherman as a senior at Yale in November, 1875; *bottom:* Father and son, San Francisco, 1876.

Above: Taken in October, 1877, when Tom was in the law office of Henry Hitchcock in St. Louis and an active member of the local Shakespeare Club.

Thomas Ewing Sherman, S. J. at the time of his ordination in July, 1889.

Opposite: With his St. Louis University students (second from left in top row).

Father Sherman as chaplain in 1898, during the Spanish-American war.

A photo from the Province of Missouri archives, taken in May, 1914.

Portrait by an unknown artist, presented to St. Louis University by Rev. Joseph R. Stack, S. J., pastor of the Jesuit church in Santa Barbara, California.

The last photo, sent to his brother, P. Tecumseh ("Cump") Sherman, by Father Stack.

CHAPTER 9

The Great Campaign:
First Phase

Assigned in the summer of 1891 to St. Louis University as professor of philosophy for the scholastics,[291] Tom was for a while involved also in family business. Some of it was decidedly unpleasant.

There was some restrained squabbling among the Sherman daughters with regard to "the fund" set up by the General's admirers as a tribute to his memory and as a recognition of the fact that the financial situation of his heirs was none too secure. Minnie and Ellie, though married to husbands who apparently could support them, thought they should share in the extra money. This conclusion was, understandably, not clear to Lizzie and Rachel. Tom used good judgment in not taking the responsibility for a decision in the matter. But he was concerned over the fact that the press had gotten hold of the story of the bickering.[292]

Not only was he handling, with Cump, all the details relating to the Sherman properties in St. Louis and elsewhere;[293] he was also, to a very important extent, contributing to the family's financial needs. Although he had, as a Jesuit, taken a vow of poverty, he had secured from his religious superiors permission to use for family purposes the money and property that he still legally owned, and which he would continue to own until he should pronounce his final vows:

My permission to exercise the right of property expired with the administration and I cannot renew it. You will have to exercise your discretion then without asking of me any action that means being proprietor. I have not taken my last vows and will not for two years to come. Meantime I can get permission for individual acts of ownership but only occasionally. Before my last vows I shall make my will and that will end practically my "right of property." I shall then be "civiliter mortuus." I have only to ask you to keep enough to finish Tom Fitch's schooling, as that permission is outstanding, and let the rest go into the pot till the last dividing, if we ever get to a dividing. Of course, it would suit me best to have my share separated before the two years are up, so that I can make my final disposition with clear conscience. . . .[294]

"If you are ever short of money," he wrote to Cump, "say so plainly and I shall see that some is forthcoming."[295] As the time of his sister Rachel's wedding approaches, he assures Cump that "all that you have of mine you may give Rachel for her wedding expenses." She is to estimate what she will need and let him know. Cump should not scruple to call on Uncle John Sherman for help since "he defeated the pension [act] [that would have added much to the family income] and is really bound to help us out."[296] Rachel must have a fine wedding; "the family honor demands it."[297]

He sends money periodically to Lizzie.[298] He is paying the tuition for Minnie's son, Tom, at Holy Cross High School in Chicago.[299] He assigns to Minnie his share of the proceeds from the sale of the family farm in Illinois.[300]

The most troublesome item of business that faced the Shermans during these years concerned the General's *Memoirs*. This venture, it seems, had been dogged by misfortune from the beginning. The book had been published by Webster's, who had done a poor job editorially and in terms of promotion and sales. There were, in brief, too many textual errors and too few books bought. The Shermans had lost money on their investment— Tom himself had paid for the first five thousand copies—and they were afraid of losing more. In the late summer and fall of 1891 they were trying to secure a release from their three-year contract with Webster's and find another publisher who would put out a new edition of the book.[301]

At this time, Tom was apparently all too willing to let Cump handle the whole problem: "My business career has terminated and you had better assume full responsibility. . . . I consider that the lesson was cheaply learned at that."[302] But a few days later he is back in the driver's seat and is urging Cump to interview one or two other "pushing" publishers. He directs Cump, also, to examine the terms of the subcontract with the view of determining whether further issues of the book are not at Webster's own risk.[303] He recommends further that Mark Twain, an ardent admirer of the General, should be asked to help, as the great author had influence over publishers.[304]

As the affair became increasingly more entangled, Tom from St. Louis seemed to be managing the strategy. "Sanction any compromise till Christmas," he wired his brother. "No open breach. Will make new contract then." And, shortly afterward, "Change if you can get plates. Sound Colliers. . . . Have notified Webster that you act with my authority."[305] The upshot of the dispute was that the change to another publisher was finally made.

What is more significant for the light it throws on Tom's character is another disagreement evoked by the larger one.

Cump, in the course of the negotiations, had lost his head and addressed some exceedingly harsh words to the Websters. For this Tom scolds his brother in a letter that bars no punches:

I am willing to stand by any agreement you may make with Webster's people for *six months* as appears your plan laid down in your last letter. I have exchanged letters with Hall who says you were insulting and hostile from the start of the controversy; quotes passages of your letters to substantiate his statement. You can't accuse a partner of "sharp practice" and expect to keep things on a friendly footing. I agree however you had a right to insist on our having a share of Granfield's profits, but you had no right to accuse them of "breach of contract" when we had made no new contract but only a verbal agreement. You had no right to say the work is "selling at $2.50 universally" when it has been sold under my own eye here at $2.00. You have gone too far and hurt the book by hurting our publishers. We all know that Blaine spoiled the sale of the cheap edition, so we needn't blame anyone else. Alfred [Hoyt] was ready to sink his money to give the people a good book cheap. Do not change the original contract till I come to N.Y. at Xmas when I shall see Hall to whom I feel bound to apologize for your remarks as quoted by him. Things are bad enough, I hope they won't grow worse, but they will if we are not more than polite. If I were Hall I would lock up the plates and let the Shermans whistle.[306]

Cump did not take the reprimand humbly. He retorted with three sharp letters to Tom in which he justified his attitude toward Webster and denied the right of his brother to criticize it. Tom was hurt and demanded an apology. It was given, and an answering letter of Tom's followed close on its heels.*

---

* TES to Cump, St. Louis, October 10, 1891. This missive, now reposing among the Cump Sherman papers, has been annotated by the recipient. These annotations are represented here in editorial brackets:

"Your manly apology is exceedingly welcome after your three painful letters, and it is accepted in the straightforward spirit in which it is tendered. You mean it to cover many imperious expressions which you think are justified by my calling you to task, but which no provocation can justify though your generous apology condones them. Were you any other person than my brother I would have taken no notice whatever of any of your letters, and as

The family was gradually learning to handle their problems without constantly calling on Tom. This was fortunate since he had plenty to do now at St. Louis and elsewhere.

An immensely important fact in the history of late nineteenth-century American thought has, by historians, been inadequately treated. The period antedated the era of swift and wide communication of knowledge and opinion. There was no television or radio, nor even the simplest kind of amplifying devices for aiding a speaker to be heard by a large audience. The news-

---

it was I could only indirectly call your attention to what I now caution you against, a manner which in Napoleon would be an extravagant stretch of authority. 'Must' and 'shall,' etc., etc. are to be suppressed or 'must' be suppressed as between men who are on a level, as all are in America.

"I did not deny [Cump: '(?) he did.'] that Webster & Co. had broken their contract; they admitted as much to me before I wrote. I deprecated your saying so to them, as after such an accusation they cannot take an interest in our book nor do I see how they can be expected to. You say now that 'I accepted the naked assertion to the contrary' etc. Hall *admits* the breach and did so before I wrote and I remember having his admission in mind.

"I did feel bound to apologize for your 'expressions' and 'conduct' so far as they go together. I think I said 'expressions,' that was what I intended and what I did apologize for, as you now do yourself to me, [Cump: 'I do not.'] and as we ought to do to inferiors as well as equals (if we wish to put our publishers in a category). In doing so I *urged* your claim and told them I '*must*' sustain you and they wrote they had yielded.

"I *revoked no authority* [Cump: '(?) he did.'], I opposed no action [Cump: '(?)'] except 'open breach,' which I should have defined as I meant it, public law-suit, and change of publishers without first securing plates etc.

"I relinquished all authority before I had a single line except two imperious telegrams, the second of which you must have receded from, the first of which made me blush for shame in presence of the man who read it before I did, and laughed at your being 'red-hot.' Spectaculum facti sumus! If you think that your tone and manner to your own brother is justified by your excited feelings in a complicated misunderstanding, I warn and caution you that you will stand in very great danger of imperilling all the interests you are now in sole charge of. You will not have a tenant to be able to make a contract unless you use at least formal politeness. We can omit it as between brothers. Business men of today will not tolerate its omission. 'Must' and 'shall' should be dropped from your vocabulary if you care to save a few dollars to support Lizzie. If you are unable to see this you should ponder it till you do, for all your true friends and those that love you see it as plain as the sun in heaven.

papers, it is true, were developing with giant strides; but there were millions of people whom they never reached. Americans were not fond of reading books. Periodicals of the more serious type enjoyed only a moderate circulation.

Under these circumstances a great burden and opportunity was placed on the shoulders of the orator, lecturer, and preacher. It was the day of the platform and pulpit. The influence exerted by the effective wielders of the spoken word was tremendous. The politicians, of course, took the lead in applying rhetoric to the services of their party and (so they claimed) the nation.

"You reported to me that you had got Websters to admit a balance of $4200 in our favor [Cump: 'I did not.'] Rachel says our losses by the Memoirs are $8700.00. Which is the truth or are both true? Am I obliged to believe such contradictory statements? I suppose I am. If you can give me a definite figure some time, without any lengthy account, a mere line on a postcard will do, I shall be very much obliged, and the harm done by Rachel's expression will be partly undone. (A bare statement is all I want, to counteract Rachel's, my latest advice.)

"While I fully and cordially accept your manly expressions withdrawing the offensive phrases that cut and wounded [Cump: '(?)'] and grieved and appalled me, I trust you will never forget the danger in which you stand by reason of the nature which we have both inherited, a nature military, imperious and commanding, therefore *very offensive* to others. My own reason for accepting the administration was my perception of the fact that that fault stood out so preeminently in your otherwise amiable character, and my fear of the consequences. If you perceive the same fault in me, so much the better for my purpose which is to say that in resigning the administration into your hands I do so with the greatest possible misgiving not because of faults unnamable to those who bear an honored name, but because of a very real palpable and glaring fault which all your affectionate brothers and sisters see and deplore and which they beg you to keep before your eyes when dealing with business matters in which they and their children are interested. A little more diplomacy won't hurt us. If I had taken the stand you imagined I had do you think your telegrams or letters would have done anything else than intensify it? If you do you are not aware of the first elements of human nature. I was too busy to write fully during September and tore up several letters written for fear of offending. I approve your whole course against the Websters up to your move about the July accounting [Cump: 'Before that move there was nothing to oppose.']; but I must strenuously disapprove of your manner and expressions. I thank you for your letter and beg you to take in good part my strong words of warning and brotherly advice.

"Affectionately your brother
T. E. Sherman, S.J."[307]

The fact was dramatized by the sudden rise to national prominence of William Jennings Bryan on the wings of a single great speech about a cross of gold.

But in another field—religion—there were practitioners of the word who rivalled the secular orators in molding the views of the populace. The proponents of the so-called "religion of humanity" which sought to retain God as a very silent partner in a system that would reconcile Darwin, Spencer, and Christianity; the evangelicals and revivalists—usually Baptists or Methodists—who with all their doctrinal errors were fighting a vigorous rearguard action in defence of the real Christian tradition; the suave and mellifluous descendants of Emerson and Channing; and last, but not least, the leaders of the Roman Catholic minority—these and many other preachers, theologians, and missionaries for their respective creeds or attitudes were decisive factors in determining the ways in which the American people would regard the really fundamental issues of morality and what Crane Brinton has called the Big Questions of human existence.

It would appear, by the historical record, to be incontestable that in orally defending the Roman Catholic religious and moral position before a wide public, Thomas Sherman, the Jesuit, was for a while among the topmost leaders in the nation. This is a claim that has never been made since his death, although at the time of his greatness it was recognized without question. The simple truth is that for a period of approximately fifteen years, with some intermissions due to ill health, he was, with a handful of other priests, the Catholic doctrinal and apologetic voice in this country. The tribute is, admittedly, great; it is no more than is warranted by the facts.

The geographical ground he covered in his preaching and lecturing tours and his constant and remarkable drawing power speak for themselves. His base of operations was, from 1891 through part of 1894, the Jesuit university and church at St. Louis; and, from 1894 till the early summer of 1896, the Order's church and college at Chicago.

He ranged literally from coast to coast and from northern to southern border. We find him giving, during the Lent of 1892, a week's mission in Chicago to twenty-two hundred young men nightly, many of them Protestants. Two weeks later, he is preaching to an overflowing church in New York City and being toasted as "the eminent Catholic divine." On that Easter Sunday he is in St. Mary's, Kansas, speaking on "Americanism." Soon afterward, he appears for talks at Minneapolis, Kansas City, Milwaukee, and, of course, St. Louis. He is called back several times to preach at Denver, St. Paul, and Nashville, Tennessee, Chicago; and—somewhat later—New York City and Philadelphia call for him repeatedly. His itinerary and activities at home from 1894 through the first quarter of 1896 tell the story succinctly. In a typical month of the former year he gave a major lecture in Chicago on February 4, returning to St. Louis for featured sermons in the Jesuit church on the two following Sundays. On Washington's birthday he lectured at St. Matthew's Church, St. Louis. Three days later he preached twice—morning and evening —at the home church. Three weeks later he went to St. Mary's, Kansas, to give a retreat to the students. During all this time he was also teaching philosophy several hours a week to the Jesuit seminarians at the university.

After an interval of about nine months spent, according to the rule of the Order, in advanced ascetical studies at Frederick, Maryland, he returned to St. Louis to increase still more the pace of his activities.

He was relieved of his teaching duties so that he could devote himself exclusively to missionary and lecture work. From January 2, 1895, until the last day of the year he was "on the road" with the exception of less than fourteen days—not continuous— spent at home in St. Louis. During this period he preached and lectured in scores of cities and towns in an area extending from northern Wisconsin to central Missouri and from Denver to Chicago. The record is all the more remarkable inasmuch as his general health at this time had begun to fail. During the first five months of the next year he repeated this schedule, except for the lecture engagements. In view of the transportation facilities of that time, the rapidity of his movements is rather striking. It is no trick today to travel from St. Joseph, Missouri, to Chicago; but to finish a mission at the former point on Wednesday of a week in 1895, and to be in a pulpit in the Windy City three days later was much more of an achievement.

He is in Bloomington, Indiana, one day, and twenty-four hours later is opening another series of sermons at Bedford, half-way across the state. Besides, he makes periodical sweeps east to New York, looks in on Philadelphia and Washington for a sermon, and, on the way back to the west, has a one-or-two-night preaching call at Harrisburg or Pittsburgh. The sequence of his departures from and returns to St. Louis, as registered in the Father Minister's diary there, gives a picture of his peregrinations:

1896. Jan. 2—Fathers Finnigan [one of his partners at this time on the mission band] and Sherman left for Denver.
Feb. 6—Fr. S. arrived a.m.
Feb. 8—Fr. S. and Moeller left p.m. [On March 17, he will speak in Cedar Rapids, Iowa, and by the end of April has covered a half-dozen towns in Indiana.]
May 4—Fr. S. arrived p.m.
May 7—Fr. S. left p.m.
June 17—Fr. S. arrived. . . .

He told a newspaper reporter at Bloomington, Indiana, in April 1896, that he had delivered three hundred public addresses in the past two hundred days.[308] He refused a complimentary ticket to the local baseball park on the grounds that "a missionary in our church has no time for games of any kind."[309] He undoubtedly inspired awe and deep respect as he swept through the West. "Father Sherman ranks high as a scholar and churchman," ran a typical newspaper reaction, "and is one of the most distinguished literary men of America. And yet, with all his attainments, . . . he is as affable, pleasant, and as approachable as a child."[310]

Wherever he goes he is greeted with churches or lecture halls crowded to the doors and is hailed as a nationally famous orator. When he preached in capacious St. Francis Xavier's in New York City in 1892, several thousand people were turned away for lack of room. It was so uncomfortable inside the church due to the crowd and the heat, that several women fainted and had to be carried out during his sermon. His audience at St. Mary's, Kansas, in the same year had been equalled in size only a few times previously. At Omaha in the year following he spoke in the great Exposition Hall to a crowd "the like of which has seldom assembled in that great structure." In the larger cities— Detroit, Chicago, Kansas City—the response was the same.

The newspaper accounts of his talks make the front pages of the Catholic journals—six full columns in the *Catholic Home*, for example, for his sermon at Chicago in the summer of 1891; and the secular papers give him prominent headlines and generous coverage. His notable lecture at Chicago in February, 1894, is awarded several columns by most of the big dailies of the city and awarded first-page spots by some of them. There is no doubt that the reflected fame of his father contributed to his power of bringing out the crowds. To behold and hear the son of Old

Tecumseh as a Jesuit priest was a dramatic spectacle and one that evoked thrilling memories. Almost always among his listeners were old Grand Army veterans who happily wallowed in nostalgia while they paid attention to his words. But this borrowed lustre was not the whole explanation for his unusual popularity.

As he stood in the pulpit or on the lecture platform he looked like nothing so much as a field commander addressing his troops. It was always noted that his spare, militarily erect figure of medium height, his snapping blue eyes, aggressive jaw, and decisive—almost impatient—gestures recalled his father's appearance. The lines of his pale face were clear-cut and refined. His voice had usually a metallic ring and great carrying power; but he had a trick of modulating it to a tense softness. He had a flair for the dramatic pose and an acute sense of theatre. At one of his public lectures in Omaha, when they told him his speech would be preceded by "Marching Through Georgia" from the band, he said he would walk to the speakers' stand while the march was being played. He spoke in vivid pictures and pulled out all the stops in the organ of the richly colored, nineteenth-century oratorical style, yet he alternated with the staccato thrusts of a hard-bitten drill sergeant. It was felt by one observer that at times his delivery savored more of the political stump than of the pulpit. Another critic said that he kept firing a 12-pound cannon with one hand and scattered flowers of rhetoric with the other. His hearers noted his "magnetism" and his "superabundant power and energy."[311] They remarked his "inborn fight, ready resentment" that "stamped the educated priest as a natural soldier."[312] When he talked, "it were easier . . . to imagine the quick return of blow for blow than the passive turning [of the other cheek]."[313] On occasion he could create the appearance of profound learning by means of references or comparisons that ranged the fields of half-a-dozen arts or sciences. He was well-read in the world's great literature; he shrewdly utilized that valuable source. As mentioned previously in this story, he had a wide stock of theological and philosophical surface knowledge which, without going deep, was excellently adapted for impressing a popular audience.

He concentrated on three types of talks—mission sermons, including short doctrinal instructions and question-and-answer sessions, the latter device being one of his favorites; sermons explaining the Church's teaching to non-Catholics; and the apologetic lecture in a public hall where his audience would be largely Protestant and his main objective was to refute charges against the Church and represent her in her true light. In his mission sermons he addressed himself to Protestants as much as to Catholics. He was, in fact, the first member of his Order to be assigned to missions intended exclusively for non-Catholics. In this work he possessed, as he never tired of telling his brethren of other faiths, a peculiar advantage: the parent who had been so dear to him had never been a Catholic. He dramatized his fellow-feeling toward Protestants when he was asked publicly about his views on mixed marriages. "It would ill become me," he replied to a packed St. Patrick's Cathedral in New York City, "to condemn my begetters."

One of the irreparable losses in the documentary materials for his life story is the record of his conversions of Protestants to the Faith. There is weighty reason to believe that the number would be amazingly large. One piece of important indirect evidence for this postulate is contained in the newspaper descriptions of what normally happened at the conclusion of one of his missions. For several days afterwards, he would be occupied with giving further instructions to those who had expressed a desire for further knowledge of Catholicism. These groups are consistently referred to as being large. It may not be too bold to suppose that if they were sufficiently interested to devote this time in addition to the week they had already given to attending the mission itself, they were thinking seriously of joining the Church.

In his sermons to non-Catholics he always insisted that the Catholic Faith was a "rational worship of a rational mind."[314] What his Protestant hearers liked was his putting his argument across the board as a straight appeal to intelligence. To them his plea for the Church was made to appear like the method of positive science applied to the field of religion. He exploited to the full the peculiar advantage of the scholastic philosopher— his inveterate and almost ostentatious grounding of argument on logic.

Yet he did not neglect the appeal to emotion and the resources of drama. At Kansas City in the fall of 1892, he presented a word-picture of the crucial confrontation of the prophet Elijah with the wicked King Ahab. Face to face they stood—the King in his majesty and wealth and brute power and the man of God, poor, in tatters, physically weak, but invincible and fearless: "As the Lord God of Israel liveth, before whom I stand, there shall not be dew nor rain these years, but according to my word!" The evil King—not to mention the audience of Father Sherman— was enthralled and sobered by the terrible sentence the prophet launched against worldliness—"What is *your* Ahab, you married man?—What is yours, you housewife?" So the modern echoer of Elijah pressed his point home to a congregation that felt deeply his power.[315]

He always gave his feeling full rein when preaching on Christ's passion, which held for him a special poignancy. At Minneapolis one evening he had many of his congregation in tears as he portrayed the taking down of the body of Christ from the cross by Joseph and Nicodemus and the tender scene of the

Burial. "When he dramatized the Passion," observed one of his listeners, "he put you under a strain just short of unbearable but somehow deeply consoling." He had the actor's ability for intensely living through and, in a way, experiencing a scene of powerful emotional appeal—the real histrionic ability. Often after one of his Passion sermons he would retire to the sacristy and quietly weep. Once when a pastor congratulated him on such a sermon Tom looked at him and said, as if in a partial daze, "For me He suffered; why should we not be willing to suffer for Him?"

In regard to the sin of Judas he presented an unusual interpretation, which in the light of some events of his later life, might seem to be significant. He felt that the apostle betrayed his Master not from mercenary motives but from ambition. Judas, he suggested, hoped by his treasonable act to win from the Jewish authorities a "post of honor equal to a Supreme Court justice of today."

His highly successful first sermon in New York City in January, 1892, was notable for a quality that in dealing with adversaries he usually did not display. His specific aim was to prove that the Gospel of St. John had really been written by that Apostle in the first century and not, as the rationalists charged, by a Christian posing as St. John many decades later. He presented with the utmost fairness, at their full strength, the arguments of his adversaries. The rationalist position was explained with great objectivity and a notable absence of mere emotionalism. In answering the charge, for example, that St. John's Gospel was nothing more than a late second-century production, he listed some of the concrete geographical and sociological details contained in the book—details that could have been known only to a man who had really lived in the period during and immediately following the lifetime of Christ.

The virtue of the sermon was that the rationalists were being answered on their own ground. Their objections were met patiently, scientifically, and with no recourse to mere generalized expressions of outraged orthodoxy. It is a pity that the preacher did not follow this method more regularly. His usual weapon in dealing with adversaries was the meat cleaver. The vitally important fact is, however, that this was precisely the approach that was most likely to convince an audience of the 1890's.

The age delighted in the devastating rhetorical sweep and did not ask for the meticulous logician's method of refutation. This New York sermon of Father Sherman was, therefore, an exception to his usual manner, but it was typical in the overwhelmingly favorable reception it won from his hearers. The bald truth was that there was something about the man that hypnotized his listeners into going along with him wherever and however he led.

Equally important were his lectures to dominantly Protestant audiences, usually assembled not in a church but in a public hall. In these talks he concentrated on two main themes: Socialism and what he regarded as a widespread plot to destroy the Catholic Church in America.

As regards the former of these topics he took a position which, as will be described later in fuller detail, marked him as one of the most vigorous opponents of the error. He may have failed to recognize the grain of truth in the Socialist argument: that the conservatives were holding a far too reactionary philosophy of property rights. Later he would attend more to the stronger argument against Socialism—the reformation of the social order by the conservatives themselves.

His address at St. Mary's, Kansas, on Easter Sunday of 1892 [or 1893], though given in a church, is representative of his stress on both these subjects.[316]

In insisting that every true American should set his heart against Socialism and anything that led to it, he declared that "first come the rights of the individual, second the rights of the family, and third the rights of the State. . . . The State is for man and not man for the State." To emphasize the proposition he gave his argument a typical Sherman touch. "I do think," he said, "that some States take away men's liberty as individuals. I do not think the State of Kansas [a 'dry' State, where, of course, at the moment, he was speaking] has the right to dictate to man what drink he shall have upon his table or prevent him from having wines or liquors in his cellar. If I were to tell them in France that when travelling through Kansas I would not be permitted a glass of wine with my dinner on the dining car they would exclaim amazed, 'And is not Kansas a free State?' The law makers of Kansas seem to think that temperance means prohibition and therefore take away your rights as an individual." Characteristic, too, was the final, not-too-happy fillip he added to this very frank slap at the government of Kansas: "The most intemperate man I ever knew was one who never tasted wines or liquor but drank such quantities of water that he died of dropsy."

But his most vigorous blasts he reserved for those who by insidious and cowardly means were attacking Catholics. This was a subject which would ever fill him with profound foreboding. He was convinced of the existence of a widespread and secret conspiracy to weaken and if possible to extinguish completely the influence of the Catholic Church in this country. That there really existed an underground campaign against Catholicism is certain, although Father Sherman seems to have exaggerated its importance.

It is certainly true that proscriptions of various kinds were imposed on Catholics in public life, and the press and even the "better" periodicals often printed attacks on the Church that would never be found in such organs today. Destruction of Catholic churches by mobs was not unheard of, even in the 'nineties and in the first decade of the present century. One might say, without fear of contradiction, that Catholics in the opinion of most of their fellow-citizens were something less than loyal Americans since, said the Protestants, they owed allegiance to a "foreign power," the Pope.

Mincing no words, Father Sherman flatly equated such accusers with Benedict Arnold. They were, he charged, guilty of treason, inasmuch as they were undermining one of the basic tenets of the Constitution—religious fredom: "A man who says [as indeed some were saying at the time] that any citizen of the United States is unfit to hold an office because of his religion sets himself against the Constitution and is guilty of treason." He went even farther: those guilty of such a flouting of the principle of religious liberty should be *punished*. Orders such as the "American Mechanics," "Junior Sons" and others dedicated to the destruction of Catholicism should be "crushed out" by every true American.[317]

But in a notable and widely publicized lecture at Omaha, Nebraska, in the early summer of 1893, Tom Sherman fired his biggest guns at what he regarded as the deep-laid plot against Catholicism. In doing so, furthermore, he linked the conspiracy with his other *bête noire*, Socialism.[318]

He spoke in the largest auditorium in the city—Exposition Hall—to about twenty-five hundred persons including most of the civil and religious dignitaries of the city. It was by no means a predominantly Catholic audience. Both sides were, as the press accounts remarked, "numerously represented." The section of the crowd that constituted the speaker's chief supporters was the group of Grand Army veterans scattered throughout the hall and occupying some places on the stage.

The speaker compared the anti-Catholic campaign to that of the Socialists. There brooded ominously over the great city of Omaha, he reminded them, the cloud of religious war. Catholics were being deprived of their constitutional right to worship God according to their conscience. And this intolerance was being exploited by Socialism to further the latter's dark ends. In that same hall on a date that should have shamed and silenced the speakers—on the previous Fourth of July——there were preached Socialistic doctrines which would "rend the ties of the nation, of home, of hearthstone and of God." And, at the same time, "blizzards of abuse" were heaped on Catholics and their Church. The conjunction of themes was not accidental. The men who hated the free American political system hated also Catholicism.

There should indeed prevail in the nation healthy differences of opinion; but these differences should be settled openly, with a regard for truth, and not in secret lodges. Religion has vested rights and should not be "thrown down as a firebrand into the midst of political life." There was, added Father Sherman, enough discord in politics already. (Laughter from the audience.)

He took up the charge that Catholics were seeking to "unite" State and Church: "I stand before you tonight as a citizen—a proscribed citizen, if you will. I might plead that my father fought for the Union (tremendous applause). . . . If the Pope imagined that he had direct political power and called upon me to renounce my allegiance as an American citizen to the President of the United States . . ., I would resist the Pope. If President Cleveland called upon me to renounce my spiritual allegiance to the Pope as Vicar of Christ and head of the Church, I would resent such an interference." That the papal delegate to the United States, Monsignor Satolli, was a threat to the country's independence was an allegation utterly ridiculous—"Why, the other day, he obeyed the summons of a Jersey judge!" The papal power is a spiritual, not a political power. It was being asserted that Catholics could not be loyal Americans. The speaker struck back vigorously at the indictment:

How about General Sheridan, Hugh Ewing, Captain Washington of Company A at Vicksburg, Luke Clark and thousands of men in blue who fought for the flag we all love so well? It was a Roman Catholic who planted the stars and stripes on the parapets at Vicksburg after three other Union soldiers had fallen in the attempt. It was a Roman Catholic who led the most dashing charge on that occasion and fell just outside the trenches of the enemy. Had it not been for Irish bayonets and the soldiers who came over with Lafayette in the revolution, how would American independence have been gained? George Washington instructed his soldiers not to speak against the Catholic religion. Had it not been for Roman Catholic assistance we would not now be a nation.

Father Sherman was pulling no punches: "At Detroit," he said, "before a crowd of these un-American people, I hurled the charge of cowardice in their teeth and proceeded to convince them that they were poltroons. No one [of them] resented it; no one answered my argument. If a man has a spark of manhood in his breast he will resent being called a coward."

Nor were his suggestions for meeting the anti-Catholic conspiracy merely the conventional ones: "In the . . . Know Nothing campaign of the past similar attacks were made, and . . . resulted in prejudicing many people against the Catholic Church until fair-minded American citizens took the platform and with two pistols on the table in front of them proceeded to talk reason to the more rabid exponents of Know Nothingism." It was the fighting technique of the great General Stanley to "get his enemy on the run, then stick a bayonet in him and keep him on the run."

This, declared Father Sherman, was the way these religious bigots should be treated. "I fired," he thundered, "the first gun in this campaign at Detroit at V. K. Booth [one of their leaders], the . . . assassin of the Constitution. I have him on the run and I propose to put the whole organization on the run."[319]

This was pretty hot shot, and doubtless it was regarded by many Catholics as being too daring. In his political conflict with South Carolina in 1832, President Andrew Jackson had asserted that he would hang the first nullifier he could find to the first tree he could find; but nobody believed that he meant it. In regard to Tom Sherman's threat no one could have a similar assurance. His pistols on the table and his bayonet in the back were to return to haunt him.

However, of one fact we are, on the evidence, certain. The address made a tremendous and highly favorable impression throughout Nebraska. The mixture of stars and stripes and two-fisted manliness had an irresistible appeal.

It was sometimes charged that in lectures of this kind he was an exhibitionist. Whatever the grounds for the accusation, they must be mitigated when applied to his preaching. If on occasion he played to the gallery in a public hall, he was too intently sincere to do so in the pulpit. There he was all on fire with the realization of the sanctity of his message; and he was not tempted to think of histrionic effects. If they came, they did so naturally. He once expressed his concern at the fact that many in his congregation were actuated by a desire to see the son of General Sherman rather than to listen to the word of God that he spoke. He termed this a "vulgarity of curiosity" and felt that it "does much to spoil the sacred character of the work."[320]

There was no type of audience he more loved to talk to than that of GAR veterans. After a sermon at Cedar Rapids in the early spring of 1896, he retired to the parish rectory to hold an informal reception for a large group of old soldiers. They each insisted on shaking his hand and he regaled them for an hour with stories of the war. Cigars and other refreshments were passed around.[321]

He was scarcely ever as contented and gay as when he was enjoying such company. His pleasure was augmented when the veterans would speak in praise of his father, as they always did. If the Sherman family as a whole came in for some compliments, so much the better. He was undoubtedly delighted when, on the Cedar Rapids occasion, one of the old men "referred to the fact that the Sherman family appear to be devoting themselves to the cause of human liberty and republican government, and cited the recent speech of Senator John Sherman on the labor question.[322] (The interesting point about this observation was that the Senator's sentiments on this specific question were rather more liberal than Tom's would have been.)

But, as there are hierarchies of preference, Tom's purest joy was to be with his father's own veterans of the Army of the Tennessee. These heroes of the war assembled annually to renew their sacred memories of the conflict and to reaffirm their undying affection for each other. They had as a special mark of devotion to their leader, re-elected each twelve-month the General as their head. To their meeting in November, 1892—a year after the General's death—they had invited his son to address their thinning ranks. The first section of his speech on this occasion made the first pages of the next morning's papers as the sensation of the hour. With a few bitterly spoken paragraphs, he had catapulted himself into an ominous struggle between two social classes.

The background for his remarks was this: At the time of the General's death the family had ordered from an Eastern stone-cutting firm a granite shaft to be placed over the tomb. The work had been undertaken by the cutters but, just as it was almost completed, a laborers' strike occurred in the industry and the Sherman monument was immobilized in the company's yards. For months the family had been trying fruitlessly to secure delivery.

Tom had taken the affair as a personal affront to the General's memory, and he was, as the press reported, "passionately indignant." He expressed his wrath to the Tennessee veterans in the following words: "The nearly completed monument stands there now, and there seems to be no power in this country, in state or nation, to move that stone from the hands of the labor union. I am told that they will not consent to let us have it moved, so I only know one way to get it, and that is to organize one of his old regiments, and go there and take it by force. . . . We [the family] feel sad and mortified to think that in our own country, which you have made so free, you cannot even move our father's simple monument from the spot where these workmen hold it confined."

The veterans approved of his stand with thunderous cheers. It was just the kind of a call to direct action that tickled them, nor did they stop to consider the very real difficulties of carrying the plan into effect. The spectacle of the ancient members of the Army of the Tennessee marching east to break the picket lines was, after all, somewhat ludicrous.

There were others, however, who did not take kindly to what they termed the arrant and dangerous reactionary views of Father Sherman. They particularly were troubled at his final blast against labor unionism: "There is a power among us, then, higher and stronger than the power that you conquered, and our generation has yet to meet the problem of conquering, or, in other words, of subduing to law that giant power."[323]

The remainder of his address was in a different vein. He told them how his father had been indifferent to honors—"I was by his side in his library on Garrison Avenue when he received the telegram . . . at the time of the Republican Convention of 1884 . . . which said substantially: 'Your name is the only one we can agree upon, you will have to put aside your prejudices and accept the Presidency.' Without taking his cigar from his mouth, without changing his expression, . . . my father wrote the answer: 'I will not accept if nominated and will not serve if elected.' He tossed it over to me to be handed to the messenger, and then went on with the conversation . . . as if the Presidency was to him nothing."

There was, however, one distinction that the General *did* crave—to preside over the Society of the Army of the Tennessee. And, by conferring upon him, year after year, this honor, the Society had underlined the fact that he was greater in loving men than in combating them, and that he was a man who valued the friendship and affection of his old comrades above all else. It was his son's duty and deep pleasure to thank them for their tribute which had so cheered his father's declining years.

The speaker then developed an idea that was dear to him—the grandeur of the quality of loyalty that seemed to be nurtured by war. There was, he thought, in the evolution of the race, one type of character that has come forth higher than any other. It is the knightly type and it is specified by its feeling of loyalty to the Chief. The trait, he felt, had been manifested in its fullness by his hearers in their attitude toward their old leader. As the son of that leader, he stood before them to thank them. He was there to surrender his heart to the Grand Old Army of the Tennessee.[324] The knightly posture, loyalty to the Chief, both of these feelings nourished by war which, as he said, "we all admire"—everything here was quite typical of Tom Sherman's outlook. Needless to say, it was exactly the tone to inspire the GAR veterans with enthusiasm.

CHAPTER 10

The Chicago Music Hall
Address

PERHAPS HIS GREATEST address during this first period of his public achievement was that given in the vast Central Music Hall at Chicago on February 4, 1894. He had come up from St. Louis to talk on a topic specially chosen by himself—"The Jesuit, Fact and Fiction." The Order, at the time, was under vicious and unfair attack from many quarters. It was high time, he felt, to reveal to the American people the true character of the Society of Jesus. Apart from its intrinsic value, the address is highly significant in view of his later career as a Jesuit.

A few hours before he spoke he was interviewed by the press on some general topics. He expressed to the newsmen his ideas on religion and politics. He was proud of the progress of the Catholic Church in this country. In Chicago there were a hundred Catholic parishes; fifty years before, there had been none. Political conditions in the United States, he believed, were the best possible for the growth of the Church. Complete separation of church and state was the most fruitful means of nourishing religion. A man's religious tenets should not be considered when he enters politics. As long as he is an honest politician, what difference does it make whether he be a Catholic, a Methodist, or a Baptist?

Broadening the scope of his remarks, he said he had a supreme faith in America. And he loved the American individual—"There is something in his character which we cannot find in any other nationality."

When asked whether he thought Cardinal Gibbons might be elected Pope, he answered with rather unusual frankness. It must be remembered, he reminded his questioners, that the Catholic Church is "the greatest factor in the world in influencing nations." Therefore it would be better to have as Supreme Pontiff a European, who would be more adept at dealing with the Great Powers of the Continent.[325]

On the following evening he addressed a multitude that packed to the doors the great Central Music Hall in downtown Chicago. It was by no means a dominantly Catholic audience. It represented a cross-section of the thinking people of the metropolis and included some of the most outstanding leaders in civic affairs. Tom Sherman enjoyed that night a superb opportunity to present his message to the most influential minds in Chicago. Probably no public lecture by a clergyman up to that time had received the wide attention as this one was destined to evoke.

His modestly confident manner, as he advanced to the rostrum to begin, showed no effects of an unpleasant incident that had occurred as he left St. Louis. His rector, Father Rudolph Meyer, contrary to what seems to have been his generally forbearing attitude, had administered to him a rudely sharp warning against pride. The remark had hurt, though Tom had been able temporarily to forget it.[326]

His appearance on the stage and his general style was variously described by the newspapers next morning. He was a "young man of spare, wiry, upright form . . . with a strong intense face and a vibrant voice."[327] (It is notable that his hearers almost invariably referred to the richness and beauty of his tones.) He held in equilibrium the opposed qualities of dash and meekness.[328] His discourse was "keenly logical," but "at times the passion of religious fervour carried him beyond the cold-bloodedness of a lecture proper, and then he stood out with splendid interest as an orator, lofty and inspiring."[329] He talked for two hours straight, referring only once to his notes.[330]

He began his lecture with an elaborate picture of the magnificent Court of Honor at the recent Chicago World's Fair. The description followed closely the current cumbrous and highly colored rhetorical style and reached its climax in a word-painting of the colossal statue of Liberty that rose out of the Court's artificial pool. He then came directly to his theme: "Liberty is the divine prerogative, colossal in proportion, springing straight from the broad basin of the soul's essence. . . . Take her away, your court of honor is meaningless; diminish her, your court of honor is not human; cloud her in secrecy or slander or unmanly plotting, and she is the opposite of divine; touch her little finger, you are guilty of outrage; cut off her right hand, you are a villain; stab at her, you are a traitor."

This, he said, is precisely what the enemies of the Jesuits have done. They have violated the principle of American liberty that a man is free to worship God as he pleases—"As recently as January 20, 1894, threats of banishment have been uttered against our Order by a noted periodical. The issue contains a cut of the burning Peristyle. It is a happy coincidence. Burn the Peristyle, banish the Jesuits! The two propositions stand closer than the writer imagined." The orator was now in full sweep:

"Would you banish Marquette, who first traversed this country from Northern Wisconsin to the Mississippi, which he discovered, and who was the first white man to set foot in Chicago? Would you banish [Charles] Carroll, who signed the Declaration of Independence? Or De Smet, who was the first to carry Christianity among its inhabitants? Think of this before you say you'll banish from free America the sons of Loyola who dare to bear the name of Jesus Christ!" (Applause.)

Refuting the charge that the Jesuits were opposed to political liberty, he recalled how the Jesuit Bellarmine had, in his writings, laid the theoretic foundations for modern democracy and had insisted that all legitimate power to govern comes from the people. He then paid a glowing tribute to the sainted founder of the Order: "Ignatius Loyola, the knightly, the loyal, the true, the father of heroes and the maker of saints, . . . the best loved and the best hated man in all the world, save only his Master. . . ." It was Ignatius who conceived the daring plan of forging the weapon to beat back the Reformation, to rekindle fervor in tepid souls, to reform congregations decayed and establish new ones fitted to do the giant work of Christian charity throughout the world. It was he who formed and inspired a Xavier, scattered colleges over Europe as our army scatters its fortresses over the prairies, gave ten thousand writers to the cause of science, letters, and the arts, revived Catholic learning, reformed real abuses, and gave to his little Company a code of laws so wise that they still remain a marvel of wisdom to the learned.

The orator insisted—in sharp opposition, be it noted, to the official and representative Jesuit view—that Ignatius had regarded Protestantism as the prime enemy, and that his followers held the same opinion: "He organized an Order expressly to fight and down Protestantism. He considered all outside the Church as doctrinally his enemies and *so do we now*. Our mission is to show our Protestant brethren, baptised with the same baptism that we have received, that in the Catholic Church alone can there be that unity for which they hope." (The interpretation of Jesuit aims was, it must be admitted, unhistorical and untrue. The main objective of St. Ignatius was to re-invigorate the spiritual life of Catholics and to convert others to religious truth; but they were not *directly* waging a crusade against Protestantism. Tom Sherman, however, never clearly perceived this fact. He never minced words about Protestantism. On that point he would strain even the amenities as when, at a dinner party one day, he suddenly turned to a lady beside him and said, "You should be a Catholic. You are too intelligent not to be a Catholic."[331])

He then went on to describe the Jesuit as he really is: "The great religious orders which did so much for Christianity . . . continue to flourish. But they differ from us in that they are less directly devoted to an active life, are not so readily modified to serve the age they live in, and therefore present a less aggressive front to the modern enemies of Christianity. We are regulars in the army of Christ; that is, men vowed to poverty, chastity, and obedience. . . . Such I take to be the Jesuit: a Christian gentleman, a scholar as far as time and occasion allow, and a priest of Jesus Christ. All sciences are reduced to one in his mind in the bright knowledge of the word of God. All virtues are summed up for him in devoted personal friendship for Christ, and all hopes and desires unified and satisfied in his blissful embrace of the spirit of his divine Master."

The Jesuit should sleep on the heights of Thabor, in Peter's tent, with his eyes ever on the sun of justice. He sees all things in the light of the good to the souls of men. The world cannot rise to understand such detachment; therefore it dreams that Jesuits are scheming ambitiously when they watch like hawks to prevent all scheming: "If anyone knows that a Jesuit is scheming let him notify our Superior and he will see how soon a reprimand falls on the offender's head." It was easy to see, therefore, that this was a most difficult and sublime life: "Inner union with God, close and perpetual; outer condescension to all manner of demands; the spirit of prayer and of labor; in the world and not of it; so that a man always sees the heights stretching above him and never dares say that he has arrived at the point of being a representative Jesuit."

As he continued, his eulogy of the Order became more personal:

It would ill become me as a member of the Order of Jesus to speak in praise of the body. It is as one deeply indebted to a mother that I speak. One who feels that he owes a debt and that, though he can never repay it, there is some small satisfaction in expressing his gratitude. What I feel toward Chicago for a splendid exhibition . . . I feel to Loyola's band for a superb exhibition of Christian virtue and for constant encouragement in treading the difficult path of Calvary. I have been for thirty years under the influence of the Jesuits, and therefore I owe it to truth and justice to say that the accusations of which I have spoken are beneath contempt; that it is the supreme honor of this life to be a Jesuit; . . . and that to condemn the Order of Jesus is not only to condemn progress and thought and culture and virtue, and all that is sweet and beautiful, but to condemn Jesus Christ Himself, with Whom and for Whom the Jesuit is crucified.

He could not forbear an expression of heartfelt affection for his fellow-Jesuits: "Comrades, loyal comrades in life and death I hail you—men true to Him Who gave us His blood and who work for Jesus in fact and not in fiction!" The climax of his eulogy evoked prolonged applause: "It would ill become me, the son of a soldier, to apologize for my obedience as a Jesuit!"

Father Sherman next considered the common allegations against the Jesuits. The Order was accused of practicing the doctrine that the end justifies the means. He turned the charge against his opponents: "We neither teach nor practice the doctrine—our foes do both. First, they teach that the aim alone makes an act good or bad, which is the same as teaching that the end justifies the means."

Moreover, he added, the anti-Jesuits and anti-Catholics put the doctrine into actual practice: "The Constitution guarantees the equal right of all in politics. Therefore they form leagues to violate the Constitution. . . . What justifies this defiance of all law? . . . Why, don't you know the end justifies the means? The end is to destroy all Catholics. First, take away their political rights, then you can take away all their rights. The supreme law says there shall be no religious test for office. These men say there shall be a religious test. Which is to stand? Which is to fall—the Constitution or this pirate crew? . . . Why this return to barbarism? Why, the end justifies the means, of course. Barbarism is better than Catholicism; therefore, crucify the Catholics, if you have to pull down the old flag to do so!"

So the reprehensible theory and application were all on the other side. "The moment it is proven to me," said Father Sherman, "that this doctrine is countenanced by the superiors of the Jesuit Order . . . then will I leave the Order!"

For the more intellectual members of his audience he threw in a bit of history and exegesis. There had been indeed an axiom favored by Scholastic philosophers and translated from the Latin thusly: "Where there is a lawful end there must be a lawful means." This of course is not a statement that the end justifies the means. But, by a dishonest interpretation, it could easily be twisted into such a meaning.

One last blast he delivered in his best hammer-and-tongs style—a retort to the ex-priests and ex-nuns who, at the time, were making a career of calumniating and "exposing" the "horrors" of Catholic convents:

Attacks upon his Order scarce cause the Jesuit an amused smile. Attacks upon the church of God rouse the lion in his breast. Attacks on Catholic womanhood make him a flame of living fire. He points the finger of scorn at those who have deserted the standard of their sublime chief, leaped over the barrier of the sanctuary, broken their vows to God, and who, with effrontery worthy of the demon their master, traipse about the land to feed a morbid, vulgar, and vicious appetite with the garbage drawn from the sewers of vice. . . . Fortunately, Catholic womanhood stands so high, holds up to the world so august an example of supreme virtue that we have but to murmur the name of the Sister of Charity or the Little Sister of the Poor, to open the heart and turn the tide of bigoted hate. By their fruits you shall know them.

The lecture was a huge success. Even that part of the audience that was not Catholic was deeply impressed. Father Sherman had utilized well an incomparable opportunity to speak to the best minds of Chicago about the religious Order he so ardently loved.

It had been said by his critics that sometimes during his speeches he allowed himself to be carried away by the applause he evoked. It had been further charged that in such instances he was easily tempted to enlarge on a favorably received argument to dangerous extremes. Stimulated by the audience's reaction he would, it was said, over-state his position or try to prove too much. After the Music Hall address, however, his friends might feel indeed that in this instance he had resisted the lure. He had hit hard at his opponents, but he had not been in any sense imprudent.

One may therefore imagine the shock produced when the next morning's *Herald* quoted Father Sherman as saying in the course of his speech the following:

For my own part I have no apology to offer for the acts of Catholics in vigorous protest against these wholesale venders of infamy the ex-priests and ex-nuns. The father who slays the corrupter of his child must be left to God Almighty, the man who shoots an anarchist at sight is a public benefactor. These ex-priests are anarchists of the worst stamp. They appeal to free speech. If free speech means the right to debauch the minds of women and children at pleasure, then I, for one, say better free bullets than free speech. If America will not draw the line between freedom and license, then America means chaos and old night. There is no right to do public wrong, and every town and village must prevent it. Sue for libel. The evil is done when the suit is begun. Of course I know you will not agree with me, but if the blight of corruption were to threaten your own you would act on the principle of prevention. There are certain questions that cannot be touched in public without doing vast harm. The state exists to preserve public morality.[332]

This was obviously dangerous doctrine which could not be squared with Catholic ethics or American law. One could legitimately scorn the religious turncoat or the anarchist, but one could scarcely shoot them on sight.

The storm broke on Father Sherman almost before he had finished breakfast that day. What had happened? Those who had attended the lecture were certain that the speaker had not delivered the paragraph. He himself denied that he had done so. But, asked the public—including his Jesuit brethren—how had the *Herald* obtained the passage? The mistake was all the more embarrassing to one such as Tom, who had at least twice warned his brother Cump about the dangers of loose talking to newspaper men.[333]

Not until that evening did the explanation become public. As he was about to board the night train for St. Louis he was met by *Herald* reporters who, under pressure of public indignation and even disbelief, insisted that he verify the words which, they claimed, they had printed in good faith. He declared that in his address he had not uttered the passage. "But," retorted the reporters, "the paragraph, as it appears in the paper, is just as it was in the typewritten manuscript you gave us."

"Yes," said Father Sherman, "but it was a portion of a speech I had prepared against certain anti-Catholic organizations. It must have accidentally gotten mixed up with the manuscript of my last night's address. The two sets of pages were placed close together on my desk while I was writing them."

"Then," urged his interviewers, "you intend to deliver this passage at some future time?"

Father Sherman was rather neatly caught. He responded rather lamely that he had written the paragraph for that purpose but he probably would modify the words before actually delivering them. Or he might not use the paragraph at all. In any case, he repeated, he had not used it on the previous night.

The Jesuit's rather awkward defense did not improve the situation. It was bad enough to have so mixed up his manuscripts. More embarrassing was his admission that he had in fact intended to deliver the passage in another address. The unfortunate error and the clumsy attempt to explain it was grist for the mill of the opponents of the Order.

Despite the regrettable *faux pas* that marred it, the Sherman speech at Music Hall was one of his finest efforts and presented the Society of Jesus in its true and splendid colors to the eyes of thousands who had hitherto been deceived about her. It was also an irrefutable testimony to his ardent devotion toward the Order. It is probable, however, that these considerations did not mitigate the rigor of his reception by his rector at St. Louis, where the *Herald* of February 6 had already arrived.

His other important work during some of these years—teaching philosophy to the young Jesuit seminarians at St. Louis University—was not meeting with as much success as was his preaching and lecturing. He had undertaken his professorial duties with enthusiasm, all the more so because the subjects he was to lecture on—law, morals, and the social sciences—were congenial to his intellectual tastes.[334] But he still lacked some of the indispensable qualities of a teacher. In his explanations in class he continued to be, as in his scholastic years, rhetorical and declamatory rather than scientific. His intense interest in contemporary issues still tricked him into linking them too indiscriminately with the material of his course. His lectures abounded just as much in detours and in forays into the striking but less important periods. Whether as a student or a teacher he had not mastered the severe art of concentration.

More serious than these intrinsic defects was an external circumstance: he missed too many classes. It was impossible that he should be travelling around the country on his preaching and lecturing tours and at the same time be able to meet his students at the assigned times so many days each week. Too often his classes filed into his lecture room at St. Louis to find he was preaching in Minneapolis or St. Paul. When he returned he would give them some really inspiring accounts of his priestly missions; but this was not precisely the teaching of philosophy. A feature of his courses was the notice that appeared with embarrassing regularity on the bulletin board: "Father Sherman will be unable to meet his classes today."

The highly difficult task of evaluating a teacher's influence over his students will not be attempted here; but one question may be asked. Did he do them more good by his example as an indefatigable and enthusiastic preacher of the word than he would have done by being a competent and conventional professor of philosophy? He would come into the classroom after a successful mission tour and pour out to them his deep consolation at what he had been able to do for souls. He would be full of the thrill that comes to the devoted priest when he feels the souls of men like wax under his hands, to be molded into a form acceptable to Christ. It was good for the young Jesuit seminarians to hear this. The difficulty was that it did not help them in examinations.

His shortcomings as a professor undoubtedly aggravated another situation that was becoming more and more serious. There was a constant, though gradual, increase in the friction between himself and his religious superiors. The problem, like every clash of temperament, is not easy to analyze. The Jesuit administrators of Tom Sherman's time were a remarkable generation. Most of them were Germans, or of German descent. They were, to their very bones, vigorous, self-denying, and indomitable pioneers. They were represented at their best by the tremendously energetic and dynamic Father Arnold Damen who, after founding the Jesuit parish and college at Chicago, set up five other churches and schools in other parts of the city. These men were totally dedicated to God's work. They never spared themselves, they overcame all obstacles, and their justification is in the magnificent results they left behind them.

But, perhaps inevitably, and as even an incident of their effectiveness, they were often rigid in their human relations. Demanding much of themselves, they demanded much of others. They had little time for the niceties of personal intercourse or for the finer perceptions. They were, of course, educated men; but the emphasis of their lives was, quite properly, on prayer and untiring labor for the good of the church rather than on cultural attainments.

Between such provincials, rectors, and deans, and Tom Sherman there was sure to be an incompatibility. On the one side was a high-strung individualist of an extreme refinement of nature and a disposition unusually sensitive. On the other side were the tough-fibred, practical, blunt, and devoted priests just described.

With the best of good faith on the part of everybody, misunderstandings and misinterpretations were sure to arise. Father Sherman, giving himself without stint to what he regarded as his specific mission—his preaching and his lecturing, would seem to some of his superiors to be slighting the "regular observance" of the rules of the Order. He would, for example, be frequently absent from the spiritual exercises held at stated intervals in the rectory at St. Louis. He could not be there if he was giving missions through half of Kansas. What irritated a rector, however, was the fact that Father Sherman seemed to be always in Kansas or at points farther west.

A reprimand would be given and, since it would seem quite unwarranted to the recipient, would be not very graciously taken. The reaction would induce two unfortunate attitudes—in the superior, distrust, and in Tom Sherman, puzzlement and bitterness at what he considered an inexcusable lack of a sense of values. A barrier was slowly growing up between the young priest and those whom it was his obligation as a Jesuit to obey. The barrier was not insurmountable nor necessarily permanent, but it was there.

Surprisingly, perhaps, these difficulties did not seem seriously to affect his spirits. He insisted that he was "not in the least depressed; on the contrary they say I am growing younger."[335] If he had his moments of extreme distaste for the world, it was in the right manner. To Cump, he wrote: "I see more and more of misery and suffering and become more and more ready to leave the planet when it pleases the Master. To be with Papa and Mama, Willie and the rest is a superb joy to look forward to."[336]

One rather remarkable admission, however, he had made at the outset of his career as a sacred orator: "Preaching is very exhaustive [sic] work and I cannot stand much of it."[337] Years later it would be noted that an hour's intensive action in the pulpit incapacitated him for several hours afterward. This fact —and indeed it is more than once corroborated—makes the extent and high quality of his sermons and lectures all the more to be wondered at.

If his health and nerves were at this time generally good, he never ceased to be solicitous about the physical well-being of his brother Cump, in regard to whom, however, he had no real cause to worry. "Don't read at night," he advises, "if you can help it, for sooner or later you will be sorry for it."[338] And again he had written from Woodstock previously: "Don't study too hard. . . . Health is worth more than wealth or knowledge, and you need *at least* four hours a day in the open air under [?] saddles [or] on foot."[339] Cump is urged also to relax in the evenings with "sprightly friends."[340] The admonitions could have been wholesomely applied to Tom himself.

His consciousness of the great family heritage of honor that he bore was as keen as ever. "The letters [of General Sherman to his family] in the January *Century* were excellent and thrilling," he told Cump, "What a name we have to carry!"[341]

During the last half of 1894 and part of 1895—as far as the date span can be calculated—Tom Sherman was undergoing what is termed in Jesuit language the "third noviceship" or "tertianship." This is an intensive course of ascetical studies and training submitted to by the young priests of the Order shortly after their ordination. It is, by intention, a time of temporary withdrawal from active duties and an opportunity for taking stock of oneself spiritually.

Basing our judgment on his own words, we might suppose that he would have found the tertianship agreeable. He had said, in the Music Hall address:

Silence, secrecy and solitude are as essential for greatness of soul as for the growth of a tap root. All that is great in this world is hidden. I mean, of course, morally great. The Order of Jesus not only teaches this, but practices what it teaches. Happiness is peace of heart. Peace is found in privacy, not in publicity. Therefore, men thrust into publicity are to be pitied and prayed for. Men who seek publicity are fools. Nothing but the need of human souls can drag the Jesuit from his sweet retirement, and he shrinks back as soon as permitted, asking only the chance to do a little good in a quiet way.[342]

It was well if he made the most of this period of recruitment of additional spiritual strength. Soon he was to face one of the greatest crises of his life.

CHAPTER 11

Repulse and Recovery

An impartial evaluation of Tom Sherman's achievements as a preacher and lecturer from 1891 through the first quarter of 1896 must place him at the topmost rank in the field. Yet something occurred in the latter part of 1895 that clouds the picture with no small mystery. All the evidence shows that at this time he was sweeping everything before him and winning unusual success, and this would continue for at least another twelve-month. But, in the first week of 1896, he was ordered by the Provincial of the Missouri Province to discontinue his lectures because of complaints that had been reaching St. Louis during the preceding several months. He had been, according to these charges, putting on too much of a "show" in his public addresses (not in his pulpit sermons) and surrounding them with entirely too much theatricalism.

There is nothing in the record up to this time to prepare us for the sudden change in his professional fortunes. Equally strange is the fact that his mission and sermon work—as distinct from his lectures—does not seem to have been any less intensive or less fruitful for almost an entire year after this setback. We are hence presented disturbingly wtih two Father Shermans—the famed and nationally courted pulpit and platform orator, and the imprudent speaker whose scope of work is sharply limited by his superiors.

His own response to the order that took him off the lecture circuit is surprisingly submissive. "I had already made up my mind," he writes to the Provincial, "that my lectures must be stopped before Father Muller [his immediate superior on the Mission Band][343] gave his command, for the simple reason that opera house performances and 'exuberant enthusiasm' of a purely natural character are not in the spirit of our work for souls, even if the reason you mention did not exist at all."

He thinks he could offer some excuses for his conduct of the lectures but prefers not to do so since, to his mind, silent acceptance of the order to stop will bring greater blessing on his future work. He adds some details about his feelings which we would never have guessed: "To be entirely frank the reason given for Father Muller's command crushed the last spark of natural desire to do well in that disagreeable business [his lecture program!], but even apart from that I was thoroughly sick of the business, and convinced that in any case it was not according to the Institute [of the Jesuit Order]." He concludes by saying, "Your letter has restored my equilibrium and I again thank you."[344]

What seems to have happened during the next twelve months is this: he concentrated strictly on his mission work, not abating in the least his rigorous schedule; but something was wrong. His old flair was missing, he derived no pleasure or satisfaction from the work, and the quality of his sermons sharply declined. The climax came with a nearly complete nervous break-down in the summer of 1896. In June of the following year he was offered a reduced preaching program by his Provincial; but, in a long letter that tells much about himself, he asks for a further prolonged period of inactivity.

He is deeply grateful for his superior's solicitude. He realizes the Provincial is bending all effort to "make everything as easy sweet and pleasant [for him] as possible." But he believes that any attempt to resume preaching at this time would bring on again a total physical and mental break-down. He is now roughing it about the frontier mission of St. Ignatius in Montana, and letting his mind relax. He hopes that in six months' time he will be ready to resume preaching; but any attempt to do so now would be disastrous.

It is with great unwillingness that he thus dissociates himself temporarily from the Mission Band. He still has much at heart the missions to Protestants and hopes that the Band will continue them. With God's help he will be back on the job by Christmas, but meanwhile—"I am fit for sleeping and eating and a few poor prayers, that is all." He realizes he has never been robust, nor can he ever hope to be so. He regrets sincerely that his condition prevents him from engaging in the work he loves. He is very much ashamed of the poor quality of his work of the year preceding—"But the truth is it was a weary drag." Only at the end does his letter hold a note of hope: "I am young yet and hope to be a missionary for a generation or more."[345]

The plea of Father Sherman was granted, and for the next several months he took a vacation in the West. In the following November or December Father Edward Purbrick, the Provincial of the Maryland-New York Province, received a request from Dr. Paul Thorndike, Tom's brother-in-law,[346] that the convalescent be permitted to spend the Christmas holidays at the Doctor's home in Boston. The meticulous Father Purbrick was somewhat puzzled. The request should have been referred by Dr. Thorndike to Father Thomas S. Fitzgerald, the Missouri Provincial, if the Doctor made the request at all. The normal procedure would have been for Father Sherman himself to make it. Father Purbrick referred the matter to the Missouri Provincial, who approved the request.

But Father Purbrick was not so easily to disengage himself from the affairs of Tom Sherman. In early January he received from Dr. Thorndike another communication that greatly disturbed him. The Doctor informed him that Tom's stay in Boston had done the patient much good but that, for his full recovery, the following additional program was required: (a) several more months of complete relaxation, mental and physical; (b) these months "should be spent as far as is possible away from the necessary routine of the houses of his Order"; (c) he should make a trip abroad under the conditions specified in "b".

This, thought Father Purbrick, was asking a very great deal. And his reaction was heightened when he read the letter from the invalid himself, arrived by the same mail. Tom began by asking permission to pay short visits to his aunt at Tarrytown, New York, to his cousin, Mrs. James Tracy at Albany, and to Archbishop Ryan at Philadelphia. He then got down to brass tacks:

This request is in pursuance of medical advice to seek complete rest and change out of our houses. My brother-in-law, Dr. Thorndike, says that unless for some months I live as if I were not a Jesuit, and seek only amusement and recreation, I shall always be a burden on the Society and never can hope to recover mental vigor. He strongly advises a trip to Europe as the most hopeful remedy and I accordingly respectfully request you to arrange for this. I feel that I cannot consistently apply to my own Provincial because I expressly requested to be transferred to you, with a view of obtaining such permissions as I felt I should need under doctors' orders to

secure my convalescence. However, I may state that Father Fitzgerald [the Missouri Provincial] does not object, as he himself hinted
at the advisability of making an effort to secure the permission when
I broke down last spring. If you send me abroad, therefore, you need
not fear that Father Fitzgerald will find fault. I cannot help feeling
that there is danger of being tied up in red tape and I look to you
to cut it and open the way to relief. Months of attempted rest in our
houses have resulted in gradual weakening instead of improvement,
and lest this should go on indefinitely and without result I beg you
to grant the permissions which physicians request, even order me to
seek.[347]

The harassed Fr. Purbrick transmitted both these epistles
to the Missouri Provincial and wrote one himself to Dr. Thorndike. He assured the latter that Tom's Jesuit superiors were well
aware of his need for further rest. They had no intention of
putting him back to work too soon. But there were real difficulties in the way of allowing him to live for an indefinite time
outside the Society's fold. These difficulties were both canonical
and psychological. The laws of the Church did not permit a
member of a religious order to be absent from the Order's houses
for more than a limited time. Furthermore, to put it bluntly,
Fr. Purbrick thought that the doctors were coddling Fr. Tom,
to his injury. "Whilst I recognize . . . the kindness of your
intention," he gently chided Dr. Thorndike, "I cannot think a
real kindness is done to him by letting him [follow the proposed
plan]. In any event the case has been given into the hands of
the Missouri Provincial."[348]

Father Fitzgerald was certainly going as far as possible to
meet Fr. Sherman's demands. It was beyond his power to concede the permission to live outside Jesuit houses. Furthermore,
such permissions had been explicitly refused to Fr. Sherman by
the Father General at Rome,[349] to whom Fr. Sherman had previously—and apparently without informing either of the two

Provincials—applied. But Fr. Fitzgerald would allow Fr. Sherman to live in any Jesuit house in the United States indefinitely, and would relieve him of all work and exempt him from much of the common rules. He would make an even greater concession: "As to a trip to Europe I also agree *in quantum possum* [insofar as I am able to do so.] With the correspondence in my· possession [from Fr. Purbrick and Dr. Thorndike] I will assume the responsibility and presume Father General's permission. He [Fr. Sherman] may sojourn for the same length of time in any European province whose hospitality I am able to obtain. For the present, perhaps, Your Reverence can assure him the hospitality of the English Province and thus save him time if he would like to set out at once. I feel I am stretching matters touching this European trip, but I consider the case as grave, if not extreme, and will make at once due representation to Father General."[350]

This double offer was duly transmitted by the Maryland Provincial to Fr. Tom, who found it extremely disappointing. He had convinced himself that his only hope of complete cure was, as he put it, "to live for awhile as if he were not a Jesuit." He failed to realize that it was decidedly too late to do that. His blind spot was encouraged—rather fatuously, it would appear —by well-intentioned medical men, beginning with his devoted brother-in-law.

Then, while he fretted at Boston or tried to forget his irritation by means of numerous visits to relatives and friends, a solution was provided—by the international situation! On February 15, 1898, the United States battleship "Maine" was blown up in Havana harbor, and on April 11 President McKinley sent his war message to Congress. He never dreamed that he was mitigating for two Jesuit Provincials an embarrassing situation and furnishing Fr. Thomas Sherman with a legitimate and highly agreeable way of securing his vacation outside the cloister walls. On May 16, 1898, Fr. Tom was mustered in as a chaplain attached to the Fourth Regiment, Missouri Volunteer Infantry.[351] Three months later, he sailed from Newport News, bound for Puerto Rico.[352]

The Spanish-American War has come to be regarded by American historians as an *opéra bouffe* affair notoriously lacking in dignity. The view has been confirmed by the recollection of such incidents as the headlong race between two regiments at Tampa to determine which should enjoy priority of transportation to the combat area; or the numerous heroic charges up hills found on closer examination to be spots of idyllic peacefulness.

The whole conflict has been latterly written off as being on the part of the United States a brutal imperialistic war of which we are now properly ashamed. We were the bullies—so runs the current interpretation—and the only respectable part of the record was that of the defeated Spaniards.

There is, however, another possible way of looking at the brief struggle of 1898-1899. In the first place, our armed intervention in Cuba and Puerto Rico actually brought permanent peace and law and order to regions where previously those requirements of civilization had been patently absent. As in the more notable instance of the Philippines, American occupation or the establishment of American hegemony over the territories produced—after the initial period of what was, to speak candidly, bulldozing—a vastly healthier, happier, and more civilized life for the native populations. This is not said to excuse all our excesses; it is meant to balance them fairly.

The Spanish-American War was, moreover, the beginning of the first experience of the United States in the governing of peoples who were not American citizens but American subjects. The lessons learned from that experience must be always an important part of our national fund of political wisdom.

Tom Sherman's involvement in the war was not as modest as one might have expected it to be. The United States Army chaplaincy in 1898 had not been organized to its present degree of competence. The clergyman assigned to the armed forces in the war with Spain had no clear-cut set of duties, nor did he have at his disposal the aids and assured position that he holds today. His opportunities for constructive service were, as a result, severely limited.

Yet, these deficiencies in the institution of the chaplaincy proved to be an opportunity for Tom in another direction. He did not by any means neglect his spiritual ministrations to the soldiers. He made frequent visits to the posts throughout the island to say Mass and hear the confessions of the troops. He established a club for the enlisted men and officers. He attended to the sick and dying men in the army hospitals. But he had abundant time for a kind of service that was of the highest value to the War Department. Indeed, it is not too much to say that his contribution in this special line was about as important as that made by any other individual army officer in the war.

Attached to the personal staff of General U. S. Grant, II, he acted as a special observer for the War Department.[353] On horseback, sometimes accompanying the General and more often alone, he covered the island from one end to the other to inspect the rapidly changing military, political, and economic situation. On one of these trips he was in the saddle almost continuously for thirty hours.[354] The final fruit of his observations, a lengthy report to Washington, is a remarkable document that reveals his keenness of perception and sound sense of the military and political necessities. The document ranks, in the present writer's opinion, with the very best of the contemporary analyses of the meaning of America's emergence as a colonial and world power.[355]

He provided his superiors with candid pictures of the lawless elements operating under the surface of Puerto Rican society and frequently breaking forth into armed banditry on the roads. Murder was for these violent men a conventional tool for the attainment of booty. Attacks on the wealthy plantation owners usually assumed the form of destroying their property by fire. Often the local governors secretly conspired with the outlaws, either through timidity or in the hope of sharing in the loot.

In a later published article, Father Sherman noted a profound sociological principle in action in the distressed regions: "A species of Ku Klux exists in this country. . . . We have let loose passions suppressed for ages and the result is hard to foresee. The worst results of war are not the wounds received in battle, but the universal alarm and unrest, the disturbance of all confidence, the violence of the unorganized, the wreaking of private vengeance and the paying off of old scores; in a word, in the reign of hate instead of love."[356] He was "appalled" at the poverty of most of the people, and at the filth of the sections of the towns where the poor lived. This situation was a breeding ground, he thought, for law-breakers.

It was his conviction that the officers and men of our army were regarded by the Puerto Ricans as "welcome guests" and were "abundantly able to preserve life and property and a normal condition of confidence everywhere." But he warned that the removal of our troops from any place at any time in the near future would be attended by disastrous consequences to the people. The Alcalde, or local governor, at Coamo, for example, said that he feared nothing so much as the departure of the American forces from his area. The people generally were showing a profound respect for American authority and the utmost confidence in the courage of our soldiers. Even the Spaniards who remained on the island rejoiced in the change of sovereignty because they saw that it brought peace and stability.

The best way of establishing good government in the country, urged Father Sherman, was to win the affection of the local rulers, build up their authority, and govern through them. The military arm should be used only as a standing reserve to be called on when necessary by the Alcaldes.

His estimate of the Puerto Rican character is sharp and discriminating. The Puerto Rican is basically a Spaniard, but he is to the latter what the American is to the Englishman. He congratulates himself much more on his differences from the parent stem than he does with respect to the resemblances. He has a touch of the handsome manner of the Old World with a great admiration for the progressive spirit of the New. He is immensely proud of his "honor"; this feeling becomes often a kind of ostentatious vanity which hardly merits the dignified name of pride. Yet, paradoxically, he has the good grace to laugh at his own foibles—probably because, despite his highly developed individualism, he puts God first. But he has not the slightest intention of correcting these foibles.

He is "gentle, docile, and kindly," but less frank in his dealings with others than an Anglo-Saxon would be; and he is naturally timid. In the case of the large property owners the latter trait has been aggravated by the paternalistic political regime on which hitherto they have too much depended for the solution of all problems. Exceptionally strong feelings for the ties of kinship and friendship lead often to the sheltering of criminals by the law-abiding and the failure to bear witness against the guilty. The Puerto Rican puts himself, his house, and everything that he has at your disposal on briefest acquaintance. He is loyal to his friends, but revengeful and double-dealing with his enemies.[357]

Fr. Sherman's concluding policy recommendations to Washington were couched in terms most solemn:

In undertaking to make Porto Rico a part of our nation, we are obviously engaged in a work new to the United States. A million people differing from us in language, literature, tradition, customs and manners welcome us by reason of political sympathy and a sentiment of confidence in our desire to govern for their good, to enlarge their liberties and to increase the substantial blessings they enjoy without imposing on them any new burdens. Porto Rico is not to be judged by the brimming excitement and manifold tendencies to unrest due to a vast political and moral upheaval nor by the acts of a few cunning marauders who avail themselves of exceptional circumstances to wreak private vengeance or indulge the barbarous instinct of destruction. Nor are we to argue their political incapacity from factional differences such as we ourselves are always subject to, but remembering that they have cities, towns, villages and are not waste lands like California and New Mexico in 1848; that they are highly civilized, have thousands of educated men, able lawyers, excellent doctors, clever merchants, manufacturers whose establishments aggregate many millions of annual output, we are bound to show them the largest measure of confidence, furnish them promptly with a civil territorial form of governing using the military arm as a protection, but not as a source of authority and holding out the promise of statehood speedily under definite conditions.[358]

That the presentation of this great opportunity to the American people had been attended by a considerable cost in our soldiers' lives is another circumstance of the war that is usually ignored. According to Tom Sherman's accounts, the mortality rate among the enlisted men was uncommonly high. Particularly regrettable is the fact that most of the deaths were due to disease. He speaks of "the throng that crowds our hospitals and relief ships," and adds, rather out of tone with his other comments on the conflict, "—the melancholy price paid for our aggressive spirit."[359] He refers again to "the field hospital where

long rows of the fever-stricken lie suffering."[360] He is consoled to
see that "every effort is being made to relieve them,"[361] and he
pays a special tribute to the gallantry and devotedness of several
of the officers' wives who are acting as volunteer nurses.[362]

Reporting in a field more properly his own, he notes the
edifying impression made on the native population by the fidelity
of our Catholic soldiers to their religious duties. The thronging
of large bodies of men to Holy Communion had been a spectacle
unknown to Puerto Rico until the American troops came.[363] This
is all the more surprising to the people inasmuch as they had
anticipated that the advent of the Americans would mean the
downfall of Catholicism in the island.[364]

As to the state of religion among the Puerto Ricans themselves,
Fr. Sherman's comments were not very favorable. This section
of his official report, together with his further remarks on the
same topic in his *Messenger of the Sacred Heart* article, raised
a small but severe storm in some quarters at home. Hence it is
important to know what he said and with what qualifications.

The condition of religion on the island, he wrote to the War
Department, is very unsatisfactory. All the inhabitants are, with
a few exceptions, nominally Roman Catholics. In every town
of any size there is a large and handsome Catholic church, yet
the services are very poorly attended. Out of a population of
forty thousand in the district of Utuado, for example, there are
barely two hundred who make their Easter duty.[365] Very few
of the men are more than Catholics in name. They are baptized,
married, and buried by the priest; that is about the extent of
their Catholicism.

There is little or no observance of the sanctity of Sunday.
Trade and other business seems to be more active on that day
than on any other. The plazas of many towns on a Sunday
morning present the aspect of a market and a fair combined.

The state of morality may be inferred from the fact that the number of illegitimate children exceeds that of those born in wedlock. Concubinage is said to be common and not sufficiently discountenanced either legally or socially. The method of burial is barbarous. At some places corpses are thrown into shallow graves, sometimes (it was reported to Fr. Sherman) without box or casket. The cemeteries are too small and horribly over-crowded. The Sacrament of Confirmation has not been administered in the island, except in a few places, for several years.[366] In this article, published at practically the same time as his confidential report was sent to Washington, Fr. Sherman summed up the situation in these terms: "Porto Rico is a Catholic country without religion, that is to say, there is little practical Catholicity here," But, he added, "Faith is not dead, but dormant."[367]

He made some surmises as to the causes of this deterioration in religious practice, and offered some constructive suggestions for reform. One of the chief reasons for the low state of Catholicity, he believes, was the undue dependence of the priests and bishops on the civil government. Two evils flow from this close relationship: the Church suffers the odium felt by the people toward the government, and the clergy indulge too freely in politics. Another unfortunate circumstance was the frequent lack of sympathy between priest and people. This was probably an incident of the strong class feeling so characteristic of the Spanish races. Also contributing to the wretched state of religion was the failure on the part of both clergy and people to apply the principle of association as a means for solving social problems.

The practical remedy, urged Fr. Sherman—and we can picture his satisfaction in presenting it—was the freeing of the Church's administration from the civil control which for years had clogged it, and the education of the clergy in ideals of sound and progressive social reform. If the terrible poverty of the people could be alleviated, they would be much more inclined to vitalize their religious practice. Most of the clergy, he insisted, were "excellent gentlemen" and good priests. Religion in the island was by no means doomed if prompt rehabilitation measures were adopted.[368]

On any fair analysis all these statements could be substantiated by the historical facts. Fr. Sherman was not exaggerating. Still less was he scolding or ridiculing. His observations, when published, however, brought down upon him considerable adverse criticism from his American fellow-Catholics. He was accused of providing ammunition for Protestants who sought to change the traditional faith of the Puerto Ricans. The Protestant press did, as a matter of fact, use his reports as a further excuse for proselytizing in the island. If, they argued, Catholicism was at such a low ebb among the Puerto Ricans, why not invigorate them with some fresh drafts from Protestantism? Some Catholic spokesmen unwisely tried to parry this line of reasoning by painting the Puerto Ricans as being excellent practical Catholics—a claim refuted by the Protestants with the greatest of ease, with Fr. Sherman's declarations before them.

There soon began to arrive at St. Louis some letters of protest against Fr. Sherman's "strictures" on Puerto Rican Catholicism. The Provincial was understandably disturbed when he saw that many of these complaints were issuing from high American Catholic ecclesiastics. To the everlasting credit of a truly great man, one of Tom's strongest defenders in the affair was Fr. John J. Wynne, the Jesuit priest-scholar of the Maryland-New York Province. It was Fr. Wynne's opinion, based on personal investigation of his own, that Fr. Sherman had reported nothing beyond the real facts.[369] The sputtering beginning of a tempest in a rather grotesque teapot soon subsided. As a matter of insurance, however, the Provincial urged Tom not to write any more on the subject.

Not all the time of the Chaplain of the Fourth Missouri Volunteers was consumed in gathering materials for reports. In at least one instance he derived some solid satisfaction from a near-participation in actual hostilities.

In the course of one of his trips of inspection through one of the wilder parts of the island he took refuge for the night in the hacienda of one Señor José Blanco. The Señor was in a state of great trepidation due to his fear of marauding bands in the neighborhood who had already destroyed one or more nearby plantations and had openly threatened to burn down his own. At dusk the household prepared themselves for an attack. Three of the civil guard appeared, armed with rifles, and posted themselves about the grounds. Lights were placed to command the approaches to all the buildings. The Señor, his young son, his servants, and his reverend guest the American army chaplain, took up positions within the main house, with loaded revolvers in their hands. His host's weapon, according to Tom, was of ancient pattern loaded with American cartridges which his son had trimmed down for the purpose: "Had it gone off at all, it could only have blown his hand to pieces."[370]

At about midnight the dogs began to bark furiously and a single pistol shot rang out on the night air. Instantly the defenders were out on the piazza, peering into the darkness as they tried to descry the expected enemy. The sky was lurid with the flames of a neighboring burning hacienda. Then came the sound of a party of men approaching the Blanco gate. The next few minutes provided one of the best anticlimaxes in a war studded with such. Whether Tom regarded it in this light is not clear from his narration: "I hallooed to them, and was answered in a tone quite distinctly American. This was comforting, but it might mean a *ruse de guerre,* so I posted myself beside the sentinel at the gate and when the advancing party came within range halted them and parleyed. They proved to be two soldiers, friends of Señor Blanco, who . . . had come to help him defend his property." The crisis ended with all the household going to bed "with the utmost confidence." Tom's later philosophizings on this experience are illuminating:

When I saw the smouldering ruins of an erst flourishing plantation, where a general officer of our army had been invited to take
breakfast that very morning, when I saw the sky reddened with the
flames of other buildings burning in the near distance, when I heard
the pistol shot which seemed to us to be the signal for an attack,
when I felt the keen alarm of those about me, guards and servants
and all, then for the first and only time in my life did I realize the
intense pleasure which there is in exposure to danger, a pleasure
which the psychologist may analyze as he chooses, the moralist
classify as he may, but a pleasure still, and one that leads all the
world of manhood to concede that fighting is the best fun in the
world. Yet the bravest men are the first to admit that they soon get
enough of it. Some two weeks later I had a long ride in a mail coach
which contained several thousand dollars and would have proved a
dainty prey for bandits; but the sensation of danger, even as we
drove through dreary jungles in the moonlight, was not in the least
comparable to that night at Señor Blanco's hacienda, a night which
I suppose must stand alone in the peaceful experience of the priest.[371]

He had, however, his more tranquil and meditative moments. Once he rode all night through what seems indeed to have been an almost idyllic and fairy scene. "I wish," he writes, "I could give a vivid description of the night ride, the tropic moon paling the stars and filling the air with silver sheen, the mountains rising black to the north, the palms and flamboyants here and there brushing the lines of the thick sugar cane, huts nestled amid flowers and fruit trees, here and there a gleam of light from a distant cottage sparkling like a fixed star on the horizon;

carts drawn by oxen and slowly wending their way to the distant market town, the road winding in and out, up and down, always veiled in shadowy splendor; a sense of peace and security balmy as the night air filling the soul with quiet joy and content."[372]

His sensitivity to his surroundings displayed itself in yet other directions. He was intensely interested in the flora and fauna that to the American eye were so strange. He seized every opportunity to talk to any of the natives who crossed his path, and manifested a keen appreciation of their so-different way of life. He noted the special manner in which the Puerto Ricans prepared coffee; "they coated the berry with sugar, and so when browned or burnt it has a coating or glazing that retains all the aroma within the berry."[373]

Only once, in a letter to his Provincial, appears the slightly ominous and familiar note: "I have been somewhat indisposed since I came to San Juan, but believe I can stand it out till my two years are up when of course I shall resign promptly, unless otherwise directed. . . . If I find my health notably impaired, I shall resign from the army without further ado."[374]

The sudden cessation of hostilities rendered these doubts academic, and made it easy and reasonable for him to return to civilian life. He headed for home, stopping over briefly at Cuba, where for a moment he dallied with the idea of staying for a while to help in the reconstituting of the sagging college of the Spanish fathers. The proposal was gently vetoed by the Missouri Provincial who, having secured a great deal out of this war, was unwilling to press his luck too far.[375]

CHAPTER 12

The Great Campaign:
Second Phase

WHEN TOM SHERMAN was appointed as a parish priest and travelling missionary in 1899, with his headquarters at Holy Family Church, Chicago, he was being placed, in a real sense, on trial. For the past four and a half years his health had been precarious. His one attempt at serious work during that period had been his military chaplaincy, the duration of which, as we have seen, had been almost curtailed by another weakening of his physical—though not his mental—powers. The assignment to Chicago was therefore to determine, both for his Superiors and himself, how much ministerial activity he could take.

The results of the experiment were not what we might have expected. Within a few months, he was giving most of the "big" sermons in the church plus frequent missions there and in other cities. Furthermore, his preaching, judged in terms of his hearers' response, was more effective than ever. The mere announcement that he was to occupy the pulpit was enough to attract crowds in overwhelming numbers.[376] He was in demand for sermons and missions throughout the city and was forced by exigencies of time and distance to refuse numerous invitations to preach that came to him from almost all sections of the country. It seemed, indeed, as if he had found himself again. Also, he was apparently deriving solid satisfaction from the work.

He found time, besides, to be the director of the parish Young Men's Sodality. Association with the young (except for formally teaching them) was always appealing to him, and they reciprocated the feeling. He salted the spiritual activities of the organization by outfitting the more athletic of them in new bright blue baseball uniforms and promoting a game in the college yard each Sunday afternoon.[377]

His reputation won him an invitation to make the main address before the Catholic Educational Association at its Cleveland meeting, July 9-12, 1906. The speech was a major contribution to Catholic educational theory. He argued vigorously in favor of the higher education of Catholic women—a position which, at the time, was remarkably progressive. He made the headlines of most of the Catholic papers of the country by his sharp criticism of what he called the submission of our nuns to "a rigid rule which seemed inconsistent with the spirit of progress in lines of personal [intellectual] endeavor."[378] In the opinion of sound Catholic thinkers of the period he had outlined a concrete program that was a generation ahead in its wise perception of the educational needs of our Catholic girls.[379] For several weeks after the address he was besieged by invitations from educational groups across the nation.

Soon it was recognized by his Superiors that his preaching talents should be utilized in a wider field. He was accordingly permitted to devote himself more and more to this work, and undertook once more the far-flung mission journeys that had built up his great reputation in the first half of the preceding decade.

This time he concentrated more and more on the aspect of mission work that was dearest to him—preaching to Protestants. No one can understand him who does not realize his intense solicitude for those whom he regarded as being deprived of the true Faith and who were—often subconsciously—thirsting for it. He was even at times in private contacts, though never in his sermons, impatient and blunt with Protestants who displayed indifference or opposition toward the arguments in favor of the Catholic Church. To what extent his passionate desire for making conversions was an outgrowth of his disappointment that his father had never become a Catholic is interesting food for speculation.

He undoubtedly had a special gift for winning the confidence of non-Catholics and a keen instinct for choosing the approach most likely to bring them over to his way of thinking. It is not surprising, then, that within three years he had established himself as one of the handful of Catholic preachers who were devoting themselves to this type of apostolate. Among Jesuits he was the first to be exclusively so engaged.

When the total score of his priestly work is calculated, this side of his activity must be reckoned as constituting one of his claims to unique preeminence. This praise is not too extreme. His achievement here was, by any objective, cold-blooded estimate, of an unimpeachable and—for his time—solitary grandeur. It will be interesting to watch him at work in this field.

At the mid-point of the first decade of the present century the most famous Catholic pulpit orator in New York City was the Jesuit Father William O'Brien Pardow. There were many who claimed that he was the outstanding Catholic preacher in the nation. It is highly significant, therefore, that in the spring of 1906 Father Pardow was superseded in his usual role as Lenten preacher at St. Patrick's Cathedral by Father Thomas Sherman, who gave the first series of sermons ever offered in the Cathedral for Protestants particularly. The success of the western Jesuit was immense. Each night he talked to crowds of 4,000 or more. His hearers were unanimous in their enthusiasm for his performance. Protestants by the hundreds thronged to the sermons, and in literally scores of instances joined the convert class that he set up before he left the city. He was attracting even many Protestant ministers. The mission was, in brief, a spectacular triumph.[380] He duplicated this success in Philadelphia, where for a full week he spoke to almost equally large crowds in the Cathedral there. The total number of his converts was steadily rising. Besides his work in the large cities, he was receiving invitations constantly from literally scores of smaller communities. He would close a week's session in Pittsburgh on Friday night and set off for another mission in Chillicothe, Ohio, or Nashville, Tennessee. After his sermons at New York City, he undertook a two-months' speaking tour through the whole state. Cincinnati, Cleveland, Milwaukee, Denver, and, of course, Chicago, brought him back to their pulpits again and again.[381]

He must have been greatly comforted by his success. Even for a priest dedicated to humility it was pleasant to hear his achievements spoken of with wondering admiration in Jesuit community rooms, diocesan rectories, and in the residences of bishops. These latter high ecclesiastical officials, it seemed, were always demanding his services. The invitations he received would have kept busy a half-dozen preachers.

For at least five years—from 1900 through 1905—he carried on from coast to coast the missions-for-Protestants campaign. No other single preacher even approached him in terms of actual results from the sermons. The evidence and the tribute is in the records of the crowds he consistently drew to hear him, and in the converts to the Church that his sermons produced.

His method in preaching to Protestants was that he drove them into a corner with his ruthless logic, and then he wooed them with the emotional appeal. His stress was always on the former means. His arguments were at once limpid and bullet-like; they caught his hearers in what indeed was a logical trap, though the trap was the way to truth.

This was not his only achievement during these years. In two important respects the American Catholic clergy did not attain success in the first decade of the twentieth century. They did not, by and large, meet aggressively enough the challenge of Socialism, and they did not exploit with sufficient energy the possibilities of the written and published word.

The usual palliation of this deficiency is based on the postulate that the bishops and the priests were too busy doing other more necessary things. It was the "brick-and-mortar" era of Catholicity in this country. The Church was still in process of being built. It was the period of foundation laying. The first requisite was the founding of schools and churches, the education of the Catholic people in the indispensable fundamentals of their Faith and the maintenance of basic Catholic religious practices. A harried pastor of a growing parish might justifiably claim that his total energy was consumed in seeing to it that his flock repaired to Mass on Sundays and went to the Sacraments regularly. To undertake a systematic defense of the Church against Socialist attacks and to develop a Catholic press were luxuries of the apostolate that simply had to wait. "First things must come first" was the axiom of the pastors of 1900-1910. But the gnawing question, as we look back to those days is: were there some first things that were being omitted?

It would be easy to exaggerate the danger accruing from the Socialist movement in the United States at the beginning of the present century. It was not a radical program. It was a distinctly minority tide of thought and direction of action. The economic state of the country was unfavorable to the movement's growth. The chief aim of the movement—the abolition of the system of capitalistic free enterprise—was unacceptable to the vast majority of the American people, including those who felt themselves to be exploited by capitalism and who were desperately seeking a reform. Here the Socialist Party was running up against the obstacle that in America has always been fatal to any really radical program. In this country, unlike Europe, there has never existed a tightly closed economic interest. As Louis Hartz has pointed out, we have never had a form of real feudalism.[382] No matter what the power and exclusiveness of the economically dominant group may be at any given time, the opportunity for the "outsiders" to secure a place on the bandwagon is never entirely lacking. The radicals, in other words, could never wholeheartedly fight against the Board of Directors since the radicals knew they had a chance for a seat on the Board. The Directors, on the other hand, were quite willing to buy off the radicals in this way.

In Europe the situation had always been different. There the radicals always had had a first-rate target provided for them in the form of some kind of thoroughgoing feudalism. It might be a powerful Church, or King, or, later, a financial or manufacturing interest. Whatever it was, it furnished the radicals with a constant *raison d'être*, a rigid economic and political stratification to be broken down. The radicals were kept perpetually in being because there was a perpetual enemy to fight against. This was the natural breeding ground for Socialist leaders like Robert Owen and William Thompson in England; Saint-Simon,

Fourier, Louis Blanc and Pecqueur in France; and, in Germany, Karl Rodbertus, Lassalle, and Marx and Engels. They could be really radical because the situation was favorable to radicalism, as it never was in the United States.[383]

Furthermore, with few exceptions, the Socialist movement in this country was not led by men of violence. The typical captains of the Party came from the middle and professional classes. Morris Hillquit, Louis Boudin, Meyer London and Job Harrison were lawyers. Daniel DeLeon was a middle-class intellectual. Charles Edward Russell and J. A. Wayland were respected journalists. Even Eugene Debs was a man of scholarly tastes who had rarely worked with his hands.[384]

Nor did the rank and file of the movement resemble in any degree the European proletariat. It is a surprising fact that perhaps a third of the American socialists were farmers.[385] The membership of the Party was much like that of the middle-of-the-road British Labourites. The American socialists were not the kind of men to frighten babies in cradles or wives at hearthstones or to flourish burning brands at homesteads. They were too busy taking care of their own wives and babies and the only brands they flourished were on their cigars.

What, then, was the real peril presented by American Socialism? The answer is to be found not on the economic but on the political and ethical plane. The deep Socialist threat was not in its direct claims but in its broader implications. The program of DeLeon and Debs was part of a wider attack against the Christian principle of justice and against the embodiment of that principle in political forms. The principle, as understood by Western civilization, was this: that a man had certain rights, including property rights, and that no other man nor the State itself could deprive him of those rights without what was called due process of law. It was believed, as an axiom of liberal political theory, that on this principle depended the security of a man's freedom.

John Locke had stated this proposition with great eloquence, and the founding fathers of the United States had assented. The idea was that for a man to be truly free, neither his person nor his spiritual or material goods could be touched in any way that was not demonstrably just. And the touchstone of the unjust was that a man should have taken from him by extra-legal means what the law of the land recognized as being his own. There was no dictate of political or economic expediency that could override this metaphysics of justice. The belief was institutionalized in constitutions and bills of rights.

The Socialists saw what none could deny—that, by an abuse of the principle of justice, men had acquired vast amounts of property and were exploiting their fellowmen. The Socialists' remedy was, therefore, a daring short-cut: the traditional Christian principle of justice should be superseded by the principle of the equal distribution of material goods by some kind of organized compulsion. The agency of distribution might be political, as in the system of Saint-Simon; or it might be by means of some kind of cooperative groups, as recommended by Fourier. The point was this: the Socialist reforms involved inevitably the denial of the claims of justice according to due process of law as understood for nineteen hundred years by the civilization of the West. And the denial was, reductively, a negation of the traditional Aquinas-Locke-Jefferson concept of freedom.

It cannot be stressed too much that the means proposed by the Socialists for the realization of their aims were compulsory, and in a particularly objectionable sense, whether in the form of an all-powerful State or cooperative groups below the State level. In either case, to establish the system, the individual was to be coerced by government or by social pressure without benefit of constitutional guarantees and other legal protections. And, for the maintenance of the regime, the same type of repressive control was obviously required.

It was at this point that the ideology of the movement merged with a highly dangerous mode of thinking that was all too prevalent in the academic circles of the time. The natural rights political theory of the American founding fathers was being replaced by a doctrine of unrestricted State or social power and a sweeping denial of the freedom of the individual. Wrote Westel Willoughby, one of the outstanding political scientists of the day:

There are in the individual no so-called innate or 'Natural Rights', that is, such rights as exist independently of the State and beyond its control. . . . From the power of the State . . . the . . . domain of private liberty . . . cannot be shielded; its boundary line will ever depend upon political expediency.[386]

In the view of Jeremiah W. Jenks, another noted political theorist, most of the best contemporary thinkers on politics (he was writing in 1919) would agree that "there is no such thing as a natural right." Each man, he felt, ". . . may do things, ought to do things that will be for the benefit of the community, but he has not the right to demand anything from the community." Moreover, said Jenks, "the criterion of what is for the benefit of the community at large must be settled by the community itself, not by any individual. . . . The citizen, then, may and must do what the community determines it is best for him to do. . . . He must not do what the State forbids . . . and *we may not properly speak of a natural right as opposed to the power of the State.*"[387]

The real danger of Socialism was that it encouraged such antilibertarian doctrines as these and brought nearer the advent of political and social tyranny disguised as humanitarianism or economic reform. In the light, therefore, of these corollaries of the movement, it was time for men of truly liberal spirit to mount the barricades. Tom Sherman, ever alert to barricade climbing, was naturally in the forefront of the counter-attack. In the fight against Socialism, it may not be too much to say, he did more than most, and as much as any of the Catholic priests in the United States.

One aspect of his anti-Socialist addresses is notable: he stressed the point that Socialism, as it was being put forward in this country, was derived from the theories of Karl Marx. This was, of course, in a sense, true; but the statement was over-simplified. Marx himself and his followers had regarded Socialism as the enemy, the dangerous and deceptive compromise that would block the realization of the ideal of the true classless society. But it was, perhaps, on Father Sherman's part, an acute insight that linked the more moderate anti-individualistic doctrine with thoroughgoing Communism. What he was always striking against was any social philosophy that denied the God-given rights of the person and of the family and of legitimate private societies. He was ever the opponent of those who sought to narrow dangerously the area of freedom. Freedom was the word most often on his tongue.

His anti-Socialist arguments could be used against the Soviet Russian fallacies of today. A recent observer has called attention to the surprising relevance of the Sherman lectures to our number one social and political problem:

The late Father Sherman, S.J. castigated the Marxists in a lecture in Chicago about forty-six years ago. His scathing indictment still stands: "Socialism in its view of matrimony reduces the state to the level of a breeding farm. Socialism asks us to vote for the dishonor of our mothers, for the shame of every drop of blood in our bodies. Are we men to permit such a party to rear its political standard in our midst? Where is American manhood and courage that they do not rise and drive the advocates of such principles out of the political field? The American man who declares himself in favor of such Socialism is hell's lowest vomit.[388]

The hard-hitting language was characteristic of Tom Sherman. He displayed more of it in his frequent addresses against the Socialists in Milwaukee, one of their chief strongholds. "Eight-tenths of all Socialists," he declared boldly in a Milwaukee talk in early 1904, "are atheists and therefore beasts. The system . . . they advance is . . . degrading, . . . base, . . . [and] vile."[389]

Yet he did not neglect to analyze and rebut the Socialist doctrine in detail. He pointed out that Socialism was not a reform but a negation. It would destroy all sound human values and give us in return only a dismal void. The weakest point of the system, he said, was its monetary theory, which would make the labor hour the unit of economic value. There would thus be 100,000 denominations of money, an idea wildly impracticable. Socialism aimed to "put money on a plane with God," and could not impart even a specious attractiveness to the blasphemy.[390]

The Socialists, he warned, were exploiting the dissatisfaction of the laboring classes. It was of the first importance, therefore, that these workingmen should be educated to an accurate knowledge of economic and social realities. Repeatedly he returned to his equation of Socialism with Marxism: "The teachings of Karl Marx and other authors of the same stamp are responsible for a growing evil throughout the country."[391] He realized that the most effective way to defeat Socialism was to convince the classes it wooed particularly that they would find their true salvation only in Christian social doctrine. The Negroes, for example, he sought to convince that they were respected and loved by their fellow-Americans. "What a grand thing it would be," he said to a Negro group in Philadelphia, "if in addition to the glory of having given you freedom from slavery, we could also free you from the errors of false reasoning and false religions. . . . St. Peter Claver became a saint through working for your race. In St. Louis for a few weeks I was pastor of a congregation of your race. I never met a gentler, kinder, or sweeter people. These are the representative qualities of the Sacred Heart of our Divine Lord and Savior, and therefore form the essence of our holy religion."[392]

He recognized also that there existed in the established economic order real defects that should be remedied. He had expressed his fears to Cump as early as 1893: "I trust for the sake of the world at large that money matters may improve, for the distress this winter is simply terrible. Those who have no bread are becoming alarmingly numerous. The problem of the distribution of wealth is a terrible one. Where is the responsibility?"[393]

Nor did Father Sherman in his lectures neglect to remind his hearers that, after all, the best answer to Socialism was the re-invigoration of one's personal religious and moral life. He had phrased the recommendation eloquently in another speech at Chicago:

The world needs a little more of the old-fashioned familiarity with the Cross; it needs a little more childlike turning to the source of all good; it needs a little more plain talk about facing eternity and despising time; it needs a little more stalwart struggling for what is best, and open condemnation of the flattery of numbers and bushels. We are weary of grain elevators and want soul elevators; . . . less said about votes and more about vows; . . . kinder judgment of one another and less bowing to scarecrows; . . . more men and women, fewer dry-goods advertisements; a little of our old-fashioned simplicity in self-help and contempt of trimmings; beautiful manners blooming on beautiful morals, not hiding moral leprosy.[394]

In this crusade for moral betterment he thought that more could be done and was being done by women than by men. He agreed with Tocqueville that the spiritual health of a civilization depends on the character of its women.[395]

Years before, in a letter to Cump, he had put his finger on the weakness in the counterattack (outside of Catholic circles) against Socialism: "Men are not fully agreed any longer on first principles. Modern thought is upsetting everything. We shall have to agree upon some basis or we can never rely upon one another in emergencies. Men may know what is right, but what binds them to do it?"[396]

The ultimate tribute to Father Sherman's achievement in fighting Socialism was uttered by the bishop who said to him, "Humanly speaking, we could not adequately guide and protect our people without you." Laudations of his work poured in from all sides. For six years there was no member of the Society of Jesus who in this field was doing more than Tom Sherman to add to the laurels of the Order in the continental United States. Wherever there were forces resisting the social and economic heresy of the day the services of Father Sherman were urgently requested. He was certainly regarded as the chief opponent of Socialism in the Middle West. No Jesuit among his contemporaries came near to equalling him in effectiveness in this field of combat. It is doubtful whether any Catholic speaker or writer of his time was more feared by the Socialists themselves.

Some of these anti-Socialist lectures were given by Father Sherman under the auspices of the Catholic Truth Society of Chicago. The story of the establishment and subsequent career of this organization is the history of another of his operations that places him in that very small but honorable rank of men who in their respective times and localities have had the vision to recognize the new and more effective tools for the communication of ideas.

The Catholic Truth Society of Chicago, founded by Father Sherman, sought to spread, defend, and nourish the Faith by means of the printing press.[397] For about eight years, from its foundation in the summer of 1901, it issued many thousands of brief pamphlets on apologetic, devotional, and social topics, with the emphasis of the latter being on Socialism. The style of the publications was frankly popular. Almost all of them were reprints of articles by outstanding Catholic writers such as Cardinal Gibbons; Father Rickaby, the English Jesuit philosopher; Cardinal Wiseman; and many others. Four of the pamphlets were original essays by Father Sherman himself. The Truth Society was aiming not at a scholarly or "intellectual" audience but the ordinary educated or lightly educated adult. The goal was to explain in simple terms the Catholic religion and to present the Catholic position on burning social issues of the day.

The original Catholic Truth Society was that of London, England. It had been established in the late nineteenth century, had enlisted the services of practically all the gifted Catholic writers of England, and had spread its publications throughout Europe and America. Other Truth Societies had, before 1901, been in existence in the United States, all of them imitating the procedure of the parent organization.

The first suggestion for the founding in Chicago of another society of the type had come from the leading Catholic laymen of the city, who had asked Father Sherman to request the Bishop for permission to initiate the venture.[398]

It is significant that these men who comprised the most outstanding names in the Catholic circles of Chicago had turned to Father Tom as their intermediary with their ecclesiastical head. The fact was that he had for some time been on intimate social terms with most of the prominent Catholics of the city, so that it was natural that they should turn to him in this instance. The Bishop had acceded, with the proviso that Father Tom himself should take charge of the enterprise. With his Provincial's cautious but explicit approbation Tom had undertaken the task.[399] The Society had been launched in what was at least superficially a very businesslike style. A legal corporation had been formed, with eight of the most outstanding laymen as its board of directors and with Father Tom himself acting as spiritual director, general manager, and "censor." His intention was that all business details would be handled by the imposing lay group, while he himself confined his activities to the editorial side of the operation. By this division of labor he hoped to avoid entangling himself or the Jesuit Order in financial matters.

Tom Sherman did not, of course, realize it, but the fact was that when he undertook to guide the destinies of the Catholic Truth Society of Chicago he was beginning an involvement which, paradoxically, would add greatly to his record as it is inscribed in the history of his times, but which would also be one of the chief instruments of the final tragedy of his life. That strange story must now be recounted.

During the years 1900 to 1909 there occurred periodically in the large cities of the Middle West and elsewhere meetings of small groups of an unusual type. These gatherings were composed of a kind of person we would with difficulty be able to duplicate in large numbers today. They could be described as being simultaneously anti-Catholic, anti-religious, and reductively anti-American, although they were all Americans by birth and loud profession.

A specimen of their attacks on the Catholic Church is the following statement made by a Protestant minister, the Reverend Doctor E. C. Oggel, with special reference to the Jesuits:

I would remind you of Webster's definition of a Jesuit: a designer, an intriguer. If the Church of Rome prevailed, the Pope would be the universal King. . . . The Jesuits are here to plot and scheme and, if possible, take from us the noble heritage of our civil and religious freedom. The rules of the Jesuit Order justify theft, licentiousness, lying, false witness-bearing, suicide and the murder of parents and other relatives. The greatest crimes in history committed against individuals and nations have been committed by the Jesuits. . . . Wherever Jesuits are they have the torch to burn, the sword to slay, the inquisition to torture. They are the enemies of Christianity. They live for conquest, fortune and glory.[400]

Not everyone viewed such effusions with the disbelief which they deserved. There was required, obviously, a reply and, particularly, a plain explanation of what the Catholic Faith and Church really is. This need the publications of Father Sherman's Truth Society tried to fill.

They were scattered widely over the Middle West and most of all in the large cities—the five-cent 20-or-30 page pamphlets that told the simple, accurate facts about Catholicism. They were read by thousands of average people on trolley cars, trains, and in their homes. They were picked up in bookstores and passed from hand to hand and talked about by people who were receiving from the little booklets their first straight ideas about the Church.

The well-intentioned but misinformed Protestant who kept a store and loved to exchange opinions with his customers, discussed frequently with them now the fresh aspect of the Catholic Church presented in the Truth Society's essays. The religious-minded man who had feared the Church as being anti-American, took a second sober thought about the matter when he read, for example, the article by Cardinal Gibbons on the harmony between Catholic and American principles. The modest CTS paper-backs were turning up in the most unexpected places; they were being read and re-read until they were worn out; and they were, over a wide area, slowly but steadily changing and rectifying the thinking of Protestants with regard to the Catholic Church.

This was not all. In this crusade of enlightenment the CTS of Chicago, while it was not alone in the field, was, by all the evidence, the chief spokesman for the Church by means of the written word in the section of the country west of the Alleghenies. Its pamphlets outsold all other Catholic publications in Chicago. In Milwaukee, regarded as a hot-bed of Socialist action, the Bishop[401] kept calling constantly for more of Father Sherman's "What Is Socialism?" brochure.

An historian of Catholic journalism in America would be forced to say that the thing that was done by the CTS of Chicago was second in importance and effectiveness to no similar effort made by Catholic publicists up to that time. He would then go on to say, if he was giving a full estimate, that without the aid of this Society the defense of the Church for the first ten years of the century would have suffered a possibly irreparable loss.

But an essential part of the CTS story involved the way in which the organization was kept alive. Despite its accomplishments, it was never operated on anything more than a shoe string. The original elaborate set-up, studded with "big names," was apparently only a facade. The financial support that Father Tom had so hopefully attempted to secure did not materialize. A year after its foundation the CTS of Chicago was a leaking ship driven on stubbornly and bailed out constantly by the single-handed efforts of Tom Sherman.

While carrying a full burden of work as parish priest and touring missionary he sandwiched into his heavy schedule numerous public lectures the honorariums from which he contributed (by arrangement with his Provincial) to the CTS treasury. This was, during its whole span of existence, the main source of revenue for the organization. All the editorial work he handled himself, with the aid of two assistants. Details of advertising and distribution were completely in his hands. On occasions when the Society's financial fortunes were at a particularly low ebb he would hurriedly improvise an "entertainment" featuring, of course, a lecture by himself and a performance by concert singers and musicians lured for the night from a parish or civic group.[402]

If there was ever a one-man show, the CTS of Chicago was such. Not the least of its achievements was the fact that it remained alive. Its most striking feature, however, was the wildly disproportionate and amazing results it produced from a rickety organization that looked as if it would collapse at the slightest touch. It was David overcoming Goliath without even his slingshot and with a half dozen other equally pressing problems on his hands.

CHAPTER 13

Gethsemane

So much for the achievement. Now for the first appearance of the cloud no bigger than a man's hand—or the handwriting on the wall. During the past several years, it seemed, Tom had secured a grip on himself. While he had confided occasionally to close friends his irritation at what he regarded as the lack of sympathy he was receiving from some of his religious superiors, there had been no serious disagreements, no acute clashes.[403] His immersion in his work, and, apparently, his improved physical health, had contributed to this happier condition of affairs.

He was less likely to "blow up" when disappointments came. He had even borne with comparative tranquillity in the spring of 1906 an unpleasant experience which, in its repercussions, provided a nation-wide sensation. The incident is valuable also as a footnote to the history of the American mind.

The trouble began—although nobody at the time perceived it— when President Theodore Roosevelt, on the day the General's statue was unveiled in the capital, gave a dinner in the White

House in honor of the Shermans. Father Tom was there, arrayed in his army uniform, and enjoying the occasion to the full. Someone mentioned, during the meal, that some West Point cadets were scheduled, for purposes of instruction, to traverse on horseback the route of General Sherman's march to the sea. The President, in a brief lapse of his sense of history and Southern psychology, invited Father Tom to accompany the young officers on their trip.[404]

A few months later the son of General Sherman was riding through Georgia accompanied by a unit of United States cavalry. The reaction of the South was immediate, sharp, and hot. The telegraph wires from Augusta and Savannah burned with indignant complaints to the White House. Rather surprisingly, the objection of the Southerners was not that Father Sherman was in Georgia, but that he thought it necessary, apparently, to protect himself with a military escort. It was not the South's historical memories but its sense of hospitality that was being outraged. "Aside from all questions of propriety," said Georgia's Senator Bacon, "such a thing as an escort for Father Sherman is entirely unnecessary. If General Sherman himself were alive he could with perfect safety and impunity march through Georgia on horseback or on foot without fear of being molested in any way. To give Father Sherman a military escort either assumes the contrary to be true or is an entirely uncalled for piece of ostentation calculated to be offensive to our people."[405]

Congressman Bartlett of Georgia was even more aggrieved. "Father Sherman," he remarked caustically, "may have trouble tracing the line of march now, but some time ago crumbling chimneys and smouldering homes would have made the path plain."[406] And from Captain J. M. Weigle, described as being one of the leading local veterans: "I wish no one harm, but I would not regret at all if some one killed young Sherman should he attempt to march through Georgia."[407]

President Roosevelt may have momentarily forgotten his American history, but he was aware of the exigencies of politics. Avoiding, apparently, any communication with Father Sherman, he at once withdrew the cavalry escort. Tom's acceptance of the repulse is reported by the correspondent of the New York *Sun*: "Stung by criticism and angered by the action of President Roosevelt in withdrawing his escort of United States cavalry, Father Sherman has abandoned his trip over the route taken by his father and has returned to Chattanooga. Father Sherman and escort reached here [Cartersville, Ga.] last night, where they learned of the President's order. So angered was Father Sherman at what he considered an insult by President Roosevelt that he took his baggage from the army wagon and had it moved into the home of his friend, Gen. Granger, who was military secretary to Gen. W. T. Sherman. . . . Father Sherman says he was an invited guest of the Federal Government. This invitation, he says, came unsought by him, was pressed upon him by one who is recognized as authorized to act for the Government in such matters."[408] (It is interesting that Tom did not reveal the fact that his invitation had come directly from the President himself. There may have been a bit of irony in his statement as reported in the last three lines of the above despatch.)

The abortive march and the furore it caused is particularly piquant when compared with a similar incident of twenty-seven years before. In March of 1879 General W. T. Sherman himself returned to Washington from a trip to the South. The journey had been undertaken as part of his duties as military head of the War Department, but he had obviously taken the occasion for some purely personal and social visits in the region of the old Confederacy. He wrote to his friend Major Turner:

If I were the devil incarnate, as many people thought me in 1865, I surely exposed myself to revenge or insult. I went to Chattanooga, Dalton, Rome, Cartersville, Atlanta, Macon, and Savannah, over which cities my army swept as a hurricane, and everywhere my coming was known . . . and the feelings of the people as manifested were respectful, not noisy—but in not a single instance was a word uttered, within my hearing, that was rude, impolitic, or offensive.[409]

At every hotel, reported Sherman, his party was given the best rooms and the best tables, and the people consorted with him familiarly and amiably. "All classes," he declared, "came to me as I walked the streets or sat in my room"; and he adds suggestively, "just as I wanted them to do."[410] It is to be noted that he traveled unescorted by soldiers.

Whatever his chagrin and embarrassment at the failure of his Georgia campaign, Tom Sherman was soon able to recall the incident without undue disturbance of his equanimity.

But, toward the end of 1908, it is clear that all is again not well with him on a more serious plane. He speaks of a letter from his Provincial having "relieved [his] burdened conscience."[411] He was troubled by scruples regarding his handling of the finances of the Catholic Truth Society. His lecture fees he had long since secured permission from his superiors to use for the support of the organization. But he has been forced to borrow other funds from laymen; he fears his inability to repay them, and in addition he has used for the benefit of the Catholic Truth Society some other money that, strictly speaking, should not have been employed for that purpose. He fears that he has been playing rather fast and loose with his solemn obligation incurred by his Jesuit vow of poverty which forbids the free use of money in one's possession.[412]

Whatever his fault, it does not seem to have caused any serious concern to Father Meyer, his Provincial, who has written him a soothing letter endorsing his actions. But Father Tom has communicated his misgivings also to the Father General in Rome, who, doubtless surprised at being drawn into a problem normally settled by local superiors, has referred the matter back to the Provincial.

Tom has proposed further to the General that he be allowed to go to Rome to explain personally his actions. This time it is Father Meyer who is somewhat disturbed, since such a procedure in an affair of the kind is considered quite unnecessary and irregular. He tries to assure Father Tom that no recourse to Rome is required, and that all doubts can be settled at St. Louis. Tom, notwithstanding, is in one of his characteristic fixations. He must obtain his solution and further directives on the highest possible level; he must carry the matter to the Father General himself. It was a *modus operandi* that sprang from his intensely military orientation and was phrased in his frequently used expression, "Always go to the Commander-in-Chief."

It is difficult not to surmise that Tom, despite his anxiety, was deriving, in a twisted kind of subconscious way, a glow of satisfaction from the negotiations with his two top superiors. Such personal dealings "at the summit" were sure to flatter his sense of involvement in affairs of moment at the highest altitudes. There is a touch of pomposity in his letter to the Provincial. He practically dictates to his superior how the latter is to handle the case. He even transmits to Father Meyer some "instructions" from the Father General which the Provincial is to follow. He announces that he is coming to St. Louis to discuss his position, and requests that in the interim the Provincial shall do nothing in the affair.[413]

Another thought which this letter provokes in the reader is that a trip to Rome was attractive to Tom Sherman on its own merits, apart from the situation which might afford immediate grounds for it.

His concluding words of the same communication strike another significant note:

I am working about eighteen hours a day . . . to try and put this little Catholic Truth Society on a genuine business basis. I confess that I am suffering a great deal from self reproach in not having done more than I have done and in not having done better. You know some of the difficulties under which I labor as a missionary, present in legal fiction in Chicago as a business manager of an important corporation. There is danger to my nerves in this, and about that, too, I have to consult you as my father. Again thanking you for your great forbearance and the tenderness characteristic of our Company [the Jesuit Order], I remain, Your obedient son.[414]

Whether Tom Sherman and his superiors realized it or not, he was moving fast toward a crisis.

During the week before Christmas he threw the community at St. Ignatius into a minor turmoil by having his CTS volunteer workers practically take over the lower floor of the rectory to prepare for the organization's holiday entertainment. His fellow-Jesuits regarded it as being highly unconventional that the "lady secretary" (as she was referred to in their reports to the Father Provincial) should have been escorted by Father Sherman to the attic of the rectory to search for pamphlets. They were even more disturbed by the fact that he remained with her there for some time with the door "securely closed." There is not the slightest evidence that there was any real impropriety attached to this circumstance, but it was a startling new mode of procedure to the priests at the Holy Family rectory—as the Father Provincial was at once informed.[415] Matters were not improved when the lady secretary remained in Father Sherman's office at her typewriter until nine o'clock in the evening.[416]

There was constant bickering between Father Sherman and the local superior, who objected to the former's "absolutely independent and high-handed conduct." He ordered the house servants around without consulting the Father Minister,[417] who alone had authority to direct them. His demand that he be permitted a telephone in his office was refused. He was accused by one of the members of the Jesuit community of wishing to supersede the rector and become superior himself.[418]

When the long-prepared-for entertainment was finally put on the boards, the behavior of Father Sherman continued to meet with disfavor from his Jesuit colleagues. The extremely observant Brother Donaghy (who, rather piquantly, had been assigned by the rector to assist in the work of the CTS) wrote a full description to Father Provincial: "At the concert he made himself very conspicious [sic] by escorting the lady singers or players off the stage by catching their hand and accompanying them back of the curtain separately. As many as three or four prominent ladies afterward sayed [sic]: 'It is too bad Father Sherman so far forgot his dignity.' A few other people of prominence who were there asked, 'What was his lecture [given as part of the presentation] on? Was it on Porto Rico or was it a lecture of compliments to General and Mrs. Grant?' "[419]

Then, less than two weeks later, matters came to a real head. Departing a few days after Christmas for a brief visit to St. Louis, Father Sherman left his office tightly locked with all its lights ablaze. The latter fact, noted by the assiduous Brother Donaghy, was made known to the Father Minister, who ordered the room to be opened by the lay watchman and the lamps extinguished. Father Sherman on his return shortly afterward found his office unlocked and flew into a rage. The privacy of his chamber, he charged, had been violated. He declared that those responsible for the act had committed a common burglary and he reported the watchman to the police. He "discharged" Brother Donaghy from the rolls of the CTS, notified the corporation's lay attorney that there were grounds for "criminal prosecution," and asserted that he would not tolerate "petty larceny under whatever cloak of religious discipline." There had been for the past thirty days, he reported to the Provincial, an "acute case of scandal" at Holy Family, although the superior was doing nothing about it.[420] (The most diligent research has given no hint as to what this alleged scandal was.)

Brother Donaghy was equally solicitous in enlightening the Provincial. He explained to the latter the origin of Father Sherman's "burglary" accusation. Some weeks before, during an absence of Father Sherman, the "lady secretary" had wished to secure some CTS pamphlets from her Chief's office. She applied to Brother Donaghy, who told her he had no key. She insisted that the pamphlets were required for immediate mailing and herself urged that the door be forced open. Brother Donaghy appealed to Father Roswinkel, who in turn had recourse to the rector, who said simply, "Force the door open." This was done with a skeleton key. Father Sherman, when he discovered what had occurred, had been very angry and had made wild charges of "criminal entrance" against the Brother and Father Roswinkel. He had also accused Brother Donaghy of having an unbalanced mind. As to the most recent breaking into the office, Brother Donaghy declared, he had had no part in it except for his notification of the Minister about the lights, which had burned steadily for forty-eight hours.[421]

The storm, happily, soon subsided. Father Sherman quite willingly retired to a hospital for a month's rest. Almost at once he wrote a much milder letter to Father Burrowes[422] to assure him that he receded from his intention of bringing criminal prosecution. A soothing reply from the Provincial strengthened him in this wise reversal of plan. It was decided that henceforth the operations of the CTS would be carried on from a private office in downtown Chicago.

Meanwhile, Father Sherman's physicians were recommending for him a long vacation in the West. He had been overworking, they said, and subjecting himself to dangerous tensions for too long a time.[423]

In mid-February, 1909, he asked the Provincial if he might go to Santa Barbara, California, for a convalescence of indefinite duration. His friend, the Jesuit rector there, had offered him the hospitality of his house. Plenty of sunshine and outdoor life, especially horseback riding, would be available in this garden spot. He would even enjoy living in a tent under the open sky if it could be arranged. He had learned by hard experience that health of body and mind go together. And—a more somber note— he wished "to avoid the danger of scandal here."[424]

The request was granted by the Provincial in a letter particularly cordial and sympathetic. He was not only willing but earnestly desired that Father Sherman take the required rest. He was anxious to do everything that was necessary for the restoration of the invalid's health for the greater glory of God. Father Sherman could start for the West as soon as his physicians wished him to do so. The best wishes and prayers of his Provincial would follow him.[425]

With this kind of careful handling (his superiors seem to have thought) his jangled nerves could be restored to normal and the unpleasant Chicago incident pushed into oblivion. But they may have been over-optimistic. On the same day on which Father Meyer was penning his gentle letter, Father Sherman wrote the following private memorandum for his own files:

Father Sherman's room was broken open ruthlessly without rhyme or reason. This *made him ill.* . . . He cannot improve while superiors

openly favor such thieves and lock-picks and employ a kleptomaniac
and his accomplice. . . .

It was at least an improvement in the situation that he was
going West for recuperation. Yet, in a letter to the Provincial a
week later, he revealed another of his swift changes of mood. He
spoke as if he had no intention of leaving Chicago. He was full
of new plans and projects for the CTS, and requested the Provincial to approve four Jesuit censors to expedite the work of
CTS publications. He pleaded guilty to having been remiss in
the matter of submitting the pamphlets to such censorship, as
the rule of the Jesuit Order demanded. He bowed very humbly
to the express wish of Father General and the Provincial that he
should no longer attempt to finance the CTS by means of fees
obtained from his lectures. Henceforth, he said, the support of
the CTS would depend entirely on Providence. The proceeds from
the sale of pamphlets, he admitted, "amount to nothing."[426]

This rather puzzling epistle he concluded by expressing his
desire to stay on the coast "even for a year or two." He felt
that his month in the hospital had not done him much good
except that it had enabled him to escape some "sources of irritation." His weight was only 128 pounds. He was quite anemic.
He estimated that it would take many months of fresh air and
exercise to put him back in condition for work in the pulpit. He
added a postscript: "It happens strangely enough that the former
President of CTS, Mr. Bremner, the present lady President and
my former clerk and assistant all are now in Los Angeles. More
of this later. No stopover is granted east of the mountains, so I
booked through. A rich friend pays my expenses of the journey."[427]

During the next two years Father Sherman stayed out west in
retirement. For a brief period in May 1909 he felt that he might
return to Chicago to do some useful work. But his proposal was

vetoed by superiors, and he himself was forced to admit that he was now a "confirmed nervous dispeptic, [sic] destined to test the indulgence of superiors everywhere."[428]

In the mid-summer of 1911 he was residing at the Jesuit rectory of St. Michael's, Portland, Oregon. There had been signs of improvement in his mental and physical health. He indulged in much outdoor exercise, especially horseback riding; he paid a number of visits to his lay friends all along the coast; and he engaged in some light mission work. The dark days at Chicago he seemed to have forgotten or at least pushed far back in his memory.

The reports of his recuperation were encouraging the Provincial back in St. Louis when suddenly the blow fell. On the thirtieth of July, while staying at Gonzaga College, Spokane, he had a complete mental breakdown, and was removed, against his strenuous protests, to a nearby sanatorium.

He himself has recorded the moment and the tragic days that immediately followed:

That day I fell before the altar, afraid to consecrate, conscious of an enormous weight of sin. The next day . . . I was . . . *forced* (physically) to take the train for San Francisco and put in a hospital. The next day I went to the novitiate at Los Gatos. I made many efforts to manifest myself [to his superiors] and make full confessions. I tried to *force* myself to say Mass. Got no peace. Had Lehmkuhl and Oswald [books of moral theology] open before me and was overwhelmed with consciousness of reserved cases. Then I tried to do away with myself and failed. Then I was put in the State Insane Asylum. . . .[429]

His sister Lizzie arrived from the east a week later to transfer him, accompanied by a Jesuit father, to the Mt. Hope sanatorium in Baltimore. After a fortnight at this institution he was again moved, this time to a mental hospital on the outskirts of Boston.

On this latter trip he was accompanied by his two sisters, Lizzie and Rachel, and two Jesuit priests from Loyola College of Baltimore.

Although when first stricken he had been quite violent, he was during these dolorous journeys "gentle and sweet and perfectly harmless." One of his few mild complaints was uttered in the course of his brief stay at Baltimore when he learned that his Provincial had been in the city for a few days and—doubtless due to lack of time—had omitted to visit him. He was in continual despair over what he viewed as his "lost" spiritual condition. "I went to perdition," he would say, "in Chicago in utter judicial blindness [blindness of judgment?] and . . . in my reckless folly accepted and spent 1,000 dollars free handed . . . without asking permission."[430]

One of the other things he kept repeating to Lizzie on the trip from California eastward was, "No matter what happens, always remember how good the Jesuits have been to me—in fact, too good!"[431] His general attitude was, however, a kind of apathetic resignation.[432]

The sanatorium at Boston—it was in the city's suburbs at Brookline—was a private one, and somewhat expensive. This latter fact was an additional source of worry to his loved ones, to his Jesuit superiors, and to himself. In the first of a series of letters sent by his sisters to Fr. Rudolph Meyer, the Missouri Provincial, Rachel (Mrs. Thorndike) gives a report of his state of mind. "He knows it is expensive and is constantly wretched about breaking his vow of poverty. I may telegraph you to write him telling him it is your order for him to stay there for a time at least. This might make him more resigned."[433]

His physical condition also is very bad. To Rachel, it is "beyond words to describe."[434] His blood, the doctors say, is "chiefly water."[435] He feels cut off forever from his Jesuit brethren and his family, and he is convinced that he has lost his faith.[436] Yet, Lizzie is sure, he is desperately anxious to get back to a Jesuit house. Again, paradoxically, he believes there is no place or hope for him anywhere in this world or the next. He is tortured also by the realization that he has been thrown helplessly on the hands of his brother and sisters, "although," Lizzie cannot forbear to add, "he knows that we would all gladly die for him."[437]

When they had reached him in California, Rachel relates, his clothes had been practically in rags. They discovered later that for several months past he had had scruples about buying anything for himself, and had also let his personal appearance deteriorate from a motive of penance for what he believed were his grave sins. He now worries at the expense incurred when his sisters forced him to accept some decent new garments.[438] For the most part, he sits in silence, looking out the barred windows, with an immeasurable sadness in his eyes.[439] Would Father Meyer please, please write to him (it is Lizzie's urgent request) to assure him that he is still a member of the Jesuit Order and that his fellow-Jesuits are praying for him? "Dear father," she concludes, "it breaks my heart to see him."[440]

Father Meyer sent the letter, which seemed to console Tom greatly. The Provincial wrote as a spiritual father. He recalled to the sufferer that none of us can understand completely God's ways: "While you were working strenuously—too strenuously, I fear, for His glory—He allowed you to be stricken down." Meanwhile, Tom was to be assured that his Jesuit brethren were thinking of him with deep sympathy and constantly praying for his return to health. He should try, in union with Our Lord, abandoned on the Cross, to bear his affliction with resignation to the divine will. He is to tell his sisters and all who are in any way ministering to him that the Provincial appreciates as a personal favor all their kindnesses.[441]

As the autumn merged into winter, Tom's condition improved to a slight degree. He received gratefully the fathers who visited him from Boston College and he went to confession and received Holy Communion a few times. He insisted that Lizzie secure for him a new button of the League of the Sacred Heart, which he had always worn but had lost in the last few months.[442]

Then one day he refused to see a Jesuit who came to see him and declared that he wished no more visits from members of the Society.[443] His new delusion was that he had sinned unpardonably against his vows in traveling around California during the past two years, and that he deserved to be repudiated by the Order.[444] He was permitted to spend a few hours at Rachel's home in Boston on Christmas Eve and during the visit talked very rationally. But he was still far from well.[445]

There was during this time a concurrent grief and deep humiliation that had to be borne by Tom's family. The Shermans were quite unable to pay all of the hospital and medical charges. Consequently, many letters on this subject passed between the sisters and the Missouri Provincial. The situation was difficult for all the parties. The family, as was well understood by the Jesuits, had naturally thought first of Tom's welfare. This had led them to remove him twice from sanatoriums where conditions were not the best to the private and expensive refuge at Brookline, where the board alone cost seventy-five dollars a month.

The Provincial and his consultors were trying their utmost to be considerate and gentle, but they felt obliged to express their view that the Society's contribution to Tom's support during his illness must, by the very nature of the situation, be limited. Hence the questions were delicately but firmly asked by Father Meyer, how much could the family pay and could not Tom be moved to a sanatorium that was less expensive?[446]

Only those who knew the intense family pride of the Shermans could appreciate their keen embarrassment at being obliged to bargain with and beg from the Jesuits. From their earliest childhood the General had impressed on his sons and daughters the impropriety of borrowing money. No one indeed had taken the lesson more to heart than had Tom. And now it was necessary to plead for funds from priests!

The financial arrangements, however, were soon agreed on. The Missouri Province assumed half of all past, present, and future expenses of Tom's illness, with assurances that the family would handle the other half. As part of the settlement, Tom was taken from Brookline and placed in Providence Retreat Sanatorium at Buffalo, where the rates were much lower.[447] Rachel reported that Tom was pathetically anxious to get some of his old sermons published so as to defray some of his expenses.[448]

Tom stayed at the Buffalo sanatorium for about a year. He seemed to be again securing mastery over himself, although he still had a long way to go before he would be altogether recovered. The doctors now allowed him more freedom. Wearing an old military cloak, he took daily walks through the city park and loved particularly to watch the multi-colored birds in the zoo. Rachel said that he had always been attracted by bright and beautiful things. During this time he was regularly visited by the Jesuits.

But the old restlessness, intensified by his illness, and his desolation of spirit continued. Toward the end of January, 1913, his longings assumed a new and in a way a more wholesome form: he wished ardently to return to a Jesuit community. His letter to Fr. Burrowes, now his Provincial, tells the story:

I am convinced superiors do not realize my extreme spiritual need. For a year I was in much despair. I did not bend a knee, make the sign of the cross, or wear a scapular. Now I am trying to drag myself back to God, hungering and thirsting to get back. I crave and implore assistance of my brethren and believe I can have it more effectually in a place like Milwaukee than here. [What he has in mind is his transfer to a Milwaukee sanatorium run by a Dr. Stack, with whom the Shermans were already acquainted. Its chief attraction for Tom was its proximity to the Jesuit Marquette University.] For instance I want someone to help me learn how to say the new offices, and all Ours are very busy here. I am really a stranger. Pity me in my extremity and use your authority to get me where I can have a right to command the assistance of someone of our own. I promise blind submission to superiors in everything. Four months [and a] year and only one night's real sleep, my poor brain is incapable of real thought. I implore your pity and assistance. From the depths, T. Sherman.[449]

A month later he sent to the Provincial another plea, which is also a description of his agonized soul:

I have not had the faintest gleam of any hope of salvation since July 30th 1911. . . . I was brought east to Mt. Hope near Baltimore, thence taken to a sanatorium near Boston (from October, 1911, to October, 1912) under a Unitarian doctor. Watched day and night like a caged animal. No sleep but snatches. No appetite for any food. . . . Brought here October 1, 1912. In five months one night's sleep. . . . Repeated confessions but *no peace.* Have said Mass the last few weeks, an *agony* to *drag* myself to the altar.

No hope whatever of eternal salvation—continual effort to choke back blasphemies against God. Blind obedience has brought no amelioration. I will have no instant of peace in time as in eternity. Of this I am most positive. Still my vows press on me and I will continue to obey blindly. . . . Do what you think you should with me. . . .

In utter despair,

T. Sherman

P.S. In 1910 no general confession. Afraid to face my conscience.[450]

He firmly believed that on the critical day two and a half years before when he had his break-down he reached the limit of God's mercy and that his eternal doom sounded at that hour. On the way to San Francisco, he recollected, he had called on the hills to cover him. From the depths of his soul he wrings the final tortured cry: "I am utterly at a loss what to do. . . . Was ever man so utterly blind and so wasteful of advantages and opportunities! My judgment will be terrific. . . . I will gladly go to a Trappist monastery, but am fully aware that *no peace is possible for me*. I already suffer the pain of loss, am damned before my time.[451]

Father George Krim, the rector of Canisius College, urged the Missouri Provincial to let Tom make the move to Milwaukee. The rector felt that the patient had improved "a hundred per cent." He was saying Mass daily, though Father Krim was forced each time to command him to do so under the vow of obedience. He periodically gave Benediction to the nuns and distributed Holy Communion. It was the rector's belief that if Tom were placed "amongst his own men" at Marquette, even though he would be a patient at the Milwaukee sanatorium, the effect on his mental health would be excellent.[452]

His religious superiors were obviously trying to satisfy all of his desires that were reasonable. Within a few weeks he was at Dr. Stack's hospital, and, after only two or three more weeks there, was allowed to take up his residence at Marquette College itself as a full-fledged member of the Jesuit community. He was given no work assignment, but every effort was exerted by his fellow-Jesuits to make him feel at home again. His devoted sisters were greatly consoled. It seemed that the worst was over and that he would now "get hold of" himself.

But everybody was too optimistic. After two months at Marquette, this was the letter he wrote to the Provincial:

I am three years without a retreat. Two years in Bedlam, abandoned by Ours. I need a retreat more than any man in the Province. Father Rector forbids. The doctor forbids; he thinks of bodily health. . . . I was taken in here out of pity on April 17th. I am desperately in the dark though in the midst of loving brethren and with my family devoted. May God inspire you to direct me. Aimless walks about a strange new city, fears of seeing anybody, sleepless nights, empty days and awful fear of God's judgment for the great scandals I have given. It is a terrible existence. You are now responsible for my soul. . . . I offer my life as a forfeit to my folly with every Consecration at Mass. Please use your authority and command me under obedience. I feel like a rat caught in a trap, my head whirling, my hand trembling. Is there not some way out of all this? Do try to help me.

In deepest distress,

T. Sherman.[453]

Then, a month later, he made one of his swift changes of mood—this time for the better. He asks the Provincial's permission to consult "a young osteopath" from whose treatment he hopes great benefits for his health. He assures the Provincial that he wishes to make every effort to become again a useful member of the Society. He is saying Mass privately, but he is not allowed to "ride, row, or do anything I consider manly." No stone will be left unturned, he vows, to render himself fit again for the active life of a Jesuit.[454]

His temporary and precarious grip on himself was, however, rapidly loosening. He quickly developed an intense dislike for the Superior at Marquette, Father Joseph Grimmelsman. The available evidence suggests the existence of no rational grounds for this feeling. It was true that there had been, many years previously, some misunderstanding between them; and the rector's nationality was never with Tom a recommendation for friendship. But Father Grimmelsman had sincerely exerted himself to make things as easy and as pleasant as possible for Tom at Marquette. What may have occurred—given the rector's blunt manner of speech and Tom's abnormal sensitiveness—was a passing remark of the former that Father Sherman was in the house by charity and that he had "no standing" in the community. This was, in a sense, of course, true; but it was an imprudent observation—if it ever was actually made.

Whatever the provocation, real or imagined, Tom, on the tenth of February, 1914, wrote out this statement and filed it for the time being among his personal notes:

Rev. Jos. Grimmelsman stated yesterday that I was in this house simply as an act of charity. This is a falsehood base deliberate and most malicious. I am in this house for the same reason and by the same right that he and any other man is in this house, neither more nor less and he knows it perfectly well. . . . I am here by right of my simple vows. . . . When I came here he ridiculed my eagerness and used it as a whiplash. . . . I have a double right here because I am a professed father and as such one of the governing body of the Society. I am here as a free American citizen, not as a slave, a servant, or a punching bag for a boor, a brute, and a bully.[455]

On the same day he packed his grip and, without notifying the rector or provincial, departed forever from Marquette College. A few days later he appeared, without previous warning, at Loyola College (then Loyola Academy), Chicago, and asked for temporary accommodations.

CHAPTER 14

Crisis at Chicago

FATHER PROVINCIAL BURROWES decided he had better go up to Chicago. What Tom's next move might be, nobody could guess. There were unpleasant and dangerous possibilities in the situation and the Provincial wished to be on the scene to prevent them.

The decision made by Father Burrowes after a stormy talk with Tom at Loyola can be both blamed and defended. Tom, he saw at once, was not in full possession of his mind. He was threatening to make public charges against what he termed the unjust and brutal treatment accorded him by his superiors. Being a Sherman, his recriminations would make news of national importance and a scandal of national scope. He could not be returned to a sanatorium except by physical force. The Provincial, for weal or woe, chose to gamble with time. Early in 1914 he offered to Tom the post of special assistant to the editor of the new Jesuit magazine, *The Queen's Work*. The assignment was a sinecure improvised on the spot and calculated to keep Tom immobilized temporarily, at least, in St. Louis, the magazine's headquarters. It seemed like a prudent way of keeping him harmlessly occupied. It might even be hoped that the new interest would bring him to his right senses.

One may therefore surmise the dismay of all concerned when a few days later in mid-February, 1914, Tom appeared at the *America* office in New York City and announced himself as eastern representative and associate editor of *The Queen's Work.* There followed an exchange of communications between a mildly shocked Maryland-New York Provincial, Father Anthony Maas, and a disappointed and sorely worried Father Burrowes. To forestall a still worse back-firing of the original plan the Maryland-New York Province agreed to let Tom remain at the *America* office, but to keep him as far as possible under watch and ward.

This latter program was more easily stated than carried out. Tom set himself up in an office of his own in the *America* building, hired a young man as secretary, and wrote to Father Burrowes for a "broadest permission to effectively prepare to help Father Edward Garesché to edit the new magazine."[456] He requested also a leave of absence "to canvass the field thoroughly in the East before settling down to the task of assisting Father Garesché permanently in St. Louis."

In order to cover his expenses while travelling, he asked the Provincial to allow him to publish "a few sketches." He adds a succinct warning: "Trust me in this, grant the permissions broadly, and all will be well. Be narrow and I will be depressed again inevitably and indefinitely." Previous misunderstandings between the Provincial and himself, he suggests, "come from the fact that we have had a different training and different surroundings. Having served in six provinces I am attached to none." He signed himself, "Respectfully yours in Christ."[457]

The new stand he had taken was fraught with dangerous possibilities. He claimed to have placed himself under the patronage of the New York Cardinal[458] who, fortunately, was then vacationing in the Bahamas. He asked Lizzie to send him "a cloak with silk lining suitable to call on a Cardinal."[459] He secured by some means a horse, and took daily rides in the park. He was enjoying some ice skating. He was paying visits to some nearby relatives.[460] He went up to New Haven for a Yale class reunion, which he enjoyed hugely.[461] He was delighted with New York City: "A day here equals a week even in Chicago!"[462]

He angrily broke off relations with Cump and Rachel when they remonstrated with him over his high tone toward his superiors. As Father Maas reported to Father Burrowes: "He is out of the house practically the whole day, and no one knows what he is doing. His relatives are all nervous about him, and afraid both for him and for themselves. They fear that he will compromise their good name, even if he does no physical harm to them. But they seem to fear even physical injury [to themselves]. . . . Two doctors . . . said about a year ago that . . . if he should show delusions after his state of depression, . . . suicide or even murder might be feared."[463]

What Father Maas feared was that Tom would fall into the hands of a "sensational reporter or shyster lawyer." In either case, "the good name of the Society and of a number of good men would be seriously compromised."[464] The deluded sufferer was charging that he had been four times unjustly and illegally imprisoned in asylums, and he was swearing to have redress. "The idea of newspaper notoriety," believes Father Maas, "does not seem to be out of his mind."[465]

Since only Lizzie, apparently, had any influence over him, she was being used by the harried Missouri Provincial to induce him to come back to his Province. The great peril was that

Tom, in his then state of mind, was capable of doing almost anything. Lizzie was "discouraged beyond hope." Tom, she says, is convinced that he has been persecuted by his superiors. He "has visions of raising large sums of money" for some undefined purpose. She fears that at any moment he may commit a violent action that will bring disgrace on the Jesuits and on the family.[466]

His relations with his Missouri superiors were rapidly deteriorating. Father Burrowes, gently but firmly, had tried to dissuade him from writing any articles or sermons for publication. Tom's retort was immediate: "Will publish with or without permission, as arrangements have been definitely made. Presume General's or [and?] Pope's permission [and] that of Our Lord—as last year."[467]

He notified the Provincial that he had appealed to Rome juridically. He had, he charged, been unjustly haled across the country as a maniac and thrust under the care of "infidel" doctors. He had been held at arm's length from the Province where he belonged and where he had a better right to be than anyone, since he had done more work and suffered more for God than anyone there. He termed Father Grimmelsman a man "fiendish in character, devoid of . . . fine feelings," who had disgraced the Province and was loathed as such by the smart set of three great cities. The series of accusations concluded bitterly: "I have had enough . . . of malice and stupidity. I appeal to the Holy Father and I go to him as a child goes home. You are one of my adversaries. I am yours. . . ."[468]

Just before writing this epistle he had been notified by Father Burrowes that his *Queen's Work* "commission" was revoked.

His attitude toward Father Maas was more moderate. (He may have sensed this superior's irritation—always kept within bounds —at having inherited so unexpectedly the Missouri Province's hottest problem.[469]) Tom informed Father Maas that he was returning to Chicago but that, en route, he wished to pay some visits within the boundaries of the Maryland-New York Province. He intended to call on his old friend Mr. Walter George Smith near Philadelphia; he would see some relatives elsewhere in Pennsylvania; and he desired to stay a few days at Georgetown College in Washington. In following this schedule, he assured the New York Provincial, he was carrying out his doctor's orders which, he added, were diametrically opposed to the instructions he had received from his own Provincial. He humbly requested Father Maas' endorsement of this program.[470]

The New York Provincial had little time to muse over the paradox of Tom's defiance of the orders of one Provincial and his scrupulous submission to the authority of another. Worried reports on the case were coming to him from other sources. Tom had been inquiring at a travel agency about rates for a trip to Rome. He was apparently still considering a direct appeal to the Holy See.[471] He had discharged his male secretary and hired a young lady typist to prepare his old *Messenger of the Sacred Heart* articles for publication. He seemed exteriorly perfectly normal, "so long as he is allowed to roam about as he pleases and is not crossed." He was roaming freely about the city from morning till after dinner.[472]

The one dim ray of light in the situation was that Tom was willing to go back to his Province. But he would do it in his own way. Once started, the journey to Philadelphia developed into a brief stay there, followed by a side trip to his niece (Mrs. Daniel Armistead) at Bethlehem, Pennsylvania, and to Marietta, Pennsylvania, to visit an old friend.[473] He then returned to the Armistead's where he so upset his niece that her husband begged Cump to take him away. "I therefore suggest," wrote Cump to Father Maas, "that you summon my brother by telegram to Georgetown or that the Western Provincial order him back to the West. . . . I fear . . . that the time has come for a definite test of his obedience."[474]

It was too late for such measures. Tom, wandering restlessly, was now, it would appear, making another detour to Columbus, Ohio, the home of some of his Ewing cousins. Cump believed that his brother intended to reach Chicago, but that he could not be hurried: "From what [he] said to me and from what others report him to have said, he has it in the back of his mind *not* to disobey orders, but to stretch the permission to travel given him in the West to its technical limit." The doctors regard his delusions of persecution as being the worst possible symptom, "particularly as his grievances are directed against those particularly who have been most truly and actively his friends."[475]

The situation, if worsened in one respect, was at least clarified in late October. Having made another sudden switch in his itinerary, Tom was with relatives at Scranton, Pennsylvania. From there he wrote a formal declaration of his severance from the Society of Jesus. The announcement was couched in the terms of a circular letter to be sent to all his relatives and friends. In it he asserted that his retirement from the Order had occurred some months ago by the action of Father F. X. Wernz, General of the Jesuits. The cessation of connections with the Society admitted of no appeal according to the laws of the Order, but called for simple acceptance and submission. He wished to insist that his departure from the Society affected in no way his standing as a Roman Catholic priest. He affirmed his zealous desire to serve under Roman and episcopal ecclesiastical authority as a priest of the Catholic religion to his dying day. He was merely, like an army officer, transferring from one branch of the service to another. Indeed, the change would leave him in some ways freer from "restricting regulations," though of course he always

would be willingly subject to the central and diocesan authorities.[476]

But this was not all. He would interest "prominent ecclesiastics, distinguished lawyers, social leaders and others" in his
case, he informed Father Burrowes, and—most inconsistently—
would fight to secure from the Jesuit General a position *in the
Society* that could not be made and un-made at a boy's whim.
He would make the Cardinals merry by telling them of his
"feigned madness." And, as a final threat: "One more blunder
on your [Father Burrowes'] part and the Associate [*sic*] Press is
invoked to tell my side of the story."[477]

Any intention of returning to Chicago was now, of course,
abandoned. By mid-November he was at Lancaster, Ohio, with
the Hugh Ewings. He was, apart from the support given to him
by his relatives, practically destitute, and was demanding of the
Missouri Province a stipend of sixty dollars a month.[478]

That which his superiors and family had feared and had tried
to prevent followed swiftly, in a particularly unhappy form.
From Lancaster, Ohio, came a letter to Father Burrowes from a
lawyer, one Ben Dolson. Father Sherman, the attorney informed
the Provincial, had employed him for the purpose of arranging
his release from the Society of Jesus. The communication, obviously dictated word for word by Tom, thus stated his case:

During the past two years he has been treated as "hopelessly insane," though pronounced perfectly sane by many alienists and ex-
perts. . . . He has not been trusted to say *one prayer* for his community or its deceased members, while brimming with zeal to do
for others.

Officially informed that "he had no standing in the Order," and
so treated, he has . . . sustained dignified relations with prelates,
high officials, and with a large family and many friends. . . . He
believes that rights and duties are reciprocal. He therefore requires
promptly: First, his dimissorial letters. Second, a pledge of sustenance

in accordance with the Canon Law. Unless this request is complied with we will have recourse to the Civil law.[479]

In a letter to the editor of the *Catholic Directory* a few days previously, Father Sherman had demanded that in the forthcoming issue of that annual the "S.J." be dropped from his name. If this were not done, he threatened, his lawyer would prosecute the publication.[480]

At St. Louis further distressing news arrived from the scene of Tom's irresponsible activity. He was circulating between Lancaster and nearby Columbus, the latter point being the residence of his cousin. He was threatening to commit suicide. He was vilifying the Society to the secular priests and general public. The Bishop of Columbus begs that the Provincial will send a priest to take him away.[481]

Father Burrowes was at the time absent in Europe, so the ticklish matter became the concern of his assistant or "Socius," Father Gilbert Garraghan.

The latter's first step was to answer Dolson. He pointed out the inconsistency of Father Sherman's demand for dismissal, inasmuch as the latter had circulated some time ago the announcement that he had been dismissed already. But, Father Garraghan declared, Father Sherman's belief that he had been released from the Order by the action of the Father General was pure delusion: "No such action is ever taken by the Order towards any of its members, without documentary evidence to this effect being placed in his hands." The Society of Jesus had no desire, Father Garraghan insisted, to discharge from its ranks a subject who was not fully responsible for his actions. However, if Father Sherman was absolutely determined to have his dimissorials, he must proceed in canonical form. He must draw up and submit to his Provincial in writing a statement of the reasons why he wishes to be released from obedience to the Order.[482] It was to be clearly understood, added Fr. Garraghan, that Father Sherman would be welcomed at any Jesuit house. This was the solution the Society earnestly desired;[483] and in this wish Father Sherman's family and relatives ardently concurred.[484]

The next move by Father Garraghan was an appeal to Tom through the agency of one of the latter's best friends in the Order. Father Francis Finn, the noted author of books for boys, was sent to Newark, near Lancaster, for a talk with the sick man. (Tom was now with the Ewing family there.) The meeting that followed between the two has been well described by Father Garraghan's emissary.

Father Finn encountered Tom at the parish church, where both had been saying Mass. "Tom said Mass beautifully," writes Father Finn, "his voice being wonderfully strong." He greeted Father Finn kindly but not effusively and, on learning that the Jesuit had come expressly to see him, invited him to call at the Ewing home, where he was staying.

Their subsequent talk was unsatisfactory from the viewpoint of both. Tom demanded to know whether Father Finn had come to him with any message from his superiors. To Father Finn's announcement that Tom's superiors considered him still to be a Jesuit and that they were asking him to return to Chicago, Tom retorted hotly that he himself should have been present at the meetings where his case was being discusssed. "I had a *right* to be there," he insisted angrily.

"That," continues Father Finn's report, "was all I got a chance to say. From this on Father Sherman occupied the stage. The rest was monologue; topic: the Society of Jesus. The language was direct, vigorous, straight from the shoulder. Never did lunatic—if he may be called one—speak more eloquently. He was cured—cured by non-Catholic doctors. He owed nothing to the Society of Jesus. He would never set foot within a Jesuit house so long as he lived; and this resolve was absolute, final, and irrevocable. One Superior—Father Joseph Grimmelsman—had actually told him that he, Father Sherman, had no standing in the Society. . . . He had still some friends among the Jesuits—dear friends—I being one of them. Then he took a few shots at Father Wernz, Father Meyer, Father Grimmelsman, and Father Burrowes, the last-named being a 'sneaking hypocrite.'

"Finally he spoke in substance as follows: 'I wrote to Father Meyer for my dimissorials, insisting on an answer. He gave none, and he died. I wrote Father Wernz, demanding an answer. I got none, and he died. I have written present Superiors, and they will die.' With this he arose and walked from the room, leaving me to solitude and to take care of myself as I pleased."[485]

After this tirade Tom most cordially invited Father Finn to have luncheon with himself and the Ewings. During the meal, to Father Finn's relief and amazement, everything went beautifully. Tom explained with the greatest calmness to Mrs. Ewing, her Protestant husband, and her married daughter the manner of electing a Jesuit General. He did it, says Father Finn, "better than I could; and, curiously enough, spoke unconsciously as though he were still a Jesuit. [Of course he was such.] He told them 'what *we* do' in this and that case."[486]

To Father Finn Tom looked to be in excellent physical shape. Furthermore, barring his hatred of the Society and his views on his right to commit suicide, he seemed to his friend to be as sane as anyone. He was living a very regular life, said Mass devoutly daily, seemed to have a great love for the Blessed Sacrament, read his Office, and indulged in long walks and much horseback riding. (He claimed that the latter exercise had cured him.) "His powers as a preacher," Father Finn could not forbear adding, "are still remarkable." He was undertaking to organize a Catholic Boy Scout troop in Newark.[487]

He has also, Father Finn must report, engaged the services of one Father Eis to represent him before the ecclesiastical courts. The Bishop of Columbus had commented wryly on this development: "How is it that one rebel naturally falls in with another rebel?"[488]

It was Father Finn's belief that Tom could never be induced to return to the Society. About the only bright spot in the situation was the assurance received from the Ewings that Mr. Dolson, Tom's lawyer, was a "decent fellow" who was merely humoring Tom and who would not actually carry the case to the civil courts.[489] A final remark of Father Finn's was significant: "Father Sherman is, I believe, naturally very proud. Kindness may help him, though he may receive all kindness as his due."[490]

Tom's family and most of his relatives were praying that he would go back to a house of the Order.[491] It was only a few of his Protestant cousins who for a time were deceived by him and were siding with him against the Society.[492]

If any defense of the attitude of the Jesuit Superiors in the whole affair is required, the testimony of Cump provides it. "I am advised," writes the latter to Father Garraghan, "that at present he complains of persecution by Father Grimmelsman and Father Maas. I know that, when in his right mind, my brother . . . entertained the most unusual veneration and respect for Father Maas, and that since my brother's illness Father Maas has manifested the greatest kindness and consideration toward him. Similarly I know of my own knowledge that Father Grimmelsman, since my brother's illness, has been to the greatest pains to assist him in his recovery, and for his care and kindness deserves to be ranked among my brother's truest friends."[493]

Cump begged Father Garraghan to pray for Tom: "I who know him best can assure you that in his right mind he would be a loyal and obedient member of the Society of Jesus."[494]

Two weeks after Father Finn's abortive visit to Newark, some encouraging news came from Mrs. Ewing. She informed Father Garraghan that Tom had suddenly announced his intention of returning to Loyola College at Chicago.[495] On his way he would stop over for a day and night at her daughter's house in Columbus, where he had left his trunk.[496]

These more favorable tidings were, however, delusory. A week later Tom is still sojourning in Columbus.[497] During the next three weeks his movements, if any, are obscure. By the first of March he has arrived in Chicago, but, refusing to go to any Jesuit house there, is oscillating between lodgings with friends in the city and a room he has reserved at the West End Hotel.[498]

One of his first acts on reaching the city was to apply for membership in the University Club. This move, fraught with so many dangerous possibilities of unpleasant publicity, was blocked by a prompt letter from Cump to the Secretary of the organization.[499]

The final dolorous crisis now broke. On March 7, Father Garraghan received this letter from Tom:

Unless dimissorials are sent me here within 48 hours, i.e., by Tuesday evening, you will prepare to stand suit in United States court for defamation of character, poisoning the minds of my dear ones, and other Missouri amusements such as unjust suspension from priestly functions. Several prominent *Protestant* lawyers are engaged and primed, my petition is ready drawn. Act now, hell hounds that you are, or we will give you a taste of the hell you delight to give to others.

P.S. His Grace asks me for dimissorial letters. Every possible means will be taken to satisfy him promptly.

From the distraught priest there followed during the next two days some briefer messages of an incoherent and mad character. Two pitiable samples will suffice:

"Put two mad dogs in the same kennel and you are responsible for the consequences. I came to the Province a Christian gentleman, it made me a mad man *deliberately*. I warned you, you would not call off your hounds. [signed] Ignatius."

"My case is at the Curia. Wernz will answer before His Holiness. God pity them as much as I scorn loathe despise detest abhor their whole damned crew. [signed] Aloysius."

The acting Provincial was in a sharp dilemma. Neither himself, the Provincial, nor the General had the power under Church law, nor the inclination, to dismiss from the Society an insane man. It is to be noted that the self-imposed obligations of a Catholic religious order toward its sick members is extremely strict. Once the order has definitely and fully received a person into its ranks she willingly assumes over him an affectionate guardianship that no physical or mental deficiencies of the person can terminate. No expense is considered to be too great, and no burden on her patience too trying as she lavishes a mother's care on those of her spiritual sons whose ailing health gives them, in her eyes, a special claim on her love and solicitude.

But, if Tom's demands for dismissal were not met, the deranged man might make a spectacle of himself, his family, and to a lesser degree the Society, in the public forum. Another alternative—forcible commitment to an asylum—would, in Tom's present belligerent state, effect the same unhappy results.

Father Garraghan, crowded by the ultimatum, acted decisively. He dispatched to Tom a "dimissorial letter" that he had no authority to give. It granted to Father Sherman his release from the Order, "subject to the provisions of the Canon law obtaining in such cases."[500] This clause made the dismissal a nullity, but the fact was totally lost on Tom. The point was that the notification kept him quiet and away from civil courts and the newspapers.

For a while, that is, he was quiet. Then he took another tack. He threatened to sue the Missouri Provincial in the federal courts for "criminal libel, conspiracy to defame character, and unlawful imprisonment." As a condition for a temporary stay of these proceedings he made the following demands: Father Burrowes should address to the Bar Association a formal apology for his treatment of Father Sherman; the Missouri Province should deposit $20,000 in government bonds or securities in a specified bank to credit of Father Sherman personally, in lieu of sustenance for loss of time, suffering, and expenses incurred.[501]

After all, there were limits to what a lawyer could be hired to do. With small difficulty Tom's attorneys were induced by Cump and the Jesuits to halt the prosecution, while retaining the plaintiff's confidence. One of the minor annoyances of the situation was Tom's habit of dropping one lawyer and engaging another and repeating the operation so many times that the Jesuits could not easily discover with whom they must deal. The conclusion of the tragic farce was bewilderment on the part of the lawyers themselves as to which one of them was handling the case for Tom.[502]

The last phase of the sorrowful story of Tom's "dismissal" is soon told. How could he now support himself? The bishops and archbishops who, a few years before, had been clamoring for his services, were quite unwilling to accept him—temporarily or permanently—now. Nobody any longer wanted him as preacher or lecturer.

There followed, consequently, a series of communications between the authorities of the Missouri Province and Cump Sherman. From this correspondence emerged a final arrangement. The Order for an indefinite time would contribute fifty dollars a month to Tom's support, and the family would do likewise. This agreement the Missouri Province honored as long as Tom lived.[503]

Before the settlement of his financial future had been consummated, Tom was seeking a chaplaincy in the army, now engaged in the Mexican "War."[504]

CHAPTER 15

Position Regained

THE "TRAGIC FLAW" has been an intriguing subject of study for a generation of psychologists. Why is it that often a man is led to disaster by reason of a character fault which, in itself, is not of the deepest gravity? What is the ineluctable law of human nature that from a man's moral defects educes consequences of such disproportionate woe?

To other observers of the human scene the more interesting problem is that of the uses of suffering. Is it true that some characters can be purified only by that means? Are there men and women who, like Melville's Ahab, can find their topmost glory only in their topmost grief?

Still further avenues of thought present themselves for exploration as one watches the awesome collapse of a personality. The proposition appears to be defensible that a human being can be ruined by a false development of his virtues as well as by a proliferation of his faults. Manly pride and self-respect may become the type of self-centeredness that destroys; the earnest pursuit of a grand ideal may deteriorate to stubbornness, narrowness of view, and mania; determination may lead to suicidal independence of will.

The Thomas Ewing Sherman story seemed to have completed its main phase in those spring days at Chicago in 1915. Yet its *finis* had not yet been written.

In November of the same year he appeared in Spokane, Washington. Years before, he had come to the Pacific Northwest as the famous Jesuit preacher; now he was there as a priest without a diocese. Sensitive as he was to situations, he must have had an acute realization of the difference. He must have harked back in memory to the old colorful triumphant days.

But he had not come this time to the coast without a plan. He was not admitting defeat. He was, as ever, looking forward to doing something big and spectacular for Christ.

He declared himself to be the founder and promoter of a project called the Catholic Colonization Society. The aim of this organization, he explained, was to recruit Catholic immigrants from the large cities and establish them as farmers in a virgin territory in the northern part of the State of Washington. Such a transplantation, he believed, would benefit these people from the viewpoint of religion as well as from that of their economic welfare.[505]

He was trying—and in retrospect the spectacle is deeply sad— to become again a missionary. He was anxious, too, to do it in proper ecclesiastical form. He must secure the necessary permission from the local bishop, he realized, and be accredited by that official to the diocese of Spokane. This involved some difficulties.

The Most Reverend Augustin F. Schinner was a kindly prelate who wished to do what he could for a priest in trouble; but on any fair estimate Father Sherman did not constitute an attractive addition to the diocese. The Bishop, as the head of a pioneer ecclesiastical territory, had often been obliged to take risks; but he was scarcely prepared for this one. He had, furthermore, a quite justifiable skepticism with respect to the possibilities of the Catholic Colonization Society. To complicate matters, Tom was now asserting that he had not yet been formally released from the Society and, in one and the same breath, was asking the Bishop to help him to secure his dismissal and to accept him as one of the diocese's priests.

But, as Tom's former Superiors at St. Louis could have told him, His Excellency was dealing with a man who moved startlingly fast. While the Bishop was still debating what decision to make, he learned that Father Sherman had already set himself up as a pastor in the diocese and had had a deed recorded for the land on which he would build a church. The site chosen, Tom informed the Bishop, was excellent for the purposes of the Colonization Society.[506]

If the Bishop could not be said to have a tiger by the tail, he certainly had a pastor he had not sought. Again, however, Tom became the beneficiary of a collaboration based on a determination not to hurt him or press him too far. The Bishop agreed to let him work in the diocese, since to refuse him would (a) probably not stop him and (b) perhaps precipitate another nervous break-down, with attendant unpleasant publicity. The Jesuits and the Sherman family would continue to bear the full burden of his financial support, though Tom should be made to believe that some of this was coming from the bishop. Another "release" from his membership in the Society was forwarded to Tom, at his insistent demand. The Bishop salvaged a further grain of comfort by insisting with Tom that the deed to the new church should be registered in the name of the diocese.[507]

These improvisations quickly made, Tom began to "colonize." The spot he had chosen was the region around a faded village called Loomis, near a place called Okanagon. It was notable chiefly for its rugged scenery and its horses. The best to be said of its agricultural potential was that it was somewhat more amenable to tilling than U.S. Highway No. 1. Particularly congenial to Tom were the trips he felt he should make to St. Louis and Chicago to recruit "settlers." The duration of these journeys soon became so long that a new problem facing the Bishop was that of knowing, at any given time, where Father Sherman was.[508] This difficulty was aggravated by the further fact that the pastor of Loomis would take periodical brief vacations in California.[509]

To nobody's surprise, the Catholic Colonization Society collapsed almost at birth, although Tom held on at Loomis—on and off—for a little less than four years. Judging from some of his letters to his family, he enjoyed the horseback riding and other incidents of outdoor life at the site of the hardly projected settlement.

By May, 1919, he had apparently become finally disillusioned with the colonization plan. He had turned restlessly to some "missionary journeys" through the State of Washington, given a "patriotic address" in a church somewhere in Alaska, and at Spokane purchased a prefabricated bungalow which followed him back to Loomis![510] Shortly afterward, he wrote this brief message to the Bishop: "I hereby resign the curacy of Loomis. [signed] Thomas Ewing Sherman, Missionary Apostolic."[511]

The next few years are the period of his most extended and most pathetic wanderings as he tried to fight out his losing battle with himself. He had long desired to go to Rome, to "present" his case to the ecclesiastical authorities there. In the spring of 1919 he fulfilled that wish.[512] They treated him with the greatest tenderness and, in summary, let him believe what he wished about the treatment he had received from the Society and about his present status as a priest. What he was not informed of (since it would only have made his mental attitude worse) was the Jesuit General's action of securing for him from the Holy See a special permission to live for an indefinite time outside of Jesuit houses. The grant was required inasmuch as he was still, and would always be, a member of the Society of Jesus.[513]

He stood one day in the great square of St. Peter's and meditated on the sublimity of the Catholic religion. He could comfort himself with the thought that, as long as he was able, he had borne witness before the world to that body of truth. He returned to America shortly afterward. The visit to the Holy City had, he felt, soothed and calmed him.

It is not necessary to detail his weary and ever-restless and shifting itinerary from here on. His movements during the remainder of 1919 until the mid-summer of 1922 are obscure. In all probability, he was making the circuit of his relatives' homes, trying vainly to find some priestly ministry to which to devote himself, yet feeling his incapacity to buckle down to any line of activity for any length of time. On July 7, 1922, he was in San Francisco for a very special purpose. It was the thirty-third anniversary of his ordination to the priesthood. He offered the Holy Sacrifice in the church where, sixty-six years before, he had been baptized.[514] He was visiting his nephew, William Fitch, at Biloxi, Mississippi, in the spring of 1923, on the eve of his departure for another of his long-desired trips—a pilgrimage to Spain. At this time he seemed to be more cheerful. He even made a special journey to New Orleans to see an old Jesuit friend there with whom he had studied theology at Woodstock. On the day he sailed he told the Fitches that he had for years yearned to kneel before the holy crucifix at Limpias in the country of St. Ignatius of Loyola, and that this was one of the chief motives for his trip.[515]

This time the months spent abroad brought him even more comfort than his Roman journey had done. A hint of his usual physical condition is given in a letter to Cump from Malaga: "I have been without bodily pain for the last two weeks, a thing I could not boast of before for years."[516]

His only source of irritation at the time was the fact that the Jesuits' usual monthly remittance was not reaching him promptly since his arrival in Europe. They have, he admits, been "usually very prompt and exact" in the matter. He asks Cump to complain to the Jesuit procurator at St. Louis University. "At canon law," he reminds his brother, "they are strictly bound to support me, especially in view of their stand in the case." If Cump will only stand by him in "pricking" them, he urges, they will be obliged to continue paying till he dies.[517] His best friend at Malaga (who probably did not do him much good) was an ex-Jesuit of 30-years' membership in the Society.[518]

On his return to the United States, he spent a few weeks again with Will Fitch. To the latter, the European trip did not seem to have improved Father Tom. He was moody, had little appetite for food, and sat in his room through most of the night brooding over a log fire that he kept always burning. He appeared to have lost interest in all intellectual matters. He was beginning to show a trait that certainly no one had ever before regarded as being characteristic of him—a gnawing sense of inferiority to those around him.[519]

Some time in the preceding year he had purchased a bungalow at Santa Barbara, California. It was a pretty little house, just large enough for one person. It had a tiny, built-in altar and sacristy, a galley-like kitchenette, and bedroom and study. After leaving Will Fitch in the winter of 1924, he repaired to this dwelling. It would be his home from that time on—except for a later significant four-month period—until his final illness.

These years at Santa Barbara—1924 through half of 1929—were for Tom a time of relative peace. In what he termed his "hermitage" he lived a life of prayerful and studious retirement. Each morning he offered the Mass devoutly at his little altar. He read much. He lovingly tended his flower garden. He cooked his own meals. He did a bit of sermon and essay writing, though for sheer amusement, and with no intention of publishing. He bought himself a small car and enjoyed short daily drives. He prayed and meditated a great deal, and thereby derived deep comfort.

His letters to Cump were almost uniformly cheerful. He admits his distaste for washing dishes, but realizes that this is the price that must be paid for enjoying such delicacies as red-snapper with onion sauce, which is one of the frequent items on his menu. He recalls to Cump some humorous incidents of their childhood: "I remember the day you reached the ripe age of three years. You ran across the house in nature's garb, to the infinite amusement of mother and some servants."[520] He returned to one of his old loved themes in insisting that what the nation needed was more patriotism. There was a dearth, he thought, of real Americans. "No such animals are known to exist hereabouts," he teases Cump, "and your village is worse!"[521]

He received occasional visits from his sisters, brother, and more distant relatives. Everyone felt that he had recovered some of his charm of manner and that he was less disturbed. They all noted, however, that he appeared old and worn even beyond his more than three-score years and ten.

Only now and then were there indications that his mind was not altogether well. He retained the delusion that he had founded long ago in Chicago an organization called the Chevron Order for the Defense of the Catholic Faith. Some of the letterheads on his stationery at Santa Barbara were inscribed, "Headquarters of Chevron Order." Also, he was still allergic to the mere mention of the word Jesuit. He usually designated members of the Society by a scornful and bitter "they," and at times spoke of them in extremely bitter terms. But, by and large, he was keeping quiet and finding a reasonable degree of solace for himself.

Before the end, he decided, he would make one last campaign, he would go on one last march. Years ago he had seen something that he had never forgotten, a sight that had haunted him ever afterward. Now at the beginning of the summer of 1929, he felt he must act in the matter.

He informed Cump that he was coming East and would reach New York City in the last week of June. Cump, so he explained to Tom, would at that time be in Canada on important business. So, "come as you planned, use my apartment, and await my return from the North." (Rather strangely, perhaps, Cump showed no concern at his brother's being on the move again and alone.)[522]

Tom followed this schedule, with some variations. Arrived in New York, he spent a few days in Cump's empty apartment, and then went to Boston for a brief visit to one of his nieces, Mrs. Joseph Hamlen, née Martha Thorndike.

He had a most enjoyable stay there. Martha's two boys, aged eight and four, fell in love with him. He told them stories of the Indian wars, and taught them how to build an Indian tent in the backyard—with one of his niece's best bed sheets! He was most affable with the many guests that came to see the Thorndikes, even though he caused a bit of embarrassment by refusing cocktails and asking for vermouth—a very scarce article in the prohibition era of 1929.[523]

It was only after he had returned to New York that he revealed the real reason for his journey East. He wrote to his favorite niece, Eleanor Fitch:

I am going to Porto Rico where I hope . . . to work a little among the very poor in the hill country. . . . I love Porto Rico dearly . . . ever since I served there in '98-'99. . . . There is need of active work among the forlorn hill dwellers whose abject condition has been a heart-break to me for thirty years. If I die in this effort I die most contented. . . . I must essay something for the cause of souls.[524]

He had offered his services to the Bishop of San Juan, Edwin V. Byrne, who had gladly accepted him as a non-incardinated missionary without salary and with no specific assignment. (These terms had been suggested by Tom himself.) He arrived at San Juan in late July and, at the moment of debarkation, showed a flash of his old fire. With a satchel in one hand and a jug of Mass wine in the other he was stopped by the customs officer. He rose to his full pristine dignity and insisted that, as a Catholic priest, he had a right to carry wine into Puerto Rico. He won the argument.

His feelings as he trod once more the soil of the island had been anticipated in his letter to Eleanor Fitch: "The Precious Blood is my favorite devotion and a coming glory in the increasing scheme of Our Lord's triumph over all souls, the price paid every moment the world over, the redeeming flood, the second and vaster deluge of divine mercy and compassion. The King of Kings still loves best the lowliest and most forlorn and to them I devote myself. Get all the prayers you can for Porto Rico."[525]

He was assigned, with his enthusiastic consent, to the chaplaincy of a shrine dedicated to Our Lady of Lourdes, and much frequented by the poor people of the island. From this as a base he also made some trips to other sections where the poor were to be found. While he lasted, he did some good work. "Soon," recounts the Bishop, "reports came to me of his great charity and kindness."[526] Added Msgr. Mariano Vassallo, the Vicar General, "During his short stay, Father Sherman did much good, sharing with the people his money and food."[527]

But he was an old man, and he was physically sick. After a few months, he himself was obliged to admit the first two of these facts. The work was too much for him. After a few weeks, too, the loneliness of a country village began to exert upon him its depressing effect. His grudging admission of defeat is registered in a letter to his cousin John Ewing: "I am not strong enough for the labor, so can't do what I would like to do in visiting the poorest in their wretched huts of cabins. . . . I shall return to Santa Barbara by the first of the New Year."[528] He had made a gallant try; but it was too late.

When, toward the end of 1929, he settled down once more at Santa Barbara, his restless wanderings—and he must have sensed the fact—were definitely over. He was now too feeble to indulge himself in visits to relatives and friends. He was tired and broken and wished only to be alone.

One matter he had very much at heart—that he should receive from the War Department a pension for his service in the Army in 1898 and 1899. During the last days of his brief Puerto Rico sojourn just described he had made a formal application to the Government for this purpose.

Writing to the Pension Bureau from San Juan, he had given as his permanent address "Headquarters Chevron Order, 1510 Olive St., Santa Barbara." He described himself as a "Catholic priest and home missionary," and offered the following grounds for his claim to disability payments: "Neurasthenia and gastritis with ulcers in the stomach at times and chronic debility, incapacitating him for regular work of his ministry." To the query "Nearest relative to be notified in case of death" he had penned a strange answer: "William Tecumseh Sherman." While the error was indicative of his then-weakened mind, it was also perhaps a final subconscious projection of one of the master thoughts of his whole life.

His claim was admitted by the Pension Department on January 11, 1930. Thenceforward until the end he received from the Government a remittance of fifty dollars per month. It meant to him far more than the mere money involved. He felt that it gave him fellowship in the ranks of the old soldiers who had fought for the Union.[529]

It would be of interest to know what his musings were in these last days in his modest home at Santa Barbara. We know that he spent much time in re-reading and re-writing (as much as he could) his old sermons and articles. He would almost certainly have meditated over his essay published in 1896. It had told of Christ's calling of two of his apostles. They had asked Him, "Master, where dwellest Thou?" He had invited them to "come and see." Each one of us, Tom had said in that article, must ask himself the question, "Have I during my whole life been seeking Christ where He really is?"

He had spoken so eloquently against human pride. The fearful effect of that vice was, he had warned, that it made good and sincere men deceive themselves. He had urged that we kneel in reverence before the mystery of God's providence—how He sometimes sanctifies a soul by permitting it to have serious faults and by letting it suffer grievously from those faults. He had spoken beautifully of Our Lord as his tent-mate, his "comrade just home from the world's war, . . . comrade . . . proved to be heaven's own anointed one." He had tried to shadow forth this divine Comrade's career. With what success?

He spent even more time now, perhaps, in puttering around in his flower garden. He loved to talk to the children who occasionally found their way to his bungalow. He could no longer ride horseback. Only seldom did he ask one of his few visitors to take him for a drive in his car.

Back in New York City, Cump, together with most other Americans, was seriously concerned about the depression. The numerous Sherman and Ewing families were working out their own calm and rewarding destinies and, naturally enough, were thinking only intermittently of the solitary, sad old priest at Santa Barbara.

Then, on the fifth of November, 1931, a telegram came to Cump from Tom's doctors: "Sorry brother decidedly worse. . . . Violent. Advise institution. . . . We feel on account of his age little hope of recovery. Still at home with nurse."[530] Cump called on Tom's favorite niece to act for him in the crisis. Within a few hours Eleanor Fitch was on her way to Santa Barbara.[531]

The fall of 1931 was pregnant with events of high and ominous moment on the international scene. Eleanor, as she rode westward, was thinking what intense interest Tom, in his normal mind, would have found in the European political picture. She wondered, rather incongruously, how Tom would have regarded the slow but persistent rise of Adolf Hitler to power. She wondered what he would have thought of the long line of unemployed, desperate men that were characteristic features of our great cities at that time. Most of all, however, she dreaded what she would meet in California.

She found him strangely calm and fearfully broken down physically. He greeted her apathetically, but appeared to be as harmless as a child. The doctors warned her not to be deceived by his temporary docility. He was subject to periodical fits of great violence and must be constantly watched. The decision was made, with Cump's approval, to take the sufferer at once to a Sisters' sanatorium at New Orleans.

The trip across the country was managed by Eleanor with

the aid of a male nurse. There had been great difficulty in finding such an attendant in Santa Barbara. The doctors had finally secured a young man who had been acting as one of the trainers of a professional pugilist. He proved to be competent and most gentle with the patient, though, as he privately confided to Miss Fitch, he was considerably frightened at his immense responsibility. He required some urging from Eleanor before he would escort Tom from the train at way-station stops and walk him up and down the platform for exercise. "What can I do if Father won't get on the train again?" he protested. "I would never touch a priest."

Tom seemed to like him and even showed interest in the young man's normal occupation, and recalled some of his own boxing days at Yale. When his niece tried once to rearrange the articles in one of his suitcases he threw them all out on the seat beside him and remarked that he had never met a woman who knew how to pack a man's grip.

They reached New Orleans to encounter what Eleanor always described as a "misunderstanding." She was, as she said, "amazed to be given a cool reception by the Jesuits."[532]

What actually happened was this: From Santa Barbara she had wired to Father James Greeley, S.J., at New Orleans and had asked him to make arrangements for Tom's reception at the De Paul Sanatorium. "His answer," Miss Fitch recalls, "was understanding and cordial. He told me to come at once [and that] all would be in readiness for Father Sherman." On their arrival at New Orleans Father Greeley had met them at the depot with an auto, driven them to the sanatorium and helped to settle Tom there. The events—or lack of events—of the days following were what hurt Miss Fitch: "From then on I did not see or hear from a Jesuit for over four days. I was alone in an hotel—forlorn and desolate, deserted [as it seemed to her] by old friends."[533]

The fact was that the Jesuit Superiors at New Orleans had not been properly briefed. Their limited knowledge of the Sherman case indicated that he had for years been out of the Society. Hence, it is understandable that their services to Father Sherman were, at first, only perfunctory. The Provincial, Father Salter, was not sure how far he should go in sharing the responsibility for the sick man's care.

The courageous Miss Fitch helped to clear up the obscurity. She wrote to her good friend, Father Edwin Mattern, the American assistant to the Jesuit General in Rome. Father Mattern cabled instructions and information about Father Sherman to Father Salter. From then on, the Jesuits of New Orleans showed every possible consideration to Tom and his family.

The end did not come at once. From that fall of 1931 until the spring of 1933 Tom was under the tender care of the Sisters of the De Paul Sanatorium. But his mind remained almost constantly disturbed and he continued to deteriorate physically. He was also growing childish, and he had lost confidence in those around him—the Sisters, and Fathers Salter and Biever, who visited him regularly. He refused to receive Holy Communion. When they would urge him to do so he would keep repeating, "It is too late, it is too late."[534]

When the weather was particularly mild they would take him into the garden and let him sit in a wheel-chair. He was solicitous to the point of scrupulosity about his personal neatness when he thus appeared in public. He would also insist on these occasions that he wear his old military cloak. His love for the beautiful things of nature had never deserted him. When they would bring him indoors after these brief airings he would often take back to his room a sprig of a flower.

If he were visited—as periodically he was—by any of his friends besides the Jesuits, there would be a flash, though dim now, of his old courtliness and grace of manner. He would be unable to converse with them for long, but he would be sure to inquire about their families. A few times his nurses tried to interest him in the newspaper. But his former keen interest in the events of the day was all spent. It was, at any rate, a new strange world to him now. He was of a generation that was being passed by and made anachronistic in that brash era of the Roosevelt Revolution of 1932-33. His father would never have understood it, nor could the son.

Whether, as his time was running out, he thought of his father, no one, of course, will ever know. It would have been strange if he had not done so. He had tried so earnestly during all his lifetime to imitate the man who, to his mind, was all that a man and an officer should be. He might even have remembered the day when, as a boy, he had watched the General ride down Pennsylvania Avenue in triumph. Only once, on an immensely crucial issue, had he opposed his father. Must he not have recalled that?

Easter Day, 1933, dawned clear and mild. During the morning he seemed to regain some strength. At the suggestion of Sister Urbana, his devoted nurse, he signed a holy card to be sent to his niece Eleanor, who was then in Rome. In a firm hand he wrote: "Father Sherman, with love. Pray for me."[535]

Many of his most notable sermons had been delivered on Easter Sundays. He had always found comfort in the fact of the Resurrection of our Lord. Many times he had told the people that, because Christ had conquered death, we should never be afraid.

Five days later, on April 29th, he suffered a massive hemorrhage of the stomach. Outside his close-curtained room the spring morning was just breaking. An hour before, the faint sounds of reveille had floated over from the nearby military post. It had been his habit, during the past few months, to listen for the sound of the bugle and to beat time weakly with the music on the counterpane.

Then he seemed to rally. Weak as he was, he began to talk more rationally. The doctors surmised that the shock of the hemorrhage had cleared his mind. The old, worn face was more peaceful than it had been for many years. For a long time he lay very quiet. Then suddenly he beckoned Sister Urbana to come closer to his bedside. "Call Father Provincial," he told her. "I wish to renew my vows as a Jesuit."

This was indeed the last surrender, and, finally, the victory. No members of his family were with him, but three of his fellow-Jesuits knelt by his bed and heard him repeat from memory, in a clear, strong voice, the long formula of the solemn vows of a professed father of the Society of Jesus: "I, Thomas Ewing Sherman, in the presence of the Virgin Mother of God, all the heavenly court, and these bystanders, promise to Almighty God and the General of the Society of Jesus . . . poverty, chastity, and obedience. . . ."[536]

There was, according to one of his oldest friends, another traditional Jesuit prayer that he might have added—the solemn offering made by the members of the Society toward the end of their annual retreat: "Take, O Lord, and receive all my liberty, my memory, my understanding and all my will, all I have and possess. Thou hast given all to me; to Thee, O Lord, I restore it."

He received the Last Sacraments with deep consolation. He begged pardon for any trouble he might have caused during his illness, and sent an affectionate message to Cump. That night he died peacefully in his sleep.

On the following day his body lay in state in the Jesuit church of the Immaculate Conception while his Jesuit brethren recited the Office of the Dead for the repose of his soul. His requiem Mass was sung by the pastor and he was buried in the cemetery of the Jesuit novitiate at Grand Coteau, Louisiana.[537] By coincidence his grave adjoins immediately that of the suddenly-stricken Father John Salter, the grandnephew of Alexander Stephens, Vice-President of the Southern Confederacy.[538]

Epilogue

Less than two weeks after the death of his brother, Cump Sherman despatched a letter to the Provincial of the Missouri Province.

After relating how he had arrived at New Orleans too late for Father Tom's funeral, but in time "to meet and thank the fathers of your Southern Province and the Sisters of Charity at the De Paul Sanatorium who were most kind to him in his last illness," he expressed his gratification at the happy ending of his brother's life. The core of the letter was this paragraph:

Now I am writing to express to you my heartfelt gratitude for the patience and charity continuously shown by you, your predecessors and the fathers of your Province toward my brother during the many long years of his illness. He was never morally responsible for his irregularities, but it was difficult for all, except those who knew him most intimately, to realize it.

Cump then referred to a matter that was affording him considerable worry. He had been, and was still unable to contribute anything of moment to the payment of Tom's doctors' and hospital bills of the last few years. He assured the Provincial that he wished to do something about this as soon as his financial means would permit.[539]

To this communication the Missouri Provincial replied as follows:

We have rejoiced at the graces granted your brother Father Thomas E. Sherman, S.J. It had been our hope and expectation that at the threshold of death his mind would be clear and he would express his confidence in and loyalty to our Society. Our Fathers are greatly consoled. We felt that your brother's manner of death was what your heart desired as it was ours.

Father Sherman never ceased to be a Jesuit, was never officially "out" of the Society of Jesus. His great affliction made it impossible for the Society to grant him a release. Hence the Missouri Province always accepted without demur its obligation to assist Father Sherman in such ways as were open to it; it regretted only that it was so wholly deprived of the assistance his talents could have afforded it. . . .

Our Fathers and Scholastics and Brothers are saying Masses, receiving Holy Communion and reciting rosaries for the repose of Father Sherman's soul. Approximately 1400 Masses will soon have been said and that many and more Communions received. . . .

For your gracious letter I beg to offer you the thanks of our Society. . . .[540]

Four years later another letter was sent by Father Horine to Tom's brother. The Provincial expressed his thanks for a gift of $10,000 made by Cump to the Missouri Province as a proof of the gratitude of the Sherman family toward the Society of Jesus.[541]

FATHER SHERMAN'S LAST WILL & TESTAMENT

I THOMAS EWING SHERMAN hereby make my last will and testament.

I bequeath the sum of $500 . . . to the Mission of Santa Barbara asking that Masses be said for my soul.

I give $500 . . . to St. Vincents' Orphan Asylum; $500 to St. Francis Hospital; $500 to my dear niece Elizabeth Thackera.

I give the bust of my father W. T. Sherman to Arthur H. Sherman of Beverley Hills. My gold chain I give to Othelia Carroll Beals of Seattle.

My books, pictures, saddle and bridle together with $500 I give to Elizabeth Thompson.

My altar, vestments, sacred vessels, linens etc. I give to the Church Extension Society.

I request the First National Bank of Santa Barbara to act as Executor and to hold my house; the principal part of my worldly effects; in trust, for purposes confided to the Bank by letter.

Thomas Ewing Sherman
Sept. 18, 1928.

Witness:
 W. F. Rhodehame
 A. B. Harmer.

The following poem was written by Thomas Ewing Sherman for a family reunion in honor of his father in April, 1884:

To Papa

What crown shall deck his brow?
Wears he the laurel now?
Weave we the holly bough,
With myrtle entwine him.

Spray of the staunch old yew,
Sprigs of the oak so true,
Broad beech and buck-eye too,
Bud to enshrine him.

Gone are his days of war,
Danger and strife are o'er,
Comes now the autumn hoar,
Sweet peace enfolds him.

Garlands must hide his sword,
Heap high the genial board,
By loving hearts adored,
Home ties shall hold him.

A longer verse in commemoration of the gallant General Macpherson, one of the heroes of the battle of Chattanooga, has distinct merit:

Kennesaw

The eagle coasts his eyrie,
The fox his covert lair,
But neither fox nor eagle
The lion's look may dare.

High on the mountain's summit
We see your guns in air.
Ho! eagle, is your eyrie safe?
Macpherson's men prepare
To scale yon beetling mountain
And battle with you there!

Now onward, Wood and Stanley!
Right up the darksome glade,
On! for the grand old Union!
On through the darkling shade
Of pine trees' gloomy covert,
Of clouds that burst in rain,
And cannons belching clouds and fire
That threaten you in vain.

No darker storm of shot and shell,
No deadlier lightning's flash,
Than the black storms of rebel hate
That 'gainst your country clash.
America! Thy banner
On mountain, sea and shore
Is rent with tear and tatter,
Is black with brothers' gore.
Then onward, Stanley, onward!
On to the mountain's crest,
Men, bare your bosoms bravely
As the Union bares her breast.

In vain they toil and struggle
Mid rock, and cliff and crag;
In vain the lumbering cannon
Right up the hill they drag.
In vain they force the lurking foe
Behind his parapet;
They may not win the summit,
Not yet, brave friends, not yet.

But not in vain your combat;
Still keep the foe at bay;
Hold fast the ground you've conquered;
Now waits a better day.
When force and courage cannot win,
A *mind* can conquer all;
A *mind* commands your army;
Dark Kennesaw shall fall!

Down eastward valleys streaming
Pour the level morning beams
And o'er a moving mass of men
The mellow radiance gleams.
'Tis Macpherson marching southward!
Now Kennesaw beware,
Tomorrow's sun shall kiss our flag
Floating in triumph there!

APPENDIX C

INVENTORY OF SACRED EFFECTS AT SANTA BARBARA

Sacred Vessels in care of Father de Rop:

3 gold plated chalices
1 gold plated ciborium
3 gold plated patens (one poorly gilded)
1 pyx and burse
1 set silver cruets and tray (small)
2 altar stones
holy oil stocks
1 wooden altar
1 chest with complete sets of vestments
altar linens
1 set chimes
4 single candlesticks
2 candelabra
2 missals
2 missal stands
several pictures suitable for a small chapel
plentiful supply of candles

List of Sources

I. BEGINNINGS ARE ENDINGS

1. For facts in this chapter not revealed by the invaluable E. Sherman Fitch primary sources, the author is indebted to two books: Anna McAllister, *Ellen Ewing: Wife of General Sherman*, New York, Benziger Brothers, 1936; Katherine Burton, *Three Generations*, New York, Longmans, Green & Co., 1947. See also the exuberant—and somewhat hysterical—newspaper accounts of the Grand Review.
2. William Tecumseh Sherman to Thomas Ewing Sherman (n. p.), October 4, 1863. [Unless otherwise indicated, primary sources such as this are taken from the E. Sherman Fitch Papers, in the possession of Miss E. Sherman Fitch, New York City. Henceforth the abbreviations "TES" and "WTS" will be used for Thomas Ewing Sherman and William Tecumseh Sherman respectively.]
3. WTS to TES, Nashville, Tenn., April 25, 1864.
4. WTS to TES, "In the Field," Kingston, Ga., Nov. 10, 1864.
5. WTS to TES, "In the Field," Savannah, Ga., Jan. 21, 1865.
6. TES to his mother, Woodstock, Md., Dec. 27, 188– [certainly during his period of theological study.]
7. Conversation with Miss E. Sherman Fitch.
8. Maria Boyle Ewing (mother of Mrs. Sherman) to Mrs. Sherman, Phila., July 6, 1858.
9. Mrs. Sherman to WTS, South Bend, Ind., Jan. 8, 1865.
10. *Ibid.*

11. Mrs. Sherman to WTS, Lancaster, O., Aug. 22, 1861; and Apr. 24, 1864.
12. Mrs. Sherman to WTS, Lancaster, May 1, 1860.
13. Mrs. Sherman to WTS, Lancaster, June 5, 1860.
14. Mrs. Sherman to WTS, Lancaster, May 16, 1860.
15. Mrs. Sherman to WTS, Lancaster, Oct. 11, 1864.
16. Lizzie Sherman to WTS, Lancaster, May 19, 1859.
17. Mrs. Sherman to WTS, Lancaster, May 28, 1859.
18. *Ibid.*
19. Mrs. Sherman to WTS, Lancaster, Apr. 29, 1862.
20. Mrs. Sherman to WTS, Lancaster, Sept. 23, 1862.
21. WTS to TES, St. Louis, Oct. 11, 1874.
22. WTS to TES, St. Louis, Oct. 23, 1874.
23. WTS to TES, St. Louis, Nov. 13, 1874.
24. Mrs. Sherman to Minnie, St. Louis, Nov. 9, 1867.
25. Mrs. Sherman to WTS, South Bend, Feb. 15, 1865.
26. Mrs. Sherman to Minnie, St. Louis, Nov. 15, 1867.
27. Mrs. Sherman to Minnie, St. Louis, Oct. 13, 1867.
28. Mrs. Sherman to WTS, St. Louis, Jan. 23, 1868.
29. Mrs. Sherman to WTS, Lancaster, July 10, 1868.
30. *Ibid.*
31. TES to WTS, St. Louis, March 10, 1869.
32. TES to WTS, St. Louis, March 20 [?], 1869.
33. TES to WTS, St. Louis, Apr. 2, 1869.
34. *Ibid.*
35. TES to WTS, St. Louis, March 10, 1869.
36. *Ibid.*
37. *Ibid.*

II. BASIC TRAINING

38. More precisely, Cump usually sat on a large dictionary to add to his height. Cf. Burton, *op. cit.*, 183.
39. TES to WTS, Washington, December 24, 1871.
40. TES to WTS, Washington, May 12, 1872.
41. *Ibid.*
42. *Ibid.*
43. TES to WTS, Washington, May 5, 1872.
44. TES to WTS, Washington, December 24, 1871.
45. TES to WTS, Washington, May 12, 1872.
46. WTS to TES, August 9, 1870.
47. TES to WTS, Washington, May 12, 1872.
48. TES to WTS, Washington, February 8, 1872.
49. TES to WTS, Washington, February 24, 1872.
50. WTS to TES, Cairo, Egypt, March 29, 1872.
51. *Ibid.*

52. WTS to TES, Vienna, June 12, 1872.
53. *Ibid.*
54. WTS to TES, Paris, July 24, 1872.
55. WTS to TES, Paris, July 26, 1872.
56. Archbishop Henry Edward Manning, second archbishop of Westminster. He was created Cardinal in 1875.
57. George P. A. Healy, American portrait painter of second rank but great popularity.
58. WTS to TES, St. Petersburg, May 25, 1872.
59. WTS to Mrs. Sherman, "Castle near Glasgow," August 25, 1872.
60. *Ibid.*
61. Minnie to WTS, St. Albans, Vt., August n.d., 1872.
62. The following account of the trip (with the exception of the passages from Mrs. Sherman's diary) is taken from a long newspaper article undated and unsigned, but obviously the work of either of Tom's two companions. The article is in the E. Sherman Fitch Papers.
63. Mrs. Sherman's diary is in the E. Sherman Fitch Papers. (The Dennis and Bradley youths were classmates of Tom's at Georgetown College.)
64. *New York Daily Graphic,* Oct. 1, 1874.
65. October 1, 1874.
66. October 2, 1874. One may imagine how feminine beauty was enhanced by the costumes of the period. Take, for instance, the case of one Miss Josie Hecker's "dress of white, with large purple pansies and trailing vines. . . ." (*Ibid.*)
67. General Philip Sheridan.
68. E. Sherman Fitch Papers.
69. Conversation wih Miss E. Sherman Fitch.

III. AT YALE

70. Undated newspaper clipping in Georgetown University Archives.
71. The original manuscript of this address is in the G. U. Archives.
72. WTS to TES, Wash., Sept. 13, 1874.
73. TES to WTS, New Haven, April 4, 1875.
74. *Ibid.*
75. TES to WTS, New Haven, September 30, 1875.
76. TES to WTS, New Haven, October 20, 1875.
77. TES to WTS, New Haven, February 27, 1876.
78. TES to WTS, New Haven, September 24, 1875.
79. TES to WTS, New Haven, September 27, 1875.
80. WTS to TES, St. Louis, September 24, 1875.
81. WTS to TES, St. Louis, September 27, 1875.
82. TES to WTS, New Haven, November 3, 1875.

83. TES to WTS, New Haven, November 4, 1875.
84. TES to WTS, New Haven, November 18, 1875. Henry Hitch-
    cock had been on the General's staff during the March through
    Georgia.
85. TES to his brother, Cump, Detroit, January 15, 1887.
86. TES to WTS, New Haven, November 3, 1875.
87. TES to WTS, New Haven, November 18, 1875.
88. TES to WTS, New Haven, June 6, 1876.
89. Conversation with Miss E. Sherman Fitch.
90. TES to WTS, New Haven, November 18, 1875.
91. WTS to TES, St. Louis, October 18, 1874.
92. TES to WTS, New Haven, October 22, 1874.
93. TES to WTS, New Haven, June 11, 1876.
94. WTS to TES, St. Louis, April 12, 1875.
95. WTS to TES, St. Louis, October 26, 1874.
96. *Ibid.*
97. WTS to TES, St. Louis, September 24, 1875.
98. WTS to TES, St. Louis, November 13, 1875.
99. WTS to TES, St. Louis, September 13, 1874.
100. WTS to TES, St. Louis, Jan. 16, 1875.
101. WTS to TES, St. Louis, Mar. 4, 1876; Same to same, Wash-
     ington, Mar. 30, 1876.
102. WTS to TES, St. Louis, Sept. 24, 1875; Same to same, St.
     Louis, Nov. 13, 1875.
103. WTS to TES, St. Louis, November 20, 1874.
104. WTS to TES, St. Louis, November 10, 1875.
105. *Ibid.*
106. TES to Cump, New Haven, February 29, 1876.
107. TES to Cump, New Haven, June 12, 1876.
108. TES to Cump, New Haven, April 27, 1876.
109. TES to WTS, New Haven, May 8, 1876.
110. WTS to TES, St. Louis, February 1, 1876.
111. *Ibid.*
112. WTS to TES, St. Louis, February 18, 1876.
113. TES to WTS, New Haven, n.d., 1876.
114. TES to WTS, New Haven, November 30, 1875.
115. TES to WTS, New Haven, December 15, 1875.
116. TES to Cump, New Haven, April 27, 1876.
117. WTS to TES, Washington, D. C., May 29, 1876.

IV. A CHANGE OF PLAN

118. Soon after the outbreak of this family strife, while Tom was still
     at Yale, the General had informed his son of the trouble. Cf.:
     WTS to TES, St. Louis, Mar. 18, 1875; TES to WTS, New

Haven, Apr. 4, 1875, in which Tom gives his reactions concerning the affair.
119. WTS to TES, Washington, D. C., October 27, 1876.
120. TES to WTS, St. Louis, October 26, 1876.
121. WTS to TES, Washington, D. C., n.d.
122. WTS to TES, Washington, D. C., October 22, 1876.
123. TES to WTS, St. Louis, February 11, 1877.
124. *Ibid.*
125. WTS to TES, Washington, D. C., January 12, 1877.
126. WTS to TES, Washington, D. C., November 10, 1877.
127. *Ibid.*
128. WTS to TES, Washington, D. C., February 27, 1877.
129. WTS to TES, Washington, D. C., April 6, 1877.
130. WTS to TES, Washington, D. C., October 19, 1876.
131. TES to WTS, St. Louis, n.d. [1878?].
132. TES to WTS, St. Louis, February 25, 1878.
133. TES to WTS, St. Louis, December 13, 1876.
134. TES to WTS, St. Louis, November 23 [20?], 1876.
135. TES to WTS, St. Louis, December 11, 1877.
136. TES to WTS, St. Louis, March 1, 1877.
137. *Ibid.*
138. WTS to Major Turner, Lancaster, Ohio, July 24, 1878. (Major Henry Turner was an old friend of the General's, and had been his partner in a banking venture in California.)
139. WTS to Minnie, Washington, D. C., June 16, 1878.
140. WTS to Ellie, Washington, D. C., June 4, 1878.
141. *Ibid.*
142. WTS to Major Turner, Washington, D. C., July 7, 1878.
143. WTS to Ellie, Washington, D. C., June 4, 1878.
144. WTS to Ellie, Washington, D. C., June 5, 1878.
145. TES to Minnie, New York, June 4, 1878.
146. Mrs. Sherman to Minnie, St. Louis, May 25, 1878.
147. *Ibid.*
148. TES to Mrs. Sherman, Woodstock, October 13, 1887.
149. TES to Minnie, Roehampton, England, March 24, 1879.
150. See also the meditation on "The Kingdom of Christ" in the *Spiritual Exercises.*
151. TES to Minnie, Roehampton, March 24, 1879.
152. WTS to the Editor, *Chicago Tribune,* Washington, D. C., October 27, 1878.
153. TES to WTS, St. Louis, n.d., [1878?].
154. *Ibid.*
155. The date of his sailing may have been June 4. In a letter to Minnie, dated June 5, Mrs. Sherman says she has just received a

APPENDIX A

The following poem was written by Thomas Ewing Sherman for a family reunion in honor of his father in April, 1884:

To Papa

What crown shall deck his brow?
Wears he the laurel now?
Weave we the holly bough,
With myrtle entwine him.

Spray of the staunch old yew,
Sprigs of the oak so true,
Broad beech and buck-eye too,
Bud to enshrine him.

Gone are his days of war,
Danger and strife are o'er,
Comes now the autumn hoar,
Sweet peace enfolds him.

Garlands must hide his sword,
Heap high the genial board,
By loving hearts adored,
Home ties shall hold him.

A longer verse in commemoration of the gallant General
Macpherson, one of the heroes of the battle of Chattanooga, has
distinct merit:

Kennesaw

The eagle coasts his eyrie,
The fox his covert lair,
But neither fox nor eagle
The lion's look may dare.

High on the mountain's summit
We see your guns in air.
Ho! eagle, is your eyrie safe?
Macpherson's men prepare
To scale yon beetling mountain
And battle with you there!

Now onward, Wood and Stanley!
Right up the darksome glade,
On! for the grand old Union!
On through the darkling shade
Of pine trees' gloomy covert,
Of clouds that burst in rain,
And cannons belching clouds and fire
That threaten you in vain.

No darker storm of shot and shell,
No deadlier lightning's flash,
Than the black storms of rebel hate
That 'gainst your country clash.
America! Thy banner
On mountain, sea and shore
Is rent with tear and tatter,
Is black with brothers' gore.
Then onward, Stanley, onward!
On to the mountain's crest,
Men, bare your bosoms bravely
As the Union bares her breast.

In vain they toil and struggle
Mid rock, and cliff and crag;
In vain the lumbering cannon
Right up the hill they drag.
In vain they force the lurking foe
Behind his parapet;
They may not win the summit,
Not yet, brave friends, not yet.

But not in vain your combat;
Still keep the foe at bay;
Hold fast the ground you've conquered;
Now waits a better day.
When force and courage cannot win,
A *mind* can conquer all;
A *mind* commands your army;
Dark Kennesaw shall fall!

Down eastward valleys streaming
Pour the level morning beams
And o'er a moving mass of men
The mellow radiance gleams.
'Tis Macpherson marching southward!
Now Kennesaw beware,
Tomorrow's sun shall kiss our flag
Floating in triumph there!

APPENDIX B

FATHER SHERMAN'S LAST WILL & TESTAMENT

I THOMAS EWING SHERMAN hereby make my last will and testament.

I bequeath the sum of $500 . . . to the Mission of Santa Barbara asking that Masses be said for my soul.

I give $500 . . . to St. Vincents' Orphan Asylum; $500 to St. Francis Hospital; $500 to my dear niece Elizabeth Thackera.

I give the bust of my father W. T. Sherman to Arthur H. Sherman of Beverley Hills. My gold chain I give to Othelia Carroll Beals of Seattle.

My books, pictures, saddle and bridle together with $500 I give to Elizabeth Thompson.

My altar, vestments, sacred vessels, linens etc. I give to the Church Extension Society.

I request the First National Bank of Santa Barbara to act as Executor and to hold my house; the principal part of my worldly effects; in trust, for purposes confided to the Bank by letter.

Thomas Ewing Sherman
Sept. 18, 1928.

Witness:
W. F. Rhodehame
A. B. Harmer.

APPENDIX C

INVENTORY OF SACRED EFFECTS AT SANTA BARBARA

Sacred Vessels in care of Father de Rop:

3 gold plated chalices
1 gold plated ciborium
3 gold plated patens (one poorly gilded)
1 pyx and burse
1 set silver cruets and tray (small)
2 altar stones
   holy oil stocks
1 wooden altar
1 chest with complete sets of vestments
   altar linens
1 set chimes
4 single candlesticks
2 candelabra
2 missals
2 missal stands
   several pictures suitable for a small chapel
   plentiful supply of candles

List of Sources

I. BEGINNINGS ARE ENDINGS

1. For facts in this chapter not revealed by the invaluable E. Sherman Fitch primary sources, the author is indebted to two books: Anna McAllister, *Ellen Ewing: Wife of General Sherman*, New York, Benziger Brothers, 1936; Katherine Burton, *Three Generations*, New York, Longmans, Green & Co., 1947. See also the exuberant— and somewhat hysterical—newspaper accounts of the Grand Review.
2. William Tecumseh Sherman to Thomas Ewing Sherman (n. p.), October 4, 1863. [Unless otherwise indicated, primary sources such as this are taken from the E. Sherman Fitch Papers, in the possession of Miss E. Sherman Fitch, New York City. Henceforth the abbreviations "TES" and "WTS" will be used for Thomas Ewing Sherman and William Tecumseh Sherman respectively.]
3. WTS to TES, Nashville, Tenn., April 25, 1864.
4. WTS to TES, "In the Field," Kingston, Ga., Nov. 10, 1864.
5. WTS to TES, "In the Field," Savannah, Ga., Jan. 21, 1865.
6. TES to his mother, Woodstock, Md., Dec. 27, 188– [certainly during his period of theological study.]
7. Conversation with Miss E. Sherman Fitch.
8. Maria Boyle Ewing (mother of Mrs. Sherman) to Mrs. Sherman, Phila., July 6, 1858.
9. Mrs. Sherman to WTS, South Bend, Ind., Jan. 8, 1865.
10. *Ibid.*

11. Mrs. Sherman to WTS, Lancaster, O., Aug. 22, 1861; and Apr. 24, 1864.
12. Mrs. Sherman to WTS, Lancaster, May 1, 1860.
13. Mrs. Sherman to WTS, Lancaster, June 5, 1860.
14. Mrs. Sherman to WTS, Lancaster, May 16, 1860.
15. Mrs. Sherman to WTS, Lancaster, Oct. 11, 1864.
16. Lizzie Sherman to WTS, Lancaster, May 19, 1859.
17. Mrs. Sherman to WTS, Lancaster, May 28, 1859.
18. Ibid.
19. Mrs. Sherman to WTS, Lancaster, Apr. 29, 1862.
20. Mrs. Sherman to WTS, Lancaster, Sept. 23, 1862.
21. WTS to TES, St. Louis, Oct. 11, 1874.
22. WTS to TES, St. Louis, Oct. 23, 1874.
23. WTS to TES, St. Louis, Nov. 13, 1874.
24. Mrs. Sherman to Minnie, St. Louis, Nov. 9, 1867.
25. Mrs. Sherman to WTS, South Bend, Feb. 15, 1865.
26. Mrs. Sherman to Minnie, St. Louis, Nov. 15, 1867.
27. Mrs. Sherman to Minnie, St. Louis, Oct. 13, 1867.
28. Mrs. Sherman to WTS, St. Louis, Jan. 23, 1868.
29. Mrs. Sherman to WTS, Lancaster, July 10, 1868.
30. Ibid.
31. TES to WTS, St. Louis, March 10, 1869.
32. TES to WTS, St. Louis, March 20 [?], 1869.
33. TES to WTS, St. Louis, Apr. 2, 1869.
34. Ibid.
35. TES to WTS, St. Louis, March 10, 1869.
36. Ibid.
37. Ibid.

II. BASIC TRAINING

38. More precisely, Cump usually sat on a large dictionary to add to his height. Cf. Burton, op. cit., 183.
39. TES to WTS, Washington, December 24, 1871.
40. TES to WTS, Washington, May 12, 1872.
41. Ibid.
42. Ibid.
43. TES to WTS, Washington, May 5, 1872.
44. TES to WTS, Washington, December 24, 1871.
45. TES to WTS, Washington, May 12, 1872.
46. WTS to TES, August 9, 1870.
47. TES to WTS, Washington, May 12, 1872.
48. TES to WTS, Washington, February 8, 1872.
49. TES to WTS, Washington, February 24, 1872.
50. WTS to TES, Cairo, Egypt, March 29, 1872.
51. Ibid.

52. WTS to TES, Vienna, June 12, 1872.
53. *Ibid.*
54. WTS to TES, Paris, July 24, 1872.
55. WTS to TES, Paris, July 26, 1872.
56. Archbishop Henry Edward Manning, second archbishop of Westminster. He was created Cardinal in 1875.
57. George P. A. Healy, American portrait painter of second rank but great popularity.
58. WTS to TES, St. Petersburg, May 25, 1872.
59. WTS to Mrs. Sherman, "Castle near Glasgow," August 25, 1872.
60. *Ibid.*
61. Minnie to WTS, St. Albans, Vt., August n.d., 1872.
62. The following account of the trip (with the exception of the passages from Mrs. Sherman's diary) is taken from a long newspaper article undated and unsigned, but obviously the work of either of Tom's two companions. The article is in the E. Sherman Fitch Papers.
63. Mrs. Sherman's diary is in the E. Sherman Fitch Papers. (The Dennis and Bradley youths were classmates of Tom's at Georgetown College.)
64. *New York Daily Graphic,* Oct. 1, 1874.
65. October 1, 1874.
66. October 2, 1874. One may imagine how feminine beauty was enhanced by the costumes of the period. Take, for instance, the case of one Miss Josie Hecker's "dress of white, with large purple pansies and trailing vines. . . ." (*Ibid.*)
67. General Philip Sheridan.
68. E. Sherman Fitch Papers.
69. Conversation wih Miss E. Sherman Fitch.

III. AT YALE

70. Undated newspaper clipping in Georgetown University Archives.
71. The original manuscript of this address is in the G. U. Archives.
72. WTS to TES, Wash., Sept. 13, 1874.
73. TES to WTS, New Haven, April 4, 1875.
74. *Ibid.*
75. TES to WTS, New Haven, September 30, 1875.
76. TES to WTS, New Haven, October 20, 1875.
77. TES to WTS, New Haven, February 27, 1876.
78. TES to WTS, New Haven, September 24, 1875.
79. TES to WTS, New Haven, September 27, 1875.
80. WTS to TES, St. Louis, September 24, 1875.
81. WTS to TES, St. Louis, September 27, 1875.
82. TES to WTS, New Haven, November 3, 1875.

83. TES to WTS, New Haven, November 4, 1875.
84. TES to WTS, New Haven, November 18, 1875. Henry Hitch-cock had been on the General's staff during the March through Georgia.
85. TES to his brother, Cump, Detroit, January 15, 1887.
86. TES to WTS, New Haven, November 3, 1875.
87. TES to WTS, New Haven, November 18, 1875.
88. TES to WTS, New Haven, June 6, 1876.
89. Conversation with Miss E. Sherman Fitch.
90. TES to WTS, New Haven, November 18, 1875.
91. WTS to TES, St. Louis, October 18, 1874.
92. TES to WTS, New Haven, October 22, 1874.
93. TES to WTS, New Haven, June 11, 1876.
94. WTS to TES, St. Louis, April 12, 1875.
95. WTS to TES, St. Louis, October 26, 1874.
96. *Ibid.*
97. WTS to TES, St. Louis, September 24, 1875.
98. WTS to TES, St. Louis, November 13, 1875.
99. WTS to TES, St. Louis, September 13, 1874.
100. WTS to TES, St. Louis, Jan. 16, 1875.
101. WTS to TES, St. Louis, Mar. 4, 1876; Same to same, Washington, Mar. 30, 1876.
102. WTS to TES, St. Louis, Sept. 24, 1875; Same to same, St. Louis, Nov. 13, 1875.
103. WTS to TES, St. Louis, November 20, 1874.
104. WTS to TES, St. Louis, November 10, 1875.
105. *Ibid.*
106. TES to Cump, New Haven, February 29, 1876.
107. TES to Cump, New Haven, June 12, 1876.
108. TES to Cump, New Haven, April 27, 1876.
109. TES to WTS, New Haven, May 8, 1876.
110. WTS to TES, St. Louis, February 1, 1876.
111. *Ibid.*
112. WTS to TES, St. Louis, February 18, 1876.
113. TES to WTS, New Haven, n.d., 1876.
114. TES to WTS, New Haven, November 30, 1875.
115. TES to WTS, New Haven, December 15, 1875.
116. TES to Cump, New Haven, April 27, 1876.
117. WTS to TES, Washington, D. C., May 29, 1876.

IV. A CHANGE OF PLAN

118. Soon after the outbreak of this family strife, while Tom was still at Yale, the General had informed his son of the trouble. Cf.: WTS to TES, St. Louis, Mar. 18, 1875; TES to WTS, New

Haven, Apr. 4, 1875, in which Tom gives his reactions concerning the affair.

119. WTS to TES, Washington, D. C., October 27, 1876.
120. TES to WTS, St. Louis, October 26, 1876.
121. WTS to TES, Washington, D. C., n.d.
122. WTS to TES, Washington, D. C., October 22, 1876.
123. TES to WTS, St. Louis, February 11, 1877.
124. Ibid.
125. WTS to TES, Washington, D. C., January 12, 1877.
126. WTS to TES, Washington, D. C., November 10, 1877.
127. Ibid.
128. WTS to TES, Washington, D. C., February 27, 1877.
129. WTS to TES, Washington, D. C., April 6, 1877.
130. WTS to TES, Washington, D. C., October 19, 1876.
131. TES to WTS, St. Louis, n.d. [1878?].
132. TES to WTS, St. Louis, February 25, 1878.
133. TES to WTS, St. Louis, December 13, 1876.
134. TES to WTS, St. Louis, November 23 [20?], 1876.
135. TES to WTS, St. Louis, December 11, 1877.
136. TES to WTS, St. Louis, March 1, 1877.
137. Ibid.
138. WTS to Major Turner, Lancaster, Ohio, July 24, 1878. (Major Henry Turner was an old friend of the General's, and had been his partner in a banking venture in California.)
139. WTS to Minnie, Washington, D. C., June 16, 1878.
140. WTS to Ellie, Washington, D. C., June 4, 1878.
141. Ibid.
142. WTS to Major Turner, Washington, D. C., July 7, 1878.
143. WTS to Ellie, Washington, D. C., June 4, 1878.
144. WTS to Ellie, Washington, D. C., June 5, 1878.
145. TES to Minnie, New York, June 4, 1878.
146. Mrs. Sherman to Minnie, St. Louis, May 25, 1878.
147. Ibid.
148. TES to Mrs. Sherman, Woodstock, October 13, 1887.
149. TES to Minnie, Roehampton, England, March 24, 1879.
150. See also the meditation on "The Kingdom of Christ" in the Spiritual Exercises.
151. TES to Minnie, Roehampton, March 24, 1879.
152. WTS to the Editor, Chicago Tribune, Washington, D. C., October 27, 1878.
153. TES to WTS, St. Louis, n.d., [1878?].
154. Ibid.
155. The date of his sailing may have been June 4. In a letter to Minnie, dated June 5, Mrs. Sherman says she has just received a

"dispatch" from Tom's friend and classmate Jim Tracy, who says he has just seen Tom off. The reference is probably to a telegram.

V. THE NOVICESHIP

156. TES to Minnie, Roehampton, Eng., March 24, 1879.
157. The small book called *The Spiritual Exercises of St. Ignatius* was written by the saint. The method of making the *Exercises* is therein outlined.
158. TES to his mother, Oct. 24, 1878.
159. Same to same, Nov. 2, 1878.
160. TES to Minnie, Mar. 24, 1879.
161. TES to his mother, Nov. 2, 1878.
162. *Ibid.*
163. TES to his mother, Nov. 20, 1878.
164. TES to Mrs. Sherman, Roehampton, November 20, 1878.
165. *Ibid.*
166. TES to Mrs. Sherman, Roehampton, October 24, 1878.
167. TES to Minnie, Roehampton, March 24, 1879.
168. TES to Mrs. Sherman, Roehampton, May 9, 1880.
169. TES to Cump, Roehampton, July 1, 1880.
170. TES to Minnie, Roehampton, March 24, 1879.
171. *Ibid.* Italics in original.
172. TES to Mother, Roehampton, October 24, 1878.
173. TES to Minnie, Roehampton, March 24, 1879.
174. TES to Mrs. Sherman, Roehampton, May 9, 1880.
175. TES to WTS, Roehampton, July 14, 1880.
176. TES to Minnie, Washington, D. C., August 25, 1880.
177. *Ibid.*
178. TES to WTS, Altoona, Pa., September 1, 1880.
179. TES to Minnie, Washington, D. C., August 25, 1880.
180. WTS to Minnie, Washington, D. C., August 26, 1880.
181. TES to WTS, Altoona, Pa., September 1, 1880.

VI. THE SPIRIT OF WOODSTOCK

182. TES to WTS, Woodstock, December 2 [22?], 1880.
183. John C. Murray, S.J., "Woodstock's Wisdom," *Woodstock Letters,* LXXIII, No. 4 (December, 1944), 282-284.
184. For information regarding Woodstock notables and details of Woodstock life the author is indebted to Patrick J. Dooley, S.J., *Woodstock and its Makers,* published by the Woodstock College Press in 1927. This work, with all its deficiencies, is the best history of the college so far published.

185. *Philosophers' Diary*, Dec. 22, 1880. (This document contains a day-by-day record of routine and extra-routine happenings of the college. It was traditionally written by the beadle of the Philosophers.)
186. TES to WTS, Woodstock, December 29, 1882.
187. TES to WTS, Woodstock, July 25, 1882.
188. TES to WTS, Woodstock, January 26, 1882.
189. TES to WTS, Woodstock, December 29, 1882.
190. TES to WTS, Woodstock, January 26, 1882.
191. *Philosophers' Diary*, November 21, 1882.
192. *Ibid.*, May 11, 1882.
193. TES to WTS, Woodstock, December 2 [22?], 1880.
194. TES to WTS, Woodstock, January 26, 1882.
195. *Philosophers' Diary*, September 22, 1880.
196. *Ibid.*, Dec. 8, 1881.
197. *Ibid.*, Nov. 25, 1880.
198. *Woodstock Letters*, issues of: Sept. 1881, Jan. 1882, May 1882.
199. The following profile of Father Piccirillo is taken from an article written by Tom Sherman himself in *Woodstock Letters*, XVII (1888), 339-350.
200. The "Father Minister" of a Jesuit house is in charge of the temporal and housekeeping and disciplinary affairs of the Jesuit community. The latter term, incidentally, refers to the totality of the Jesuits in a given house.
201. TES to WTS, St. Inigoes Villa, July 9, 1882. "Villa" is Jesuit terminology for "vacation house." St. Inigoes was in St. Mary's County, Maryland, at the junction of Chesapeake Bay and the St. Mary's River.
202. TES to WTS, Woodstock, December 29, 1882.
203. TES to WTS, Woodstock, n.d. [1882?].
204. TES to WTS, Woodstock, February 11, 1883.
205. TES to WTS, Woodstock, n.d. [1881?].
206. TES to WTS, Woodstock, July 25, 1882.
207. TES to WTS, Woodstock, January 26, 1882.
208. TES to WTS, Woodstock, April 15, 1883.
209. TES to Cump, Woodstock, May 3, 1883.
210. TES to WTS, Woodstock, Jan. 26, 1882.

VII. THE YOUNG TEACHER

211. Documentary materials covering this period of Father Sherman's life are scarce. Consequently the first few pages of this chapter constitute an imaginative reconstruction based, however, on numerous interviews with his contemporaries and those who spoke with his contemporaries.

212. TES to WTS, Detroit, December 29, 1886.
213. TES to WTS, Detroit, October 30, 1886.
214. TES to WTS, Detroit, January 6, 1886.
215. TES to Cump, Detroit, June 9, 1887.
216. TES to WTS, Detroit, January 23, 1887, recalling the earlier event.
217. The "status" is the official notice of changes in posts.
218. Such corrections in the interest of good housekeeping are perfectly normal incidents of life in a religious order. The incident was related to the author by Father William Nash, S.J. of Holy Family Rectory, Chicago, Ill.
219. Fr. L. Kenny, S.J. to Eleanor Sherman Fitch, St. Louis, July 26, 1955, quoting *The Diamond Jubilee Volume of St. Louis University, 1829-1904*, by Rev. William W. Fanning, S.J. On page 296 is a photograph of the Phalethic Debating Society, with pictures of Tom Sherman and Cump.
220. TES to WTS, Detroit, September 16, 1886.
221. TES to WTS, Detroit, December 29, 1886.
222. TES to WTS, Detroit, January 6, 1886.
223. TES to Cump, Detroit, June 27, 1887.
224. TES to WTS, Detroit, September 16, 1886.
225. *Ibid.*
226. TES to Cump, Detroit, September 20, 1886.
227. General Orlando M. Poe, noted engineer.
228. TES to WTS, Detroit, September 16, 1886.
229. TES to WTS, Woodstock, February 15, 1883.
230. TES to WTS, Detroit, March 16, 1887.
231. TES to WTS, Detroit, September 16, 1886.
232. TES to WTS, Woodstock, April 15, 1883.
233. TES to WTS, Detroit, May 4, 1887.
234. TES to Cump, Detroit, September 20, 1886.
235. TES to Mrs. Sherman, Detroit, n.d.
236. TES to Mrs. Sherman, Detroit, March 27, 1887.
237. TES to Cump, Detroit, June 9, 1887.
238. TES to WTS, Detroit, June 10, 1887.

VIII. THEOLOGY; DEATH OF A GENERAL

239. TES to WTS, Woodstock, October 24, 1889.
240. TES to Cump, Woodstock, February 24, 1890.
241. *Ibid.*   241a. *Ibid.*
242. TES to Mrs. Sherman, Woodstock, n.d. [1886?].
243. TES to WTS, Detroit, January 6, 1886.
244. TES to Cump, Detroit, June 9, 1887.
245. TES to WTS, Detroit, December 29, 1886.

246. TES to WTS, Woodstock, January 28, 1889.
247. TES to WTS, Woodstock, April 7, 1889.
248. TES to Cump, Woodstock, February 24, 1890.
249. TES to WTS, Woodstock, May 2, 1889.
250. *Theologians' Diary*, December 22, 1887 and December 24, 1889.
251. TES to WTS, Woodstock, January 13, 1889. The offer came from Colonel John M. Bacon, a friend of his father.
252. September 28, 1881. (The Provincial is the Jesuit superior in charge of a "Province," one of the major administrative divisions of the Order.)
253. *Infirmarian's Diary*, Woodstock, entry of February, n.d. 1888; also entry of November 2, 1887, regarding treatment given to him for malaria.
254. TES to WTS, Woodstock, May 31, 1888.
255. TES to WTS, Woodstock, May 27, 1888. Roscoe Conkling had died of an ear abscess.
256. TES to WTS, Woodstock, May 2, 1889.
257. TES to WTS, Woodstock, March 23, 1889.
258. TES to WTS, Woodstock, November 8, 1888.
259. TES to WTS, Woodstock, January 20, 1889.
260. TES to WTS, Woodstock, November 28, 1887.
261. TES to WTS, Woodstock, January 13, 1889.
262. TES to WTS, Woodstock, March 23, 1889.
263. TES to WTS, Woodstock, January 28, 1889.
264. TES to WTS, Woodstock, January 12, 1888.
265. TES to WTS, Detroit, January 6, 1886.
266. TES to WTS, Detroit, October 30, 1886.
267. TES to WTS, Detroit, January 6, 1886.
268. TES to WTS, Woodstock, November 1, 1889.
269. TES to WTS, Woodstock, January 13, 1889.
270. TES to WTS, Woodstock, May 2, 1889.
271. TES to WTS, Woodstock, January 28, 1889.
272. Mrs. Sherman died on November 28, 1888.
273. TES to WTS, Woodstock, February 20, 1889.
274. TES to WTS, Woodstock, January 7, 1889.
275. See TES to WTS, Woodstock, June 23, 1889.
276. TES to Cump, Woodstock, February 24, 1890.
277. *Ibid.*
278. *Press* (Philadelphia), July 8, 1889.
279. TES to WTS, Woodstock, October 24, 1889.
280. *Theologians' Diary*, November 28, 1889.
281. TES to WTS, Woodstock, Ocotber 24, 1889.
282. *Ibid.*
283. TES to WTS, Woodstock, November 18, 1889.
284. TES to WTS, Woodstock, November 1, 1889.

285. TES to WTS, Woodstock, September 12, 1889.
286. Ibid.
287. TES to Cump, Woodstock, February 24, 1890.
288. Ibid.
289. TES to WTS, Woodstock, October 24, 1889. Ellie had been married in 1880 to Lt. Alexander Thackara, U.S.N.
290. TES to WTS, Woodstock, February 24, 1890.

IX. THE GREAT CAMPAIGN: FIRST PHASE

291. "Scholastic" is the term applied to a Jesuit who has not yet been ordained to the priesthood.
292. TES to Cump, St. Louis, June 9, 1891; see also TES to Cump, St. Louis, April 20, 1891.
293. See letters from TES to Cump, St. Louis, May 21, 1892; September 22, 1892; October 2, 1892; June 1, 1893.
294. TES to Cump, St. Louis, June 14, 1892.
295. TES to Cump, St. Louis, January 6, 1892.
296. TES to Cump, St. Louis, August 29, 1891.
297. TES to Cump, St. Louis, August 20, 1891.
298. TES to Cump, Marquette College, July 14, 1892; TES to Cump, St. Louis, January 6, 1892; TES to Lizzie, St. Louis, December 22, 1892.
299. TES to Cump, Marquette College, July 14, 1892; TES to Cump, St. Louis, March 12, 1892.
300. Ibid.
301. TES to Cump, St. Louis, August 29, 1891; TES to Cump, St. Louis, May 8, 1891.
302. TES to Cump, St. Louis, August 20, 1891.
303. TES to Cump, St. Louis, August 29, 1891.
304. TES to Cump, St. Louis, September 18, 1891.
305. TES to Cump, St. Louis, September 30, 1891; October 2, 1891; October 3, 1891.
306. TES to Cump, St. Louis, September 28, 1891.
307. TES to Cump, St. Louis, October 10, 1891.
308. The Bloomington Telephone, April 28, 1896.
309. Ibid.
310. Ibid.
311. Omaha Bee, reprinted in unnamed St. Louis paper of June 10, 1893.
312. Ibid.
313. Ibid.
314. Minneapolis Times, n.d., 1892.
315. The Kansas City Journal, September 5, 1892.
316. Newspaper clipping, n.p., n.d., in E. Sherman Fitch Scrap Book.

317. *Ibid.*
318. *Omaha Bee,* reprinted in unnamed St. Louis newspaper, June 10, 1893.
319. *Ibid.*
320. TES to Cump, St. Louis, May 21, 1892.
321. *Cedar Rapids Evening Gazette,* March 16, 1896.
322. *Ibid.*
323. *Proceedings of the Society of the Army of the Tennessee,* St. Louis, November 17, 1892.—It should be noted that this anti-union position is by no means the traditional or official attitude of Jesuits.
324. *Ibid.*

X. THE CHICAGO MUSIC HALL ADDRESS

325. *Chicago Record,* February 3, 1894.
326. Conversation with Fr. William Nash, S.J., Chicago, Ill.
327. *The Daily Inter Ocean,* February 6, 1894.
328. *Chicago Herald,* February 6, 1894.
329. *Ibid.*
330. *Ibid.*
331. Conversation with Mr. John Bremner, Chicago, Ill. (Mr. Bremner was a contemporary of Father Sherman's.)
332. *Chicago Herald,* February 6, 1894. (It is to be noted that this controversial passage was not published in any other paper. The Chicago journals reporting the speech without the passage were the *Inter Ocean, Times, Tribune,* and *Record.*)
333. TES to Cump, St. Louis, March 10, 1893; TES to Cump, St. Louis, n.d., [1891-1893].
334. TES to Cump, St. Louis. August 29, 1891, and May 21, 1892.
335. TES to Cump, St. Louis, December 17, 1893.
336. *Ibid.*
337. TES to Cump, St. Louis, May 21, 1892.
338. TES to Cump, St. Louis, June 1, 1893.
339. TES to Cump, Woodstock, February 24, 1890.
340. TES to Cump, St. Louis, December 17, 1893.
341. TES to Cump, St. Louis, January 6, 1892.
342. From the Music Hall address; cf. p. 142 and following of this chapter.

XI. REPULSE AND RECOVERY

343. The "Mission Band" was the technical name for the small group of priests assigned exclusively to the work of giving missions.
344. TES to Missouri Provincial, Denver, Colorado, January 8, 1896.

LIST OF SOURCES

345. TES to Missouri Provincial, St. Ignatius Mission, Montana, January 28, 1897.
346. Rachel's husband. They had been married in 1891. Tom had performed the marriage ceremony.
347. TES to Fr. Purbrick, S.J., Boston, January 7, 1898.
348. Fr. Purbrick to Dr. Thorndike, New York City, January 8, 1898.
349. The "Father General" is the chief Jesuit superior.
350. Fr. Thos. Fitzgerald, S.J., to Fr. Purbrick, Chicago, January 12, 1898.
351. 4th Regt. Missouri Infantry, Field and Staff Muster-In Roll, Fr. Thomas Ewing Sherman, Chaplain. National Archives, Washington, D. C.
352. TES, "A Month in Porto Rico," *The Messenger of the Sacred Heart*, XXXIII (December, 1898), 1074. (The accepted spelling is now *Puerto Rico*, but Tom's spelling was correct at the time he was writing.)
353. TES to Missouri Provincial, San Juan, Porto Rico, December 31, 1898; U. S. Grant, III, to Eleanor Sherman Fitch, Washington, D. C., February 26, 1954.
354. *Ibid.*
355. Confidential Report of TES to War Department, from Headquarters, District of San Juan, P.R., November 30, 1898. National Archives, Washington, D. C.
356. TES, "A Month in Porto Rico," 1079.
357. Report to War Dep't., *supra cit.*
358. *Ibid.*
359. TES, "A Month in Porto Rico," 1077
360. *Ibid.*, p. 1076.
361. *Ibid.*, p. 1077.
362. *Ibid.*, p. 1078.
363. *Ibid.*, p. 1076.
364. *Ibid.*
365. Report, *supra cit.*
366. *Ibid.*
367. "A Month in Porto Rico," 1080.
368. *Ibid.*; cf. also Report.
369. Father John J. Wynne, S.J. to Father Thomas S. Fitzgerald, New York, Feb. 6, 1899. Cf. also: *Baltimore Methodist*, Jan. 8, 1899; *The Church News*, Washington, D. C., Jan. 28, 1899; *Baltimore Mirror*, Dec. 31, 1898.
370. "A Month in Porto Rico," 1078-1079.
371. *Ibid.*, p. 1079.
372. *Ibid.*, pp. 1076-1077.
373. *Ibid.*, p. 1077.
374. TES to Missouri Provincial, San Juan, December 31, 1898.

375. Cf. letter of Rector of Cuban college asking for temporary services of Father Sherman: Rev. J. M. Palang [?] to Fr. Fitzgerald, Havana, Feb. 16, 1899.

XII. THE GREAT CAMPAIGN: SECOND PHASE

376. Church Bulletin, Holy Family Church, Chicago, 1899-1907, *passim*.
377. Church Bulletin, Holy Family Church, August, 1899.
378. *Report of the Proceedings and Addresses of the Third Annual Meeting of the Catholic Educational Association*, [published at] Columbus, Ohio, by the Secretary's Office, 1906, 94.
379. *Ibid.*, pp. 90-101.
380. Cf. *New York Catholic News*, March 10, 24, 31, 1906.
381. For tracing Father Sherman's mission itineraries reliance has been heavily placed by the author on the Diaries of the Father Ministers at Holy Family Church, Chicago, which was officially Father Sherman's headquarters.
382. Louis Hartz, *The Liberal Tradition in America: An Interpretation of American Political Thought since the Revolution*, New York, 1955, 3-20.
383. *Ibid.*
384. David A. Shannon, "The Socialist Party Before the First World War," *Mississippi Valley Historical Review*, XXXVIII (Sept. 1951), 283.
385. *Ibid.*, pp. 280; 283.
386. Westel W. Willoughby, *An Examination of the Nature of the State*, New York, 1896, 181.
387. Jeremiah W. Jenks, *Principles of Politics—From the Viewpoint of the American Citizen*, New York, 1909, 40-41, 44. Italics inserted.
388. *The Catholic Forester*, March, 1949, n.p.
389. *The Milwaukee Journal*, January 22, 1904.
390. *Ibid.*
391. *The Pittsburg Gazette*, Jan. 5, 1903.
392. *Catholic Standard and Times* (Philadelphia), n.d.
393. TES to Cump, St. Louis, December 17, 1893.
394. Lecture at Music Hall, Chicago, February 4, 1894.
395. Talk to women at St. Xavier parochial school hall, Indianapolis, Indiana, reported in *The Catholic Columbian-Record*, December 26, 1903.
396. TES to Cump, Woodstock, December 29, 1882.
397. Prospectus of Catholic Truth Society, E. Sherman Fitch Papers.
398. TES to Father Joseph Grimmelsman, S.J., Chicago, June 13, 1901.
399. Father Joseph Grimmelsman to TES, St. Louis, June 18, 1901.

400. *Chicago Herald,* February 11, 1894.
401. Bishop S. G. Messmer.
402. Details furnished from files of CTS now in possession of Mr. John Bremner, Chicago, Ill. These consist exclusively of financial reports. They are impressive on the score of the meagre sums therein indicated as the sole income of the CTS.

XIII. GETHSEMANE

403. Conversation with Mr. Edward L. Ryerson, Chicago, Ill. (Tom had often visited with Mr. Ryerson and the latter's father.)
404. Conversation with Miss E. Sherman Fitch, who was present at the dinner.
405. *New York Herald,* n.d., clipping in Woodstock College Archives.
406. *Ibid.*
407. *New York Herald,* May 2, 1906.
408. May 2, 1906.
409. General Sherman to Major Henry Turner, Washington, D. C., March 9, 1879, E. Sherman Fitch Papers.
410. *Ibid.*
411. TES to Father R. J. Meyer, S.J., Chicago, December 23, 1908.
412. TES to Father Meyer, Chicago, Feb. 28, 1909. Cf. also: TES to Father Meyer, Chicago, Dec. 15, 1908, containing further description of the financial difficulties of the CTS.
413. TES to Fr. Meyer, Chicago, Dec. 23, 1908.
414. *Ibid.*
415. Brother Daniel Donaghy, S.J., to Provincial, Chicago, January 4, 1909.
416. *Ibid.*
417. Father J. R. Roswinkel, S.J.
418. Fr. Burrowes, S.J., to Provincial, Chicago, January 2, 1909.
419. Brother Donaghy to Provincial, Chicago, January 4, 1909.
420. TES to Fr. Meyer, Chicago, January 4, 1909.
421. Brother Donaghy to Fr. Meyer, Chicago, January 6, 1909.
422. Father A. J. Burrowes was rector of Holy Family parish and St. Ignatius High School (attached to the parish).
423. Fr. Burrowes to Fr. Meyer, Chicago, January 6, 1909.
424. TES to Fr. Meyer, Chicago, February n.d., 1909.
425. Fr. Meyer to TES, St. Louis, February 22, 1909.
426. TES to Fr. Meyer, Chicago, February 28, 1909.
427. *Ibid.* (In Santa Barbara December 20, 1909, Father Sherman slipped on ice and fell under the train, hitting his head. He was taken to Santa Barbara Hospital. Many friends considered this a cause of his later brain troubles.)
428. TES to Provincial, Santa Barabara, May 22, 1909.

429. TES to Fr. Burrowes, Buffalo, February 15, 1913. (Father Burrowes had been made Provincial of the Missouri Jesuits on January 16, 1913.)
430. *Ibid.*
431. Lizzie to Fr. Rudolph Meyer, Boston, November 15, 1911.
432. Rachel to Fr. Meyer, Boston, October 28, 1911.
433. Rachel to Fr. Meyer, Boston, November 5, 1911.
434. Rachel to Fr. Meyer, Boston, November 21, 1911.
435. Rachel to Fr. Meyer, Boston, November 5, 1911.
436. Rachel to Fr. Meyer, Boston, November 12, 1911.
437. Lizzie to Fr. Meyer, Boston, November 15, 1911.
438. Rachel to Fr. Meyer, Boston, November 12, 1911; November 21, 1911.
439. Conversation of author with Miss Eleanor Sherman Fitch, New York City, spring, 1956.
440. Lizzie to Fr. Meyer, Boston, November 15, 1911.
441. Fr. Meyer to TES, St. Louis, November 18, 1911.
442. Rachel to Fr. Meyer, Boston, [n.d.] 1911.
443. Fr. Thomas Gasson, S.J., to Fr. Meyer, Boston, December 15, 1911.
444. Cump to Fr. Meyer, New York City, December 29, 1911.
445. *Ibid.*
446. Rachel to Fr. Meyer, Boston, November 5, 1911; Fr. Purbrick to Rachel, Chicago, November 16, 1911; Rachel to Fr. Meyer, Boston, November 27, 1911; Fr. Gilbert Garraghan, S.J., to Fr. John B. Eis, St. Louis, November 19, 1915.
447. Rachel to Fr. Meyer, Boston, [n.d.] 1911.
448. Rachel to Fr. Meyer, Boston, November 12, 1911.
449. TES to Missouri Provincial, Buffalo (Providence Retreat), January 24, 1913.
450. TES to Missouri Provincial, Buffalo (Providence Retreat), February 15, 1913. Italics in original.
451. Postscript to *ibid.* Italics in original.
452. Fr. Krim, S.J., to Fr. Burrowes, Buffalo, January 26, 1913.
453. TES to Fr. Burrowes, Marquette College, July 14, 1913.
454. TES to Fr. Burrowes, Marquette College, August 10, 1913.
455. Dated Feb. 10, 1914.

XIV. CRISIS AT CHICAGO

456. Fr. Anthony Maas, S.J., to Fr. Burrowes, New York City, March 1, 1914.
457. TES to Fr. Burrowes, New York City, March 5, 1914.
458. Cardinal John M. Farley.

459. Fr. Grimmelsman to Fr. Burrowes, Marquette University, March 6, 1914.
460. Ibid.
461. TES to Fr. Minister at Marquette, New York City, March 6, 1914.
462. Ibid.
463. Fr. Maas to Fr. Burrowes, New York City, March 1, 1914.
464. Ibid.
465. Ibid.
466. Fr. Grimmelsman to Fr. Burrowes, Marquette University, March 8, 1914, quoting Lizzie's letter to him "of a few days ago."
467. TES to Fr. Burrowes, New York City, March 14, 1914.
468. TES to Fr. Burrowes, New York City, March 18, 1914.
469. Tom was not a complete stranger to Father Maas. They had been classmates at Woodstock in the early 1880s.
470. TES to Father Maas, New York City, March 20, 1914.
471. Fr. Terence Shealy, S.J., to Fr. Hearn, S.J., New York City, March 20, 1914.
472. Fr. Michael O'Connor, S.J., to Fr. Maas, New York City, n.d., 1914.
473. Cump to Fr. Maas, New York City, March 29, 1914.
474. Cump to Fr. Maas, April 2, 1914; Fr. Maas to Fr. Burrowes (telegram), Washington, D. C., April 3, 1914.
475. Cump to Fr. Burrowes, March 24, 1914.
476. TES to Thomas Ewing, Scranton, Pa., October 28, 1914.
477. TES to Father Burrowes, n.p., n.d., certainly 1914.
478. Fr. John B. Eis (rector of Sacred Heart Church, Columbus, Ohio, and acting as Tom's canonist and intermediary with the Jesuit Order), Columbus, November 16, 1914.
479. Ben Dolson to Fr. Burrowes, Lancaster, January 5, 1915. Italics in original.
480. TES to the editor of the Catholic Directory, Lancaster, January 1, 1915.
481. Fr. Theodore Van Rossum, S.J., to Fr. Garraghan, S.J., Columbus, January 8, 1915.
482. Fr. Garraghan to Ben Dolson, St. Louis, January 8, 1915.
483. Hugh Ewing to Fr. Garraghan, Lancaster, January 10, 1915.
484. Cump to Fr. Garraghan, New York City, January 14, 1915.
485. Fr. Francis Finn, S.J., to Fr. Garraghan, Cincinnati, January 14, 1915.
486. Ibid.
487. Ibid; see also, Hugh Ewing to Cump, Lancaster, January 21, 1915.
488. Fr. Finn to Fr. Garraghan, Cincinnati, January 14, 1915.
489. Ibid.
490. Fr. Finn to Fr. Garraghan, Cincinnati, January 18, 1915.

491. Hugh Ewing to Cump, Columbus, January 21, 1915; Cump to Fr. Garraghan, New York City, February 5, 1915.
492. Hugh Ewing to Cump, Columbus, January 21, 1915.
493. Cump to Fr. Garraghan, New York City, March 16, 1915.
494. Cump to Fr. Garraghan, New York City, January 23, 1915.
495. Mrs. Hugh B. Ewing to Fr. Garraghan, Lancaster, January 27, 1915.
496. *Ibid.*
497. Cump to Fr. Garraghan, New York City, February 5, 1915.
498. Cump to Fr. Garraghan, New York City, March 2, 1915.
499. Cump to Secretary of University Club, New York City, March 5, 1915.
500. Fr. Garraghan to TES, St. Louis, March 8, 1915.
501. Legal "Brief" of TES *contra* the Society of Jesus. 1915.
502. Cump to Fr. Garraghan, New York City, April 8, 1915; George Ewing to Fr. Garraghan, Lancaster, January 16, 1915.
503. Lawyer John F. Lee to Fr. Burrowes, St. Louis, August 3, 1915; Cump to Fr. Burrowes, Harvard, Mass., August 8, 1915; Lawyer E. V. P. Schneiderhahn to Clare and Christensen, St. Louis, August 20, 1915; Schneiderhahn to Clare and Christensen, St. Louis, September 11, 1915; Clare and Christensen to E. V. P. Schneiderhahn, Chicago, September 15, 1915; Cump to Fr. Garraghan, New York City, January 23, 1915; Lawyer Ben Dolson to Fr. Garraghan, Lancaster, February 3, 1915; Cump to Fr. Garraghan, New York City, January 18, 1915.
504. Cump to Fr. Garraghan, New York City, April 8, 1915.

XV. POSITION REGAINED

505. *The Spokane Review,* Nov. 15, 1915.
506. TES to Bishop Schinner, Loomis, Wash., February 21, 1916. Archives of the Chancery of the Diocese of Spokane, Washington. Cf. also, for the incidents above: TES to Bishop, n.p., Apr. 26, 1916; Bp. to TES, Spokane, May 1, 1916; TES to Bp., Loomis, Feb. 21, 1916; Same to same, Loomis, March 5, 1916; Bp. to TES, Spokane, Mar. 9, 1916, (Spokane Diocese Archives.)
507. Father Burrowes to Bp., St. Louis, Dec. 5, 1917; Bp. to Fr. Burrowes, Spokane, Dec. 11, 1917; Fr. Burrowes to Bp., St. Louis, Jan. 20, 1918 (Spokane Diocese Archives.)
508. TES to Bp., Loomis, Apr. 19, 1917: "I shall be absent a good deal in the meantime in connection with the settlement" (Spokane Diocese Archives.)
509. Bp. to Fr. Burrowes, Spokane, Jan. 11, 1919 (Spokane Diocese Archives.)
510. TES to Bp., Loomis, May 27, 1919 (Spokane Diocese Archives.)

511. TES to Bp., n.d., n.p. (Spokane Diocese Archives.)
512. TES Chronology (written by himself during his sojourn at Santa Barbara in the 1920s.)
513. Cf.: Father Joseph Mattern, S.J. (American "Assistant" to the Jesuit Father General) to ESF, Rome, Jan. 4, 1932.
514. ESF Date Book.
515. Ibid. Cf. also: TES Chronology.
516. TES to Cump, Malaga, Spain, November 2, 1923.
517. Ibid.
518. Ibid.
519. ESF memorandum, 1924.
520. TES to Cump, Santa Barbara, May 31, 1929.
521. Ibid.
522. TES to Cump, Hermitage (Santa Barbara), May 31, 1929.
523. Mrs. Joseph Hamlen to ESF, Boston, Nov. n.d., 1953.
524. TES to ESF, New York, July 16, 1929.
525. Ibid.
526. Archbishop E. V. Byrne of Santa Fe to ESF, April 2, 1954.
527. Rev. John F. Mueller, S.M., to Miss Mildred Mehren, San Juan, Puerto Rico, December 21, 1953.
528. TES to John Ewing, Lourdes P.O., Trujillo Alto, P.R., November 1, 1929.
529. The complete correspondence relating to his securing his pension are in The National Archives, Washington, D. C.
530. Drs. Vanpaing and Burkard, Santa Barbara, November 5, 1931.
531. Conversation with Miss E. Sherman Fitch.
532. ESF Memorandum.
533. ESF Memorandum.
534. Sister Urbana to ESF, New Orleans, Apr. 24, 1933.
535. E. Sherman Fitch Papers.
536. Sister Urbana to ESF, Dallas, Tex., Jan. 7, 1947.
537. ESF Memorandum.
538. Ibid. Cf. also: Richard Reid, art. in America, Oct. 7, 1933.

EPILOGUE

539. Cump to Father S. Horine, S.J., New York City, May 11, 1933.
540. Father Horine to Cump, Florissant, Mo., May 26, 1933.
541. Same to same, St. Louis, March 26, 1937.

Acknowledgments

To Father John LaFarge, Jesuit, humanist, and scholar, I am deeply grateful for the initial suggestion that this story be written. His always wise advice and his bolstering of the author's morale during the progress of the work was indispensable, particularly at some periods.

Three other of my fellow-Jesuits contributed so generously and competently to the enterprise that without their aid the book might have suffered the fate of Minnie Sherman's mare (see page 30). Father Francis J. Heyden, Director of the Georgetown University Astronomical Observatory, was an expert and ever-affable guide in the processing of photostatic materials. Father Stephen X. Winters, Administrative Assistant to the President of Georgetown University, read the proofs with an eye that was both discriminating and discrete. Father William Nash (lately deceased) of Holy Family Rectory, Chicago, discovered, arranged, and supplied to the author documentary materials of the highest importance. It is the author's keen regret that this venerable priest-librarian is not now alive to receive these thanks.

Fathers Harry J. Sievers and Joseph V. Hamilton had already done some research on the Thomas E. Sherman history, as tangential to other scholarly work in which they were engaged. They graciously made available to the author their valuable transcripts.

The charming and venerable nonagenarian Father Laurence Kenny had been a contemporary of Tom Sherman. During a hot week of a St. Louis summer two years ago, Father Kenny talked with the author and made the subject of the book seem almost to be sitting in the room with us. This revered friend and benefactor of the author died at about the time the first proofs of the book were finished.

Most cordial in their help at important stages of the author's research were Father Louis J. Hanlon, Assistant to the Provincial of the Missouri Province of the Society of Jesus, and Father Raymond J. Fussner, Assistant to the Provincial of the Chicago Province of the same Society.

Father Bartholomew F. Fair, librarian of the Seminary of Saint Charles Borromeo, Overbrook, Pa., placed at the author's disposal what is probably the richest collection of Catholic diocesan newspapers in the United States.

Miss Joan Maloney and Mr. Paul Lupone, both of the Georgetown University Graduate School of Arts and Sciences, proved to be excellent editorial assistants.

Mrs. Gladys Kekenes and Mrs. Edgar Hummel did the typing of important sections of the manuscript. Mr. and Mrs. George Boehrer read the final proofs.

One final remark: among editors, there could scarcely be one more understanding, competent, and even diplomatic, than Mr. Robert Giroux, editor-in-chief of Farrar, Straus, and Cudahy.

Joseph T. Durkin, S.J.

Georgetown University,
January 17, 1959.

Index